A PASSION FOR
DONKEYS

A PASSION FOR
DONKEYS

ELISABETH D. SVENDSEN MBE

DAVID & CHARLES
Newton Abbot · London

Uniform with this book

A PASSION FOR CATS
The Cats Protection League
Forewords by Desmond Morris and Beryl Reid

A PASSION FOR BIRDS
Tony Soper

THE JOY OF ANTIQUES
Ronald Pearsall

*A series of outstanding value, practical, fun books
with extensive text, lots of smaller features and
snippets, and lavish colour.*

British Library Cataloguing in Publication Data

A Passion for Donkeys
  1. Pets: Donkeys
  I. Svendsen, Elisabeth D.
  636.1′ 8
  ISBN 0-7153-9252-2

Designed by John Youé & Associates Ltd
Typeset by Character Graphics,
Taunton, Somerset
and printed in Portugal
for David & Charles Publishers plc
Brunel House Newton Abbot Devon

Contents

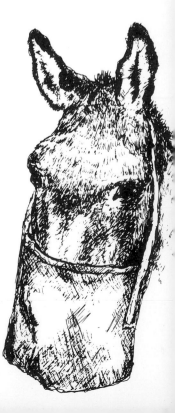

DEDICATION

*This book is dedicated to all the donkeys and mules
in the world. For those lucky enough to have good
homes and happy lives, long may this continue, but I
hope this book will draw attention to the rights and needs
of the silent, massive majority of donkeys patiently and
humbly toiling to help man under the most desperate
conditions. May they secure human respect and a
better life in the future.*

AUTHOR'S NOTE

I would like to give special thanks to
Mal Squance for her invaluable help in
producing this book, to Sue Hall of David & Charles
for being such a kind and understanding editor, and to my
friend June Evers for her encouragement
and never-ending patience during times of stress!

Foreword

Twenty years ago Elisabeth Svendsen began her work with donkeys, work that was to become famous all over the world. Old and young, large and small, ill, maimed, neglected – no donkeys have ever been turned away from the Donkey Sanctuary in Devon, which she founded in 1973. Here, expertly treated and handled with love and understanding they can, in tranquillity and with the companionship so necessary for their well-being, live out their allotted span.

Mrs Svendsen's devotion to the donkey led her to an awareness of the plight, worldwide, of thousands of these animals and her concern and outrage at the way the donkey is abused and exploited set her on the path which has become her way of life. Donkeys have always been used by man as beasts of burden, as a means of transport, as a 'tool', and in some countries as victims of 'fun' at local festivals. Lack of understanding about the donkey's physical and mental requirements can lead to neglect and premature death. Ignorance, often accompanied by lack of money, means that the life of most donkeys in poor communities and Third World countries is desperately hard and pitifully short. Until the Donkey Sanctuary, and later the International Donkey Protection Trust came on the scene, nothing of any significance was being done to research the problems and improve the health of these hard-working, intelligent and delightful animals.

I wonder if we realise what dedication to a cause really means? It sounds idealistic and noble, but of course just to care about something isn't enough, especially when you have three charities to run. (Mrs Svendsen also created the Slade Centre, where donkeys and handicapped children work together.) Dedication requires total single-mindedness, the virtual end of your private life, organisation on the highest level and, in the case of this particular commitment, the ability to blend practical, emotional, research and veterinary aspects into a realistic and harmonious way. However, as is so touchingly illustrated in this book, it is not only the donkeys that need care and love. Not all the animals come to the sanctuary because they have been ill-treated. Sometimes it is because their owners can no longer look after them in the way they wish – they themselves are perhaps too old or have become infirm. Knowing, as they do, that the sanctuary will give their much-loved old friend all the attention and affection he needs, it is nevertheless a poignant goodbye, and such partings are handled with true understanding by the sanctuary staff, leading sometimes to new and lasting friendships.

I have never owned a donkey or mule but, strangely enough, my introduction to these marvellous animals took place only last year, when I was making a documentary film in India. Walking in the Himalayas we were required to trek along narrow stony mountain tracks – sometimes only eight inches wide – with a raging river a sheer drop below us, to ford icy gushing streams, climb rocks and boulders and cross snow-bridges. And, of course, everything we needed, our tents and equipment, was carried by the team of mules.

The mules, for me, were the heroes of the story. Patient, uncomplaining, stoical: they navigated paths that seemed impassable and picked their sure-footed way over landslides and down ravines, until the sun went down and camp was reached and, burdens unloaded, they could roll and kick on the mountain grass. Contrary to what I had previously heard about the temperament of mules, it was the sweetness of their disposition which has remained a lasting impression. This book has done nothing to dispel it. I have learned so much from *A Passion for Donkeys*. The history of the donkey, his place in various cultures, his natural behaviour, his role in wartime, the inconsistencies of our human attitude towards him. And, of course, about that haven for donkeys known as the Donkey Sanctuary.

And the centre, the heart of this donkey world, is Elisabeth Svendsen. Indefatigable, passionate, inspiring, practical and loving, she summed it up in a letter to me, very simply and perfectly: '. . . my whole life is dedicated to the needs of the donkey.'

Nothing more should be said.

Virginia

Virginia McKenna
May 1988

Why a Donkey?

Early Donkeys

It is said that in early days horses and donkeys roamed the valleys and hills but the horses were much stronger and claimed the lush pastures. Gradually the donkeys had to retreat up the hillsides each side of the valley. So that they could keep in contact with each other they developed loud voices to shout with and big ears to hear with, thus the loud bray and delightfully sensitive large ears.

The donkey must be the most overworked, abused and frequently mistreated animal in the world. Over 40 million work in an agricultural capacity worldwide, plus 15 million mules helping the poorest of mankind in the most primitive conditions; and because of their basic simplicity and contrary to popular belief, obedience, they contribute to the very well-being of humanity. To their poor owners they are beasts of burden but to many, Europeans particularly, the donkey evokes different feelings.

Who can fail to be won over by those large limpid eyes; those huge ears and the soft warm muzzle; the sheer humility of the donkey evokes attention and, once attracted, the mutual relationship lasts for life.

Owning a donkey creates a very special form of companionship, a mutually shared joy of regarding life from a different level. Suddenly the necessity for the rush and bustle of today's pressures vanish; a slower more peaceful pace can be enjoyed and the beauties of a ramble along a country lane appreciated, as perhaps long ago we were able to do as children. A donkey is not an impatient animal always wanting to be in another place, as perhaps a horse would. He will stand happily pulling at the hedgerow or quietly grazing, or even just looking into space with a contemplative stare whilst you gently delve into the hedgerow.

The attraction of the donkey is magnetic. You can take the children around the seven wonders of the world, cover the four corners of the earth, sail across the sea and be driving home quietly when suddenly, in a field, two donkeys appear! The shouts of real pleasure, the emotive response from both old and young are almost beyond understanding, and suddenly you realise that these quiet, patient, gentle animals have the most unique attraction. There is no doubt that donkeys really do like humans and will willingly come up to be talked to, stroked and petted, whether titbits are offered or not. This generous part of the donkey's character has helped make him such an appealing pet.

A very special time to enjoy the donkey is, surprisingly, at night. If ever you get the opportunity, slip quietly into the donkey's stable and sit comfortably, so you will distract the donkey as little as possible. Almost immediately he will walk over, and an enquiring soft, warm muzzle will be pressed against you. You will be aware of his gentle breathing and a slightly sweet odour of hay, and then, satisfied you are not going to disturb him, he will return to his manger of hay. The quiet satisfied munching is almost hypnotic and time passes as in a dream before you are aware of the real world outside the stable and the precious moments of pure companionship and peace are gone.

Walk in the moonlight through a field of donkeys and they appear almost ghostly! Demonic shapes on the horizon, far away. Turn, just for a moment and hearing a slight noise look back and find yourself totally surrounded by enquiring eyes and pricked-up ears, yet you have not heard a sound. On recognising you, their friend, their triumphant brays echo through the still night and then peace falls again as they quietly disperse.

Ask any visitor to the Donkey Sanctuary in Devon why they love donkeys and you will receive a large variety of valid reasons. Ask how they first came into contact with donkeys and over 75 per cent will remember them from childhood. To many it was their first experience of riding, generally on the beaches of Britain or 'in grandmother's paddock'. Despite references to donkeys' bad behaviour and stubbornness, their memories are always happy and frequently accompanied by tattered, browning photographs.

The writer must now hold the record for meeting donkeys throughout the world and what an interesting experience it is The difference in attitudes between religious communities and

Heavy Burden

As it is with most children, my introduction to donkeys was through pictures; but my real interest in them must have been aroused when I saw a picture of Jesus sitting on a donkey, his dangling feet almost touching the ground, and I remember thinking: He's supposed to be kind, and He's too heavy for that little donkey.

My attitude must soon have changed somewhat for, when kneeling before the Christmas crib, it would be the nice little donkey I would sort out from the other animals. However, years later, on a beach, I was to see a row of donkeys standing mournfully waiting to be ridden and there was no sentiment mingling with my thinking then and I experienced real anger when their rumps were walloped with a stick.

I think it is for this reason I have never ridden a donkey; perhaps it was the helpless feeling in my mind that I could do nothing about it. But one day I happened to read about Mrs Svendsen's sanctuary and I became interested in helping in my own small way.

The Christian belief is that we should never hate. Well, I hate all those people who are cruel to animals, especially those who mutilate donkeys and those who needlessly throw out their dogs from their cars on their way to the airport to start their holidays. I feel strongly that no punishment is severe enough for such people who deliberately hurt an animal.

Catherine Cookson, OBE, MA

Princess Victoria (in carriage, left) and Princess Maud (standing) of Wales, with Mrs Harvey (wife of the rector of Sandringham) and her daughter Alexandra, and a donkey carriage c1888 (Copyright reserved. Reproduced by gracious permission of Her Majesty The Queen)

animal welfare is painfully obvious and many donkeys suffer torments through religious beliefs and practices. It is hard to make headway to improve conditions in these countries when religious festivals become the excuse for direct cruelty and Muslims refuse to allow an animal to be mercifully released from agonising inhumane conditions by euthanasia.

Ethiopian donkeys suffer terrible sores carrying impossible loads incredible distances with the minimum food and water. Greek donkeys are forced up hundreds of steps overloaded by heavy tourists far too many times a day and the travel guides state: 'We know they've installed a funicular but it's much more fun on a donkey'. In Ecuador the donkeys are killed and eaten at ten years old, their useful working lives finished because they are full of parasites. The meat has to be smoked so that the peasants do not become sick themselves when consuming it. These donkeys in Ecuador and many throughout the world could live much longer, healthier and happier lives with a simple annual dose of worm paste.

Muffin

THE HISTORY OF THE DONKEY

The catalogue of ill-treatment, abuse and ignorance could go on, but for now, let us look at the history of the donkey and where he comes from. Look closely at a group of donkeys. You will notice how they differ in size, shape, colour, markings, and even in the texture of their coats. So, it would be surprising if they shared one common ancestor or originated in one region of the world. A short history of the donkey can only be in general terms, but before finding out who their ancestors were, where they lived and what they looked like, you need to know something about the features of the donkey today.

Grey in various shades is the predominant colour. Brown donkeys are fairly plentiful. Other colours are black, roan (which is a mixture of white hairs and another colour, usually brown) and piebald or skewbald or broken coloured, (a combination of brown and white or black and white markings) which were very popular in the late sixties but are less so now. Finally there are the rarer colours of pure white and chestnut. The 'cross' which is immediately associated with the donkey is most clearly visible on greys and browns, less distinct on lighter colours, invisible on blacks and missing on white and broken-coloured donkeys. But, as with most things connected with the donkey, there are always exceptions!

Size is important and it is useful to have some idea of the height of the donkey. This is measured in 'hands', which is the average breadth of a person's hand, 10cm (4in). The measurement is taken at the withers. This is the highest point of the donkey's shoulder, where the neck joins the back, and most of the donkeys which you will see will be between 9.2 and 11 hands, 38 to 44in or 96.5 to 111.8cm.

The donkey's ancestors were wild asses from Africa and Asia. In Africa there were two separate species. The Nubian, standing 12 hands, from the north between the Mediterranean coast and the Sahara Desert; and the Somali, standing 14 hands, from further east to the south of the Red Sea. The Nubian wild ass had a shoulder cross which was not very marked, being either

OPPOSITE
Coats of many colours

Did you know. . .

A team of sixty-four mules pulled the hearse bearing the corpse of Alexander the Great from Babylon to Alexandria.

The Emperor Nero's mules had shoes of silver. His wife, the Empress Papiya, used to bathe in asses milk and she kept five hundred female asses that were milked regularly for this purpose. Her mules wore golden slippers.

A remedy from olden days for whooping cough in children was to pick a few hairs from the cross on the donkey's back and hang them in a bag round the child's neck.

In the Middle Ages the cure for eye trouble was to smear fresh asses dung over your eyes.

The cure for gout was to bind a donkey's hoof on the bad foot.

The Irish say 'There are three things that cannot be ruled, a mule, a pig and a woman.'

It is said that anybody who kisses a mule will be immune to scarlet fever.

THE DONKEY IN RELIGION

The donkey has numerous religious connections. The cross was said to have been put on the donkey's back as a reminder to all that he was chosen to carry Jesus on Palm Sunday. The Bible always refers to the donkey as 'ass'; the name 'donkey' being given to the animal centuries later.

Unlike the Somali wild ass (the swift ass), the onager bowed its neck to the yoke, and this is why in biblical times it was given the name 'Pereh' (wild) – a term now commonly applied to any creature that cannot be tamed.

> Who hath sent out the wild ass free?
> Or who hath loosed the bands of the wild ass?
> Whose house I have made the wilderness,
> And the barren land his dwellings.
> He scorneth the multitude of the city.
> Neither regardeth he the crying of the driver.
> The range of the mountains is his pasture,
> And he searcheth after every green thing.
> Job C39 V5–8

In early days two asses were used to carry a traveller, the asses walked side by side and a seat was slung between them in a double harness. In biblical times it was always the ass who carried the kings. Before the time of David it was not the done thing to ride a horse rather than an ass. In fact it is interesting to note that up to the Reformation English churchmen of high rank travelled by mule on affairs of state. The ass probably entered domestication around 3500 BC while the horse was domesticated, it is believed, a little later. Many references are made to the ass in the Bible:

> And the king said unto Ziba, 'What meanest thou by these?' And Ziba said, 'The asses be for the kings household to ride on . . .'
> II Samuel C16 V2

> The king also said unto them, 'Take with you the servants of your lord, and cause Solomon my son to ride upon mine own mule, and bring him down to Gihon.'
> I Kings C1 V33

> Six days thou shalt do thy work, and on the seventh day thou shalt rest: that thine ox and thine ass may rest, and the son of thy handmaid, and the stranger may be refreshed.
> Exodus C23 V12

> Rejoice greatly, O daughter of Zion; shout, O daughter of Jerusalem: behold the king cometh unto thee, he is just and having salvation, lowly and riding upon an ass and upon a colt, the foal of an ass.
> Zechariah C9 V9

> And he said to his sons, 'Saddle the ass for me.' And they saddled it. And he went and found his body thrown in the road, and the ass and the lion standing beside the body. The lion had not eaten the body or torn the ass. And the prophet took up the body of the man of God and laid it upon the ass, and brought it back to the city, to mourn and to bury him.
> I Kings C13 V28–9

> And the Lord blessed the latter days of Job more than his beginning; and he had fourteen thousand sheep, six thousand camels, a thousand yoke of oxen, and a thousand she-asses.
> Job C42 V12

> And when they drew near to Jerusalem and came to Bethphage, to the Mount of Olives, then Jesus sent two disciples, saying to them, 'Go into the village opposite you, and immediately you will find the ass tied, and a colt with her; untie them and bring them to me. If anyone says anything to you, you shall say, "The Lord has need of them", and he will send them immediately.'
> This took place to fulfil what was spoken by the prophet, saying, 'Tell the daughter of Zion, Behold your king is coming to you, humble, and mounted on an ass, and on a colt, the foal of an ass.'
> Matthew C21 V1–5

Mules were used to convey postal messages:-

> And he wrote in the King Ahasuerus' name, and sealed it with the king's ring, and sent letters by posts on horseback, and riders on mules, camels and young dromedaries.
> Esther C8 V10

There were many religious stories written and the birth of Christ must be the most popular of these; the part the donkey played was fully acknowledged. Joseph's donkey must have been absolutely vital to him to carry Mary to the stable when the birth was approaching. The donkey was, of course, also present at the birth of Christ as, most probably, were the shepherds who watched their flocks of sheep and saw the star and rode their donkeys to follow the star to the stable.

Again Joseph's donkey was absolutely necessary to him when he heard of Herod's decree with regard to male babies. Joseph hastily placed Mary and the babe on the donkey's back and fled through the narrow dark alleyways of Bethlehem to freedom.

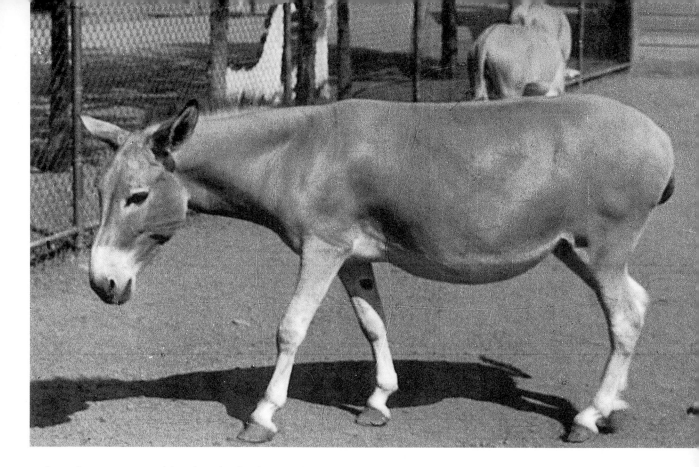

rather short or very thin, but he had no stripes on his legs. In contrast the Somali wild ass had no shoulder cross, but very prominent leg-stripes, reminiscent of the zebra. The regions where they lived were hot and dry, so that there was little difference between the thickness of their winter and summer coats. In winter both were grey, in summer the Nubian had a reddish and the Somali, a yellowish tinge.

The Asiatic branch of the breed came from a much larger area stretching from the Red Sea to northern India and Tibet where the ass had to adapt to differences of climate, terrain and altitude. Consequently there is no single type of Asiatic wild ass. The further east the ass was found, the larger, heavier and stronger the animal became. The Syrian wild ass measured under 10 hands. His neighbour to the east was the light-coloured swift-footed onager, which measured 12 hands. East again was the kulan, standing half a hand higher, darker in colour, with a very marked broad stripe along his back and growing a thick winter coat. Like all Asiatic wild asses, he does not have a shoulder stripe. Then comes the largest and heaviest of all the Asiatic wild asses, the kiang, standing 14 hands, living on the Tibetan plateau to the north of the Himalayas and adapting to extremes of climate. He has certain features more like a horse than our domesticated donkey, such as shorter ears and a rounder foot.

Through all these countries ran the trade route from the Pacific Ocean to the Mediterranean given the romantic name of the Silk Road. The journey lasted several years and no single animal completed the entire journey. Donkeys were among the draught animals used and with unplanned matings, while passing

*Nubian wild ass (*Equus africanus africanus*) in Catshill Game Park, New York State, bred in Munich Zoo from a stock imported from northern Eritrea by Heck in 1937*

IN FRONT OF HIM THE PATH LED TO A BEAUTIFUL TABLE

Donkeys never *misbehave in church!*

13

A kiang (Equus hemionus holdereri) *with newborn foal in Tierpark, Berlin*

through the territories of the various Asiatic wild asses, some mixing of the breeds occurred. Carrying the valuable bales of silk, the donkeys arrived ultimately in Alexandria. Through Asia Minor donkeys arrived in Greece where they proved to be ideal animals to work on the narrow paths between the vines. Their use in the cultivation of grapes spread through the Mediterranean countries to Spain whose coast, at the southern tip, is separated from North Africa by only a few miles.

With the Roman army the donkey travelled throughout the Roman Empire as a pack animal and later was used in agriculture and in the new vineyards which the Romans planted as far north as France and Germany. With the Roman invasion of Britain, donkeys came to England. For 1,500 years no one bothered about them as was the case, though for a shorter period, in the twentieth century.

Popularity Increases So why did the donkey begin to attract attention and why was he suddenly needed? The answer was 'war'. For hundreds of years the demand for horses as cannon fodder had been difficult to meet. They were either requisitioned by the army or taken in payment of taxes. By the sixteenth century horses had become scarce and expensive. The desperate farmer needed a replacement and in England and Wales the replacement was the neglected donkey. Years later, at the end

WORKING DONKEYS IN THE MID-NINETEENTH CENTURY

Two miles north of Ross-on-Wye, Herefordshire, is the village of Brampton Abbotts. From the *W I Village History* (1955) and parish registers is culled the following true story.

A villager, John Wilmott, made his living in the mid-nineteenth century by using his donkeys and cart for hauling coal and grains and taking luggage to and from Ross railway station. His father, of the same name, was a brickmaker at Mr Harris's brickyard in the village near the present house, 'Highfield'. John was also employed by the Ross Union to deliver pauper coffins by donkey cart in the district. On one occasion he caused a great fright because he was found asleep in one of the coffins.

At one time, when driving his two donkeys in tandem, the animals lay down in the middle of the lane and refused to pull the cart. It happened on Slade Pitch, a 1 in 4 hill, 2 miles north of Brampton Abbotts on the lane that follows the east bank of the River Wye. (Even with its modern surface, donkeys would prefer to take this gradient zigzag fashion.) John began to cry and curse at the donkeys all to no avail. Fortunately passing in the fields were the Misses Wilton, two

daughters of the Vicar of Foy whose parish they were now in. John's plea was: 'Please, please Middies Comen! Will you come and help me up th'ill wid dese 'ere brasted donties?'

On 17 April 1865 John aged thirty-eight years, a bachelor, married Mary Powell aged twenty-nine years, a spinster, the daughter of a Ross-on-Wye shoemaker at Brampton Abbotts Church. They began married life in a cottage which was scarcely habitable and which was later condemned and demolished. On the occasion of the wedding, the church was full (about a hundred people) and it is remembered that the Rector, Rev William Hulme, had a difficult time as neither of the couple could read or write! The witnesses as well, as was not unusual at that time, signed the register with their mark, a cross. An arch of flowers was erected over the churchyard gate especially for the wedding and the donkeys, dressed with flowers, joined the procession. Overjoyed with the day, John is reported to have declared: 'It was the prettiest wedding ever held in Brampton Abbotts.'

Allan Ricketts
Donkey Breed Society Magazine

of the nineteenth century, Welsh-bred donkeys were much sought after and commanded a high price.

There has been no mention of Ireland which many people think of as the home of the donkey. Once again it was England's wars – this time with the Irish – which brought the donkey to Ireland with the army of occupation. In this country, too, the army began to buy cheap horses required for other wars and the Irish farmers were more than happy to take cash, replace their horses with cheaper donkeys and put the surplus cash under the bed!

In Scotland the donkey has never been so commonly used. Two reasons for this are the cold winters unlike the mild, though damp, climate of Ireland, and Scotland's extensive area of forests, very different from the donkey's original habitat.

Whilst the donkey, particularly the white ass, had some aristocratic and even royal owners, nevertheless in England and Wales he remained the 'poor man's horse'. He was cheap to keep, at least until the end of the eighteenth century, when the Inclosure Acts abolished certain commons rights and deprived commoners of their free grazing. The farmers complained that there was no money in breeding donkeys a cry to be heard from donkey breeders again in the seventies!

Breeding mules by crossing a donkey stallion with a horse or pony mare showed more profit. The New Forest in Hampshire was a centre for this activity, since it was near the port of Southampton from which the young mules were shipped to the USA. However, they were small and not of good quality and to produce a bigger animal, the New Forest jackass was replaced as a stallion by the larger Spanish or Maltese ass.

*Somali wild asses (*Equus africanus somaliensis*) in Hai-Bar Eilat, the desert reserve in southern Israel. They derive from stock imported from the Afar country, Ethopia*

*Iranian onagers (*Equus hemionus onager*) in Hai-Bar Eilat*

JACQUOT

Queen Victoria's love for donkeys apparently influenced their driving potential in England. She had a special preference for them in her later years and it is known that at this time she owned at least three. One of these, a brown donkey named 'Jacquot', she bought from a peasant whom she saw driving him in a cart when visiting Aix-les-Bains in 1887 and she promptly decided that in future this should form her mode of transport.

Jacquot became a great favourite and travelled everywhere with Queen Victoria. This greatly astonished the inhabitants of Italy who felt, when she visited their country in 1895 and took her donkey with her, that it was an insufficiently impressive equipage for a Queen and Empress!

This carriage, however, continued to be her chosen conveyance for in addition to Jacquot she owned a white donkey which she took to both France, as well as to Dublin, the year before her death. Mostly, however, Queen Victoria used her donkeys for excursions in the grounds of her estates at Windsor, Balmoral and Osborne on the Isle of Wight but, unknown to the Queen, this caused two of her ladies-in-waiting to record in their diaries that the effort of keeping up, when walking alongside was extremely tiring.

Queen Victoria's liking for donkeys continued with her family for her son, King Edward VII, when he was Prince of Wales owned a giant white donkey stallion which was exhibited at Islington Show and there is a photograph in the royal archives of her granddaughter, the Princess Victoria, driving a donkey at Windsor accompanied by her sister, the Princess Maud.

Royal interest in donkeys undoubtedly made its mark on society, for after Queen Victoria's death in 1901 the fashion for driving them increased and there is scarcely an album of family photographs compiled during the late Victorian and Edwardian periods that does not include several with donkeys harnessed to gigs, governess carts and small phaetons.

One well-known lady driver of donkeys was the banking heiress, Miss (later the Baroness) Angela Burdett-Coutts who, although she owned a large stud in north London which bred thoroughbred horses and hackneys, entered a smart pair of donkeys harnessed to a miniature waggonette at the 1865 Islington Show.

From singles, people soon became more adventurous, pairs and one or two tandems making their appearance. Four-in-hands too have been used from time to time and make a splendid sight.

Donkeys were also considered suitable for children and several old photographs depict youngsters at the reins of donkeys and this includes one of the late Earl Mountbatten of Burma taken when he was a small boy of eight in 1908 and a photo of Charles Edward, Duke of Albany.

Queen Victoria would have been proud to know that the Driving for the Disabled Scheme was first thought of by a member of the royal family – HRH The Duke of Edinburgh.

Marylian Watney
Donkey Breed Society Magazine

Queen Victoria in a donkey carriage, Viceregal Lodge, Dublin, in April 1900
(Copyright reserved. Reproduced by gracious permission of Her Majesty The Queen)

Charles Edward, Duke of Albany, riding on a donkey, July 1890 (Copyright reserved. Reproduced by gracious permission of Her Majesty The Queen)

The heyday of the donkey in Britain was during the last century when it was used on farms and increasingly in towns as a pack animal. In Ireland the donkeys carried the peat from the bogs and drew the carts loaded with potatoes or with flax to be woven into Irish linen. In fashionable spas, donkeys transported corpulent ladies to take the waters. On the sands, the donkeys gave rides to young visitors. In the mining areas, it was the coal miners who rode their donkeys to work at the collieries. Donkeys pulled lawn-mowers on the lawns of prosperous houses and the rubbish carts of the local councils. They carried the laundry and delivered the milk. In fact, donkeys also supplied the milk! In London a herd of milch-asses made a daily milk round of some smart residential districts where the donkeys were milked in the street to produce asses milk for the children of well-to-do families. For the successful tradesman and the London coster-monger the donkey barrow came to replace the baskets and the hand carts. Hundreds of donkeys were drawn up at the markets for the carts to be filled with fresh fruit, vegetables and fish and on bank holidays the donkey would be used to take the family for an outing. With all this activity

The Bideford donkey stone

Prank Goes into History

A friendly prank has been accepted as part of Bideford's folklore. It started at the turn of the century when shipbuilders at the former Whitfield repair yard painted a caricature in tar of a local orange salesman who travelled the area on a donkey.

Twenty years later the caricature was copied for a carving in stone which was placed on a corner of the yard that became known as 'Donkey Quay'. The carving was removed several years ago when new Western Counties offices were built on the site alongside the River Torridge. It was presented to Bideford Town Council and preserved and now builders working on the quayside site have agreed to incorporate the primitive carving into a new development.

Western Morning News

Poster of prize mules and donkeys at the Great Exhibition at the Crystal Palace in 1851.

there was a thriving trade in donkeys. At Islington cattle market thousands of them found new owners each year and a steady demand for donkeys for a few weeks or even a few days ensured that hiring was a flourishing business. Donkeys were shown at the International Horse Show and at the Royal Show and special donkey shows were held at Islington. But changes were on the way.

Decline In war there were no more cavalry charges, so the slaughter ceased. Horses became more plentiful and donkeys were no longer needed to replace them. But it was the invention of the internal combustion engine which signalled the end of the donkey's role as a working animal. It was estimated about fifty years ago that the donkey population numbered about one hundred in England. This was surely nonsense if only because of the number of seaside towns where beach donkeys were still a popular attraction. The significance of this casual estimate was the indifference it showed, obtaining a more accurate figure was too much trouble. The donkey had once more become a neglected animal.

Change of Role This state of affairs continued until about 1963 when something unexpected happened. Hundreds of Irish donkeys were imported to meet the demands of a new market, people eager to own a donkey. To work? No. For the first time in thousands of years the donkey was no longer required as a working animal. He had become a popular pet. Usually the donkey was the first equine which these purchasers had owned. But their enthusiasm to learn soon overcame their lack of knowledge of how to look after the donkey. They bought books; they attended lectures; they joined the recently formed Donkey Breed Society (then called the Donkey Show Society); they learned about feeding and grooming, and the care of the donkey's feet; they were entranced by donkey foals, so they looked around for a suitable stallion for their mare and found out what special care she would need when in foal, and later how to look after the foal. All this newly acquired knowledge was responsible for an impressive improvement in the fitness and condition of the donkey. Owners showed their animals at horse and agricultural shows, which had now begun to hold classes for donkeys and they had them inspected and registered in the new stud book in order to acquire a pedigree. Children rode them, adults drove them, sometimes to elegant carriages far grander than the donkey had ever known before. The donkeys were proving hugely popular and giving untold pleasure to their owners, their families and friends and to the public.

Unfortunately when times are hard, the future of an animal which is a pet is more at risk than an animal that works and earns its keep. Unemployment and redundancies caused by the recession brought a drop in the number of donkey owners and a reduction in breeding has corrected the excesses of earlier years. This new situation, which has already lasted several years, is not unsatisfactory. Although fewer in number, today's donkey owners have shown themselves to be responsible, committed, caring and dedicated animal-lovers.

Acquiring a Donkey

A donkey is a donkey is a donkey, to misquote. To the average member of the public this would, no doubt, be a satisfactory description and with some justification. Although colour and size may vary, the image presented in ninety-nine cases out of a hundred is one of a quiet, amiable beast with friendly eyes and a long pair of ears. However, if the time has come when you are actually going to choose a donkey of your own, you should be clear in your mind as to the purpose for which you want him. The donkey will be referred to as 'he' rather than 'it'.

The donkey's roles are many and different types suit different roles best. Perhaps you may have wanted a donkey for years, in which case his age and appearance are not of importance; you may want to acquire 'something to keep the grass down in the paddock'; a ride for young children; a companion for a pony, thoroughbred or retired hunter; an animal to drive between the shafts or just a large pet. The donkey will fulfil all of these functions more than satisfactorily if selected for the part he is to play. One thing must be stressed, however, before you read on – donkeys are sociable animals and are not suited to living on their own. If space is limited his companion doesn't have to be another donkey but something else living in the same area will be much better than nothing. A lonely donkey will bray and try to make contact with others in the neighbourhood and he may well mope. To quote a horse-lover describing her horse without realising the contradiction in her words, 'after all he is only human'! One can appreciate exactly what she meant.

GRAZING

Space is essential if you keep any equine. With even the most careful management, .2 hectare (½ acre) per animal is the absolute minimum on which to manage. The area is needed not only for food but, even supposing you feed hay all the time, for exercise. You will find that donkeys tend to stale (urinate) in one area which they will not then graze; take over another patch for rolling and thereby very soon rub away the grass; the water supply and its well-trodden approach will account for a few more square yards of unproductive ground, as will the gate or the part of the fence where he stands while you scratch him behind his ears; add to this the area of his shelter and you will find that in a small enclosure there is not much space left in which to graze and walk about and have the occasional frolic.

It is preferable to divide your land into a minimum of two paddocks so that one half can be rested to allow the grass to

---

Travels with a Donkey

Blessed be the man who invented goads! Blessed the innkeeper of Bouchet St Nicholas who introduced me to their use! This plain wand, with an eighth of an inch pin, was indeed a sceptre when he put it in my hand. Thenceforward Modestine was my slave. A prick and she passed the most inviting stable door. A prick and she broke forth into a gallant little trotlet that devoured the miles. It was not a remarkable speed, when all was said; and we took four hours to cover 10 miles at the best of it. But what a heavenly change since yesterday! No more wielding of the ugly cudgel; no more flailing with an arching arm; no more broadsword exercise, but a discreet and gentlemanly fence. And what although now and then a drop of blood should appear on Modestine's mouse-coloured wedge-lime rump? I should have preferred it otherwise, indeed; but yesterday's exploits had purged my heart of all humanity. The perverse little devil, since she would not be taken with kindness, must even go with pricking.

Robert Louis Stevenson

regrow. A donkey requires a supply of not particularly high-quality grass but sometimes they seem to be expected to live on fresh air as, not infrequently, you can see them confined to a paddock eaten down to the earth. On the other hand, deep, lush pasture will quite certainly lead to disaster in the form of colic, laminitis or obesity followed by heart disease. As well as liking grass, he is very fond of browsing and enjoys tackling bramble patches and keeping hedges in trim. Be warned too, because he likes the bark of trees, so keep precious specimens securely fenced off. Also beware of planting poisonous shrubs too near his perimeter fence as a donkey's neck and head stretched out horizontally reach quite a long way! So for his own safety's sake, if for no other reason, check up on what is within reach of the fence.

SHELTER

All donkeys need access to shelter. Remember the donkey is not native to this country and has less resistance to rain and inclement weather than native ponies. Contrary to what may be

Your donkey will be a true friend

Social Behaviour

Somali wild asses move in herds consisting of females and young animals. Each adult male marks out a territory for himself which may be as large as 4–6 sq km (1½–2⅓ sq miles) and within which he will not suffer the presence of any other adult male. (In this respect they differ from the male Asian wild asses who do not mark out their territories but live in the vicinity of the female herds either singly or in small groups.) Fights between males are extremely cruel and, in captivity, may end in death. In the wild, the defeated male will run for his life.

The herds of females and adolescents may freely enter and leave the males' territories. If one of the females is on heat, the territory owner will start courting her at once. Courting in its initial stages is a very brutal business, the female kicking her hind legs, the courting male inflicting bites all over her body.

After a gestation period of some thirteen months, the female gives birth not far from the herd. Already within an hour of birth the foal is able to follow his mother, who takes care to shield him from predators and after several more days he is able to accompany her back to the herd. The foal is weaned when four months old. On reaching maturity at the age of two, the foal leaves his mother to try and establish his own domain.

Bill Clark
(from the booklet of the 'Hai-Bar' Organisation, Nature Reserve, Israel)

Make sure that your donkey has plenty of space – and company

generally supposed, shelter is as necessary for the animal's comfort in the summer as for his well-being in the winter. The reason for this is flies. Field animals can be tormented by flies: horse-flies as well as the more common variety that cluster round their eyes and the occasional warble- and bot-flies which send them into panic. Flies are part of every warm sunny day and only leave off their attentions in rain or dark. A shelter provides the necessary gloom that gives relief. In summer many donkeys prefer to stay out in the fields at night and come to stand in the shelters before mid-morning where they remain until the end of the afternoon. Cold, frost and even snow do not seem to worry donkeys unduly but a heavy penetrating downpour is something for which donkeys are quite unadapted. A soaking may well pave the way to a chill, bronchitis or pneumonia. You can hardly be responsible for seeing that the donkey is always brought indoors if it is raining but provide him with a field shelter and he will go under cover himself. See page 66 for further details of stable construction.

A SUITABLE DONKEY

Donkeys live a long time: thirty years plus is quite normal for an animal that is well cared for, so bear this in mind when you are choosing and try to plan for his future when you are planning for your own. An animal that is already old is suitable for all the roles mentioned except for riding and driving. He will, however, need a little extra food and as his molars tend to become pointed with age and therefore cannot grind food properly, his teeth need to be rasped occasionally by the vet to ensure that he can eat comfortably and digest properly. An old donkey, like a foal, may also be a little more susceptible to chills after cold rain.

A young animal should not carry weight regularly and is not suitable for riding until he is four years old. Geldings are generally stronger than mares and are ideal for riding and driving but please remember the maximum weight suitable for the average donkey to carry is 50kg (112lb). If you want a youngster and are offered a foal, it is important that he should not leave his mother before the age of six months at the very earliest and nine months to one year is a far better age. If your donkey is a male he should be castrated as no stallion will make a suitable pet even if kept with a mare. An entire male, however friendly, may sometimes be unpredictable in his behaviour and is best kept by a professional. Otherwise there is little to choose between mares and geldings and a combination of either will live happily together.

CONFORMATION

Conformation is the name used for the physical build of the animal. Buy your donkey in warm weather if you possibly can as the best time to pick out a donkey is in midsummer when, except for foals, his long coat of winter hair has been shed. The best donkey can be hidden under a thick mat of winter hair and the worst one will be disguised into cuteness. If you absolutely must pick your donkey in full, shaggy coat, you will have to rely on a careful visual and tactile examination of the head, backline, depth of body, width of chest and quarters, line of neck, legs and rib-spring.

Your donkey can improve in appearance after you have cared for him with good food and given him adequate exercise. A young donkey, once he has grown and filled out, may look considerably better. All donkeys go through a really gangly 'teenage' stage, sometimes in their second and sometimes in their third year, where they look pretty bad! When they mature in their fourth year they look quite different and usually the owner heaves a sigh of relief!

The best donkey for you, is the one who gets along with you and who fulfils *your* requirements. If you see a roached backed, droopy eared, ancient gelding who immediately loves you and whom you immediately love and you ask nothing more of him than to be your pet and companion ignore anything anybody might say and take him, not the fancy priced one, with whom you have nothing in common!

The Donkey Breed Society will supply you with details of studs in the country where first-class donkeys can be purchased. You can, of course, also purchase donkeys from markets but care must always be taken when buying from these sources as the donkey may have been under severe stress or may have some form of illness. Selected donkeys are also available from the Donkey Sanctuary on a foster basis. These are healthy donkeys that the sanctuary feels would benefit from a more personalised environment. A donkey is always sent out with a companion; if the new home already has a donkey or pony which needs a friend, we send out a pair of donkeys as companions. Of course,

Fern

Smallest, Largest and Oldest

The smallest donkeys come from the Mediterranean islands of Sicily and Sardinia, the smallest recorded, fully grown, is 61cm (24in) measured to the shoulder.

The largest donkeys are from the Poitou region of France, the largest recorded being 167.5cm (66in) measured to the shoulder.

The oldest donkey, according to records, lived to fifty-seven years. The average life span in the UK is thirty-seven and the average life span abroad is eleven years.

LESSONS FROM EEYORE

Eeyore, Smartie and the rest of the group went into a large airy barn at night and on the first night at Slade House Farm I sank gratefully into bed knowing all were safely shut up for the night.

Eeyore found a way to open the door! Although it had been latched firmly, by the little teeth marks around the latch the next morning the truth was clear. Sometime during that night Eeyore had let himself out and Maud, a very elderly donkey who had assumed a type of 'grandma' role, managed to follow him before the door swung shut again. Off trotted Eeyore determined to explore his new surroundings!

Smartie's desperate braying woke me and I realised who was missing. The top of the stable door had to be shut when I went to look for Eeyore and Maud or a desperate Smartie would have launched herself over the top! I stood quietly by the track and listened. There in the woodland area was the mournful sepulchral bray of Maud. Armed with a torch and accompanied by son Clive, I followed the sounds and soon found a, by now, very grateful Eeyore and Maud lost in the woods and led them home!

By the next morning Eeyore was apparently quite happy to graze peacefully but I was a little angry to see that the donkeys' water butt was empty. Herb had been with me for years and assured me he had filled it that morning and that the bung at the bottom must have come out. He refilled it carefully and all was well until teatime when, once again, the butt was empty. This time we put the donkeys away for the night after refilling the butt and it was still full of cool clear water in the morning. Next day I idly leant on the fence watching the donkeys enjoy their early morning roll and then Eeyore left the others and sidled up to the trough. He didn't want a drink, oh no. His little teeth closed around the plug, he braced his little hoofs, pulled and stood in delight watching the water run between his legs and down the field!

Eeyore had a fascination for water. The nursery unit used to go out with the geriatrics in the paddock by the intensive care unit where there was a lovely shallow duck pond with gentle sloping edges. One day there was a shout from the yard staff and we all had to rush out and rescue Nellie, an elderly donkey, who had somehow got herself into the middle of the pond and couldn't get out. She seemed fine after her ordeal and not a bit concerned and we thought little more of the incident until one afternoon, a little later, I was in the office and through my window I could see the geriatrics. This time Gertrude was by the side of the pond with her ears twitching. Up came Eeyore. He was standing very close to Gertrude and seemed to be leaning on her. I sprang from my seat and flung the window open shouting 'Eeyore' but it was too late. As though in slow motion, Gertrude tottered on the edge and then splash! It took three of us to get her out. Eeyore was confined to stables for the rest of the day!

Gertrude, wet and dripping, after her rescue from the pond

Getting used to another member of the family

before a donkey is delivered, an inspector visits to ensure that the new owners will be knowledgeable and have all the facilities required, ie adequate land, fencing, shelter etc. Once the donkeys have been placed in the foster home the inspector visits every three months and frequently becomes a firm friend and adviser to the new donkey owners. The Donkey Sanctuary guarantees to pay veterinary bills should the foster home incur severe financial difficulties. The donkeys still remain under the ownership of the Donkey Sanctuary and if, at any time, for any reason, the new owners are unable to continue caring for the donkeys then they return to the security of the sanctuary.

THE NEW ARRIVAL

Make a little fuss of the new arrival, see that he is wearing a head collar with a detachable leading rein, and take him to his new quarters. What you do then must depend on whether his field is already occupied by another animal and you will have to use your commonsense. If there is a resident donkey or donkeys, allow all parties to sniff each other across the gate before you introduce the newcomer into the field. The resident donkey should be more than ready to receive the stranger but the excitement will very likely lead to a bit of a chase-around for a few minutes. The same will apply if the resident is a pony, but should your donkey be brought face to face with a horse, especially a young one, the introduction should be gradual. The horse may never have seen a donkey before and may be inclined to make the point by careering about and snorting. In this case, secure the donkey close by to graze or eat a little hay, while you stay nearby. If the horse is very excitable and it is possible to keep the two animals separate for twenty-four hours or so, so much the better, but when you do introduce them make sure that you hold the horse's head until the donkey has got well into the field and looked round and make sure that no leading rein is left trailing from his head collar. Once the animals have touched noses it should be all right to let the horse loose. Many horses grow to be inseparable from their donkey companions, seeming to find a sense of security in their small even-tempered companions.

If some other kinds of animals are already living in the field, such as cows or bullocks, there will probably be far less excitement. However, with animals that are smaller than donkeys, such as goats, sheep or geese, it is as well to introduce the

Donkeys make ideal companions for another donkey or horse. The favourite for the 1988 Grand National, Lean Ar Aghaidh, has a donkey friend called Jenny Brown (Reproduced by kind permission of the Daily Telegraph)

'What on earth is this?'

TRANSPORT LAWS

The requirements for transporting your donkey by trailer are as follows:

Every receptacle shall be of substantial design and so constructed and maintained as to withstand the action of the weather and the weight of any animal which may be thrown against it.

Requirements for the protection of animals carried in receptacles:

Every receptacle shall be so designed, constructed and maintained and shall be of sufficient size and height, as to ensure that:
(a) each animal carried therein can be properly accommodated without being caused unnecessary suffering;
(b) feeding and watering can be effected without removing the animal from the receptacle;
(c) each animal being carried therein is able to stand in its natural position;
(d) adequate and suitable ventilation is provided for each animal carried therein;
(e) suitably placed apertures are available to enable the interior thereof to be readily inspected;
(f) easy access to the interior thereof is available;
(g) each animal carried therein is protected from exposure to the weather;
(h) the interior thereof does not contain any sharp edges or projections which are likely to cause injury or unnecessary suffering to any animal being carried therein;
and
(i) the receptacle can be adequately cleansed and disinfected in the manner prescribed in this order.

Every receptacle shall be so designed, constructed and maintained as to prevent any leakage of liquid matter therefrom or any escape of waste feeding stuffs or animal droppings.

The floor of every receptacle shall be fitted with suitable foot battens or provided with a suitable anti-slip surface.

Every receptacle shall be so designed, constructed and maintained as to ensure that it is capable of being properly and effectively secured to the vehicle on which it is to be transported.

Every receptacle shall be subject to the requirement that there shall be a minimum distance of 1.98m (6ft 6in) between the floor of the vehicle and the roof.

It is not necessary for a vehicle or receptacle to have a ramp for loading and unloading providing the floor of the vehicle is not more than 31cm (12in) above ground level.

donkey into their field where he is pre-occupied with the novelty of the place as well as with his new companions. If the opposite procedure is followed, and smaller animals are let into the donkey's own field, he may well chase them about for a while until familiarity is established. In any case, when putting a new donkey into new quarters detach the leading rein but leave the head collar on for a few days as should he turn out to be shy or nervous it will be easier to catch him if there is something on his head to get hold of. Do not leave the head collar on permanently, in case it rubs against the head.

Meeting the family dog

Donkeys do not take kindly to strange dogs so be sure your family pet is restrained from making himself at home in the donkey's field for the first day or two until they become well acquainted or he will almost certainly be chased and a small dog can be badly hurt. Dog and donkey invariably become accustomed to each other and even good friends but strangers' dogs should beware. The dog-following characteristic can be quite useful in seeing off stray dogs from your property!

Try to find out before the donkey arrives whether he has had tetanus injections and, if in doubt, ask your veterinary surgeon to remedy this as soon as possible. Ideally, the donkey should be wormed before he is introduced into his new domain to avoid contamination of his own pasture. It is also important to make contact with a farrier. This contact should really be made before you acquire the animal as his services are essential. The horn of a donkey's foot grows surprisingly quickly and as most farriers are very busy it is unwise to wait until the hoofs need paring before getting in touch with one. Explain that you would like him to visit on a regular eight-weekly basis it will make it easier for everyone. It is a good plan to pick out your donkey's feet every day both to remove anything that may be troubling him as well as to familiarise him with the handling of his feet.

TRANSPORT

When you have chosen and purchased your donkey, arrangements will obviously have to be made to transport him to your home. The seller may be able to assist you in arranging transport for your new donkey for a fee. Your actual presence when the donkey is unloaded will help create the right psychological effect in his new surroundings. Alternatively you will need to arrange for a livestock haulier to transport him or you might borrow or hire a trailer. If you are towing the trailer yourself then you must ensure that it is roadworthy and complies with transport and safety regulations, ie check the floor is sound, check tyres, brake lights, etc.

Before trying to load your donkey, lay some straw in the trailer as this helps to reduce the noise of the donkey's hoofs on the floor which might alarm him. The chances that you will buy a trained donkey who jumps into a waggon or trailer without turning a hair are probably rather small.

The first thing to remember about loading a donkey is that they are naturally very cautious, especially about where they put their feet. This is logical even though frustrating to the human in charge. If your donkey refuses to load straight away let him smell and examine the vehicle. When he is through he

> **Street-wise**
>
> One spring morning on walking through the office I found a visitor having a rather embarrassing bruise treated. Apparently she had been nipped by a donkey in a rather unfortunate place whilst walking through the fields which prompted the following lines:
> When walking through fields in which donkeys reside,
> Keep your face to the donkeys and not your backside.

will let you know either by losing interest and trying to walk away or by loading promptly. Only when he has thoroughly examined the vehicle do you attempt your persuasion.

The second thing to remember about loading a donkey is do not frighten him. You can try to entice him by putting some hay in the vehicle, well forward, or by placing a bowl of his favourite treats and moving it forward as he feeds. If his hoofs make a noise on the loading ramp try putting down rubber matting or an old carpet to deaden the sound. Use a long lead rope attached to the halter and walk your donkey to the ramp. Loop the lead rope around something strong at the front of the trailer and bring the end back to you, where you stand beside the donkey. Keep the rope taut and his head towards the vehicle. If someone can put the donkey's front feet, one at a time, on the ramp or floor of the vehicle this will help. Many donkeys will go only so far and then stop. When this happens be sure to keep the rope tight to hold the ground you have gained. Then put your shoulder under the donkey's rump and simply heave

CONFORMATION POINTS

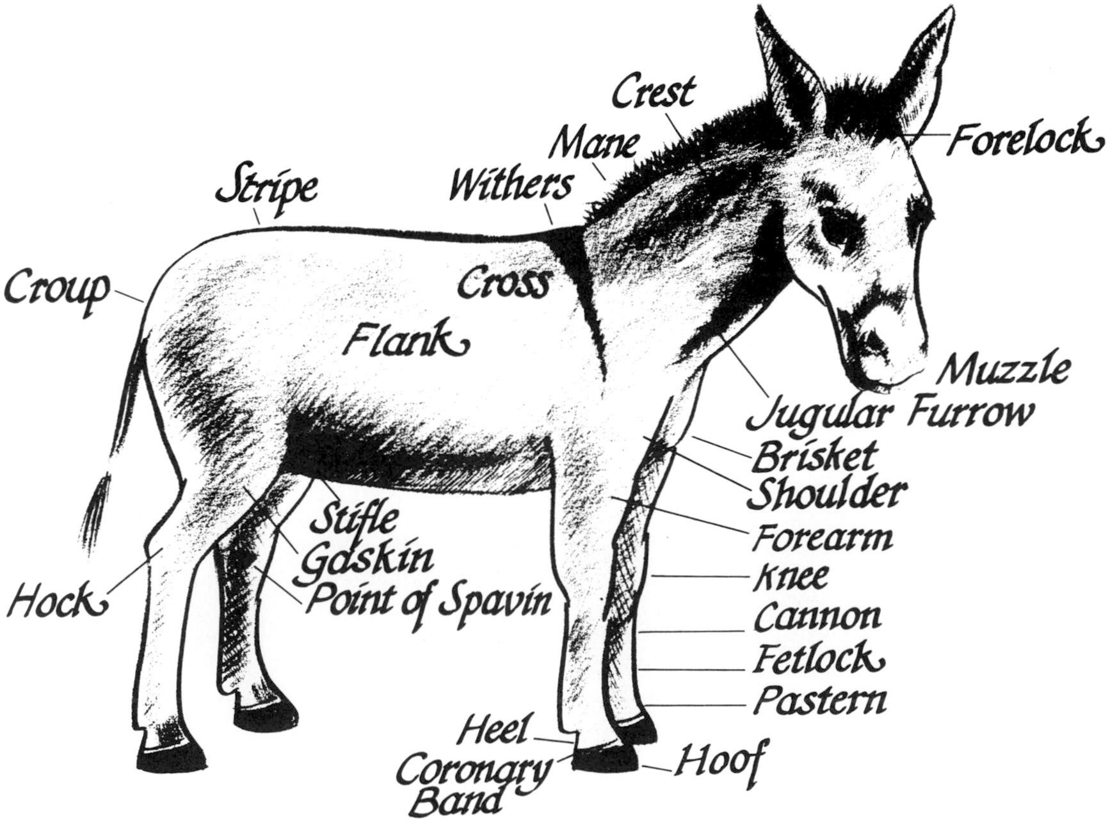

Crest
Mane
Withers
Forelock
Stripe
Cross
Croup
Flank
Muzzle
Jugular Furrow
Brisket
Shoulder
Stifle
Gaskin
Point of Spavin
Forearm
Knee
Hock
Cannon
Fetlock
Pastern
Heel
Coronary
Band
Hoof

him into the trailer – it helps to have an assistant pull from the front, of course. Give him verbal encouragement all the time and when you have loaded your donkey make sure you give him plenty of praise.

If the donkey is particularly difficult, two strong people simply link hands behind the donkey's rump and heave him in that way. Alternatively, two people can hold both ends of a rope, or lunge rein, put it around the donkey's thighs and then around a strong point in the trailer and heave him in. It is best to have a third person to put the animal's feet on the ramp or floor if this method is used. Remember to allow yourself plenty of time and keep calm.

Once the ramp is securely fastened your donkey will be happier untied so that he can move into the most comfortable position. Drive smoothly and cautiously, particularly around bends and do not brake suddenly. Check your donkey periodically and ensure that he is travelling well. If you have to undergo a long journey then do not forget to offer him water.

BODY

When first looking at a donkey, stand back and look for balance and symmetry in his general appearance. Everything should blend well: head length and proportion; length of back and legs; length of rump; depth of body; length of neck, etc. If the animal looks unbalanced because he is thin you can make allowances for that.

The withers (top of shoulder where the cross is) do not protrude in donkeys like they do in horses, but if some wither shows it is so much the better as a saddle will sit better if you want your donkey for riding. The back should be strong, whether long or short, and have a gentle dip. A donkey's back is straighter than a horse's back. A donkey will sometimes have a very dipped back and this is usually from many years of foal bearing or from a severe injury perhaps from being ridden much too early. Sometimes the line of the back will stick up in a convex manner, this is called a roach back and must be avoided in a riding or show donkey but for a pet or driving animal is acceptable. The length of the back should be in proportion to the animal's height. Many donkeys have backs that seem too long to a horseman's eye. It has been discovered by actual measurement, that if that particular animal had upstanding withers such as a horse has, the back would appear short! So just make sure the loin area is fairly broad and strong and not dipped and weak.

The line of the flank should be low and the tail set fairly high. The top line of the croup (top of rump) should not slope down at an acute angle in a 'goose rump' to the tail setting and should not have a high peak at its highest point. Such peaks are usually disguised fairly well by fat if the peak is not very pronounced. This is a typical donkey feature and is due to the pelvis of the donkey being a different shape from that of the flat-crouped pony or horse.

The shoulder area should be clean cut (not smothered in fat) and as sloping as possible although straight shoulders are normal in donkeys as they are in draught horses. The chest and ribs should be deep and rounded for heart and lung room. Flat sides are a very common defect in donkeys. The breast, the part of the chest seen from the front, should be relatively wide in proportion to the animal, a weak and narrow chest is a common fault and undesirable from the point of weight-carrying ability and endurance.

HEAD

The head should be short rather than too long and in proportion, wide between the eyes with a tapering muzzle and firm lips with large open nostrils. The profile should be straight or slightly dipped. Jaws and teeth must meet properly and not be under- or overshot (parrot mouthed). Features should be well defined and the eyes large, free of blemishes and of a kind or mild expression unless the animal is frightened. Eyes should be set low, wide apart and be clear and healthy looking. Upper jaws should be strong, generous, open and round with good width between them on the underside. The head should be deep through the

Continued overleaf/

Conformation Points cont'd

jaws, tapering to a fairly small muzzle. Remember that donkeys have larger heads in proportion to their size than horses or ponies but the head should look correct on the donkey and not be so big as to be out of proportion. Ears should be long, clean cut, set upright and firm. Notched ears, lop ears or broken ears should be avoided for show donkeys but do not stop a donkey from making a suitable pet.

NECK

The donkey's neck is entirely different from that of the horse. Due to a difference in muscle structure the top line of the neck in the normal mature donkey is straight. A truly arched neck is not normal as it would be in the horse. Young animals' necks may be more arched due to less muscle development. The donkey will also have a 'sausage roll' of muscle on the very top of his neck. In fat or older donkeys, or donkeys that have been obese and lost weight, this roll will get very large as it is a storage area for fat. If allowed to grow too big the 'crest' will be inclined to fall over to the side. The condition breaks down the cartilage that holds this area in place and if allowed to go too far cannot be corrected even if the donkey loses weight. The neck and head should be in proper proportion to each other and to the don-key. A heavy head needs a thicker neck than a light head. The neck should tend towards being long and refined rather than short and thick. A short, thick neck makes the animal more difficult to control when turning and stopping.

Some donkeys have a 'ewe' neck. That means it is too thin to be in proportion to the head and has a pronounced concavity in the top line. Do not buy a donkey with this fault as it is a real weakness besides being highly unattractive. A few donkeys have a very pronounced dip in the neck just in front of the withers. This is quite unsightly and shows a lack of muscle development but if your animal is not going to be a show donkey it does not matter in any practical way. A well shaped and strong neck will allow the animal to hold his head up alertly. When the donkey you are inspecting is walking on the lead at his ease, or in the pasture, watch the natural head carriage closely. Do not buy a donkey that walks with his head down all the time or with his neck stretched out but look for one that holds his head up and looks alert and active.

HINDQUARTERS

These should be as long from hip bone to point of hip (just by the tail where the bone sticks out) as possible and as flat on top as is consistent with normal donkey conformation. Viewed from the

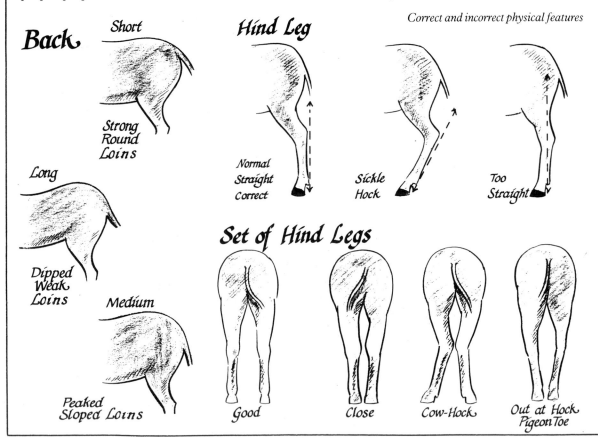

Correct and incorrect physical features

Back — Short, Strong Round Loins, Long, Dipped Weak Loins, Medium, Peaked Sloped Loins

Hind Leg — Normal Straight Correct, Sickle Hock, Too Straight

Set of Hind Legs — Good, Close, Cow-Hock, Out at Hock Pigeon Toe

Correct and incorrect physical features

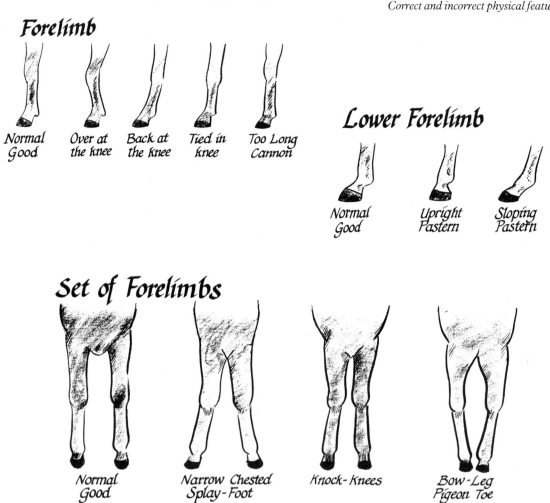

Forelimb

Normal Good

Over at the knee

Back at the knee

Tied in knee

Too Long Cannon

Lower Forelimb

Normal Good

Upright Pastern

Sloping Pastern

Set of Forelimbs

Normal Good

Narrow Chested Splay-Foot

Knock-Knees

Bow-Leg Pigeon Toe

rear the wider and thicker all parts of the quarters and upper legs are, the better. Many donkeys have upper thighs that are flat and lack any decent muscling. This is commonly found in most working donkeys in the Middle East but you still do not want to see it in your donkey.

LEGS

Legs are very important in working equines and also in ones that will be shown in halter classes. The straighter the legs and the heavier in bone the better. Keep in mind that even baby donkeys should have their hoofs rasped and kept level from birth so that they do not grow up with preventable leg faults that would have been kept at bay by proper vitamins and nutrition and proper foot care! If the animal has long overgrown hoofs, it is possible that over a period of time they can be corrected by a good farrier but much depends on the amount of leg twisting and bone damage the neglect has allowed to take place. If you are in

doubt have the animal examined by a vet and/or a good farrier before you purchase. If you are purchasing the animal for riding purposes then it would be most advisable to look for hoofs of good quality.

The hoofs should be rather narrow with a good cup in the sole, a good healthy frog and note that the donkey stands at a much more upright angle on his hoofs than a horse does. The hoofs should be hard yet elastic, clean, smooth and tough. They should be in proportion to the size of the donkey. Donkey hoofs are narrow but adequate with no tendency to low heels. The front foot should be oval, the hind foot more elongated, the frog small but well developed and not trimmed away except to take off ragged edges.

Donkeys' legs should be straight and true with adequate bone in proportion to the animal. Knees should be flat and wide; cannon bones short; hocks set low and strong, clean and correct in shape.

Thereby Hangs a Tail

ALFRED

One of the donkeys collected from the Reading sanctuary after the death of the owner, Miss Philpin, was one I named 'Alfred' after Alfred the Great. At that time he was the biggest donkey we had taken into the sanctuary and apart from his hoofs, which were badly in need of a trim, he was in fairly good condition. Although large, he could be described as almost elegant. He had excellent manners, always carried himself well and was a perfect gentleman with the farrier.

Shortly after his arrival, my ideas for putting handicapped children and donkeys together for their mutual benefit got under way and Alfred, partly because of his size and partly because of his good manners, was chosen for the trial. He proved absolutely wonderful. The children adored Alfred and Alfred adored the children.

In those days, before we built our centre, we would take the donkeys out to the children at their schools. We had a wonderful team including Alfred, Violetta, Solo and Pedro. An excellent horsewoman called Vanadia Sandon-Humphries agreed to take charge of the riding on the visits. Volunteers from the village of Salcombe Regis and from Sidmouth joined us to make a team, and because our farm was Slade House we decided to name the new charity the Slade Centre. We visited five schools in the Exeter, Exmouth and Honiton districts and each visit was quite a day for us all!

The children shrieked with joy when the waggon ramp came down and the donkeys came out. To many it was the event of the week. Noddy (as we all affectionately called Vanadia) was patience itself, tacking up the donkeys and organising the rides. We were very careful to give the donkeys plenty of rest and Alfred found one way to get his reward.

We had not realised that Violetta was in season and were happily relaxing having a cup of coffee with the staff at Withycombe House, Exmouth, when one of the children said, 'Look, Miss, Alfred's having a ride.' We all looked at the donkeys, loosely tied and grazing, still tacked up under the shade of the hedge, and there was Alfred, front hoofs neatly tucked into Violetta's stirrups, attending to his male instincts! Although a gelding, no one seemed to have told Alfred, but he was most dignified in his retreat!

The children's joy turned to sadness in the winter when the rides had to stop, but in December 1978, the Slade Centre opened, with its super play area and riding arena designed for the comfort of donkeys and children alike. Now the rides can take place six days a week, fifty-two weeks of the year. There is a team of fifteen donkeys who are all specially trained and who really enjoy giving rides, but Alfred is still the favourite.

One day, the supervisor, Mrs Pat Feather told me a fantastic story. Alfred was the second in line of five donkeys giving rides to children from Ellen Tinkham School. The children were severely disabled and to encourage them to bend and to co-ordinate arm and eye one of the many games we use had been set up. Propped against the rail on the left-hand side of the arena were a number of addressed envelopes and on the other side of the arena was a letter box. The child had to stop the donkey, pick up the letter, ride around the arena and post it at the other side.

Alfred's rider was severely crippled and, despite very real attempts, the child could not pick up the envelope. After the child had failed at the third attempt, Alfred turned his head round and grasped the envelope firmly in his teeth then, to everyone's amazement, he carried his rider to the letter box and stopped with the envelope only inches from the hole! After a ride, each child is encouraged to love their donkey and Alfred had a very special 'love' that day.

The Grass is Greener

In County Mayo there is a legend with regard to a donkey owned by an old lady. The only food the donkey received during the week was the grass he could find by the roadside.

However, on Sundays the moment the donkey heard the bell for mass he would run to the gates of the church grounds. The gates were only open during the service but it gave the donkey ample chance to have a feast of fresh green grass! The donkey became well known and was always allowed to enjoy his Sunday lunch.

Eeyore on another adventure

HOW GREEN WAS MY MISSUS

Dear Ethel

Another year gone by, another birthday. Thirty-six and still going strong. I felt I must drop you a line to let you know I'm still in the land of the living. Teeth not exactly pearly, tail a bit moth-eaten, eyesight not what it was, but who cares? The men folk around now just don't give a thrill like they used to do. Good food and a warm bed are what I go for these days.

Remember, Ethel, when we were younger – we showed them didn't we? We've trained a few humans in our time. My Missus was about as green as they come, donkey-wise. It's taken quite a while for her to twig all the tricks. Now when I want an extra mouthful she says: 'Give over putting on "the poor old donkey act". I know what you're after, and it won't work.'

When Paddy, my youngest, got to the adolescent stage and sex raised its ugly head, Missus sent for the vet. 'Oh, give the little fella a chance,' says he. 'Chance,' I thought, 'you don't know much.' I knew his dad's family, all the same they were. Two foals Paddy got himself and him still wet behind the ears. Green as the hills of Killarney. They thought because I gave him the edge of my teeth when he tried anything funny I could keep my eye on him all the time. Teenagers are all the same these days, nothing but a worry. That vet's come to his cake and milk, I can tell you. He caught on early. I heard him say:

Pick your own!

Drunken Donkeys

A publican wanted his donkey to come to the sanctuary as the field at the back of the pub had been taken over by the council for road widening. It wasn't the fact that the donkey had to come in that brought a smile but the request that the donkey should be given a pint of beer each day as he had developed a tremendous liking for it and wandered into the pub regularly for his pint.

The staff at the sanctuary could not believe it but after the donkey arrived his frequent braying told us that something wasn't quite right. We tried him with his pint of beer and what a change, he became gentle and placid and everybody could handle him. However, within twenty-four hours he was ranting round his stable again and impossible to cope with. Once again a pint of beer produced a gentle placid donkey and we realised that we had our first genuine alcoholic on our hands!

It took three months to wean the boozer from his beer by gradually giving him less and less each day and then adding water to make it weaker. But we managed; since then we have had two more alcoholic donkeys, including one called Bracken who could drink a whole pint without taking his lips off the glass and no matter where he was in the field he would gallop across at the clink of a pint mug.

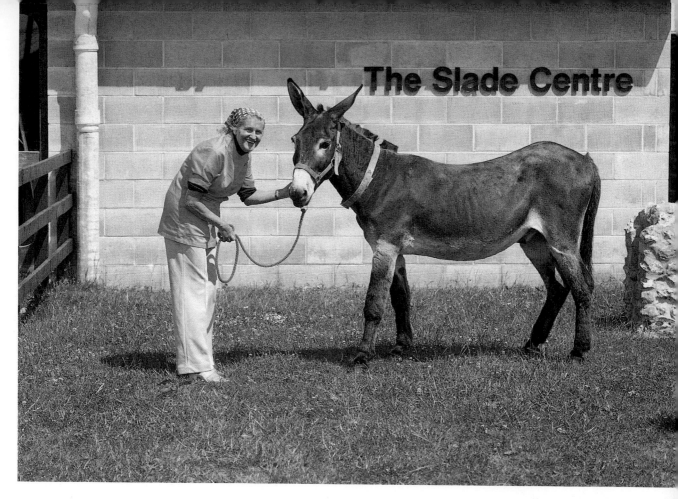

Alfred the post-donkey with Elisabeth Svendsen

'Everytime I come to this place I learn something. I always did think donkeys worked things out.' Thinks I: 'You don't know the half of it Buster.' Does he Eth?

I used to be very good at the toe-crushing game. I'm not so accurate with the footwork myself now but I've trained some right good hoofs among the younger end to judge by the howls that go up. They haven't got the 'whose foot?' expression right yet – but I live in hope!

Missus learned pretty quick about not leaving loaded barrows and tools around. Will you ever forget the gang of Irish labourers who came to put up that fence across the top field for the county council? I felt they would know about us from the brogue I heard. Missus did warn them but they took no notice. I thought she was a bit of a spoil-sport really. I can see them now when our mob got to work. Young Seamus was a credit to me with that box of nails. He fairly hurled them across the field and Paddy's grip on their hammer handle had to be seen to be believed. I didn't do so badly myself, but I was more subtle. I waited till they'd finished before I did my back-scratching act. I always was partial to new posts. Those weren't up to standard actually, they practically all collapsed before I'd got halfway through my routine.

I don't give rides anymore when the children come, but I insist on taking part. After all, if I didn't walk up and down beside them some of the younger donkeys might go too far and give longer rides. That would never do. Sixpenny worth is what they got when we were young and not a step more. Never mind

Sparkle enjoying a good joke

that we're doing it for love, give an inch and they'll take a mile. Inflation is for girths not donkey rides. That's another trick Missus is on to as well and I used to love seeing the saddles slide to the ground!

My greatest triumph I reckon, was the night Missus got home and we'd demolished that post and rail round the copse. I did keep her company though, she wasn't what you'd call sweet tempered and she didn't seem to appreciate the loving butts I kept giving her. When it was nearly finished, the phone rang and she rushed off to the house. I only went inside the rails to see what it was like from the other side, how was I to know it was hard to see a brown donkey among the trees when it was nearly dark? I didn't tell her to finish the fence with me inside. I was really crushed when she left me there, and when she'd counted noses in the stables and came back to find me, she

BARNABY

My name is Barnaby, I was born in May 1970 and six months later I joined the Jefferson family at Woodlands Kennels. Their donkey Rebecca had just died and was badly missed; as they fell in love with me on sight I became theirs. It was winter, so I was given a little barn knee deep in straw in the kennel yard and was not put out to join the family pony until spring. That was their undoing! I learned all about dogs during these months as I was allowed to 'help' with the chores. I inspected each kennel every morning and drove the kennel maids mad by picking up their bucket or brush and wandering up the yard swinging it expertly.

I got on well with all the family dogs although the boarders were sometimes a little taken aback, never having seen a donkey before. My mum always says I think I am a dog! Father reckons I am a clown (I wonder what he means), I know I am the most handsome adorable treasured creature in the world because Mum never tires of telling me. It was great fun when I was put in the field with Billy. I loved racing up and down the hilly bits but I soon tired of this and would put on my 'poor little deserted me' voice and, sure enough, someone would come running over to take me back into the garden. Eventually the children outgrew the pony and he was sent to live with a family with younger children. I was given another donkey for company, I ask you! Do I need any more company?

Dusty was an escapologist! He taught me to get through the eye of a needle (so Mum said). He led me across the river and we lost count of the times the family had to come and collect us. Dusty left and things went back to normal.

Time passed and the children left home. Last year Mum and Dad (probably feeling their age)

decided to semi-retire and we all moved 5 miles to a country filling station. It's super, most days I am tethered on the front lawn where everybody can make a fuss of me. Mum was a little worried at first as I'd never been tethered before but I took to it like a duck to water and am very proud of my new collar made especially for me by the blacksmith.

A neighbour rides her hunters past our garden and the first time they heard me these huge creatures nearly jumped out of their skins. I can't understand why as I was only giving them a cheery greeting in my sweetest voice. They're used to me now and I don't call so loudly.

Of course my family needed my help on the forecourt and the editor of our local newspaper was delighted to print a picture of me in action on the front page! One of the nicest things to have happened recently was the arrival of a little grand-daughter in the family. We are all quite besotted and I am very happy to have her sit on my back. As she's only nine months old I'm not allowed to carry her on my own but soon we will have great fun together. Who knows, there may be several more to carry around the lanes on summer days.

I celebrated my thirteenth birthday recently. It doesn't seem so long ago since I went on picnics with the children – me eating jam butties, and the children eating the carrots! Happy days.

Barnaby (The Silkman), Mr and Mrs J. B. Jefferson, *Donkey Breed Society Magazine*

Barnaby helping out at the family's garage forecourt

wasn't at all pleased that she had to take down a whole section to let me out. After all, how could she expect a poor old donkey like me to step over anything higher than six inches. Well, not unless there was something really green and lucious like roses on the other side and those words she used – not for lady donkeys' ears!

Still and all, Ethel old friend, our humans will never take away our finest *pièce de resistance*. Is there a more delicious sensation when we've been washed and brushed and curried and combed than that glorious wet mud?

Happy rollings, old girl, and many of them.
With love – your friend

Tara

MISTY

Donkeys generally hate living alone, they love company of their own sort and they love the company of people. As young animals, they are very active and play for hours. In the wilds of South America the behaviour of the younger members of the feral herds is entrancing. During the cooler hours of the day, they form into groups and the young stallions will play out the battles which will become real in later life. They spend an amazing length of time on their hind legs, forelegs locked round each

Misty – dreaming about his favourite television programme!

WAS IT ALTERNATIVE MEDICINE?

Christmas Day 1977 arrived and my husband and I were confined to bed with influenza. In our house it was customary to exchange presents as soon as we woke up on Christmas morning. My husband said, 'I know you think I have not bought you a present, but if you can crawl to the window, you will see your present.' I could not believe it, standing underneath the bedroom window with the farmer from down the lane stood this little donkey. As it was Christmas Day there was only one name for him, Joseph.

My husband knew nothing about donkeys and had experienced difficulty in trying to buy one at this time. He was offered one in foal if he could catch her but he finally heard of a dealer who had a young gelding for sale about 45 miles away. He had only seen the young donkey by the light of a lantern. The dealer's story was that he had come over from Ireland with two other donkeys for a medical school and he was the wrong blood group – a dealer's sales talk, no doubt.

Arrangements for the donkey's journey from the dealer on Christmas Eve were uneventful, he was quiet, the only acclaim he made was a loud hee-haw outside a well-known prison. He spent the night at the neighbouring farm with the cows; this was where his attachment to cows started.

Some years ago I had a fracture involving my left knee joint. The movements in this joint have never been perfect since. About two and a half years ago it became very stiff and painful with limited movement. I was referred to a well-known London hospital, investigations and X-rays were carried out, and the consultant orthopaedic surgeon said it was worn out and nothing could be done for it.

Eighteen months passed and one evening I fetched Joseph in from the field where the farmer allows him to be with the cows. Routine general health care was being carried out as usual on Joseph and, most unusual for him, he kicked out with his left foot and made a direct hit on my worn-out knee! The pain was excruciating, I leaned up against the stable wall and as I live alone I wondered how I would get back to the house. After a while I gently put my foot down, to see if I could bear weight on it, and to my surprise I found it was much easier to bend and straighten the joint. Gradually it improved as the days passed and although it is not 100 per cent, it is great to be able to walk up and down stairs correctly, to get in and out of the bath and to be able to kneel to pray.

Was Joseph meant to have a hand in medical matters? Was the knee manipulation alternative medicine and surely a saving on the National Health Service?

Irene Williams, *Donkey Breed Society Magazine*

Joseph

Eeyore Does it Again

It was 7.30 on a fine mid-July evening. Most of the visitors had left for their respective homes and on the way down to the goyle I was met by a rather red-faced gentleman of about twenty-five years of age, obviously out of breath. 'Oh dear,' he said, 'this is most embarrassing. One of your donkeys has taken my wife's t-shirt and we can't get it back.'

Together we went down to the goyle. It was no surprise to see the remains of a white t-shirt stretched out between the teeth of Eeyore and Pancho who both looked extremely pleased with this new game. It was a little reluctantly that I took the t-shirt away from the pair of them and spoilt their fun. Turning to the now calmer gentleman and asking him where his wife was, he pointed to the field shelter. There, amongst the donkeys, stood a young lady, equally as red-faced as her husband and the reason for their embarrassment was obvious – she was naked from the waist up!

They had enjoyed a walk down to the beach and finding themselves alone the wife had decided to sunbathe topless. It was their first visit to the sanctuary and not having heard of the exploits of Eeyore they had innocently stood talking and stroking the donkeys when Eeyore had pounced, taken the t-shirt and galloped away.

In reply to their thanks for services rendered I told them the pleasure was all mine!

Neil Harvey
Donkey Sanctuary employee

other's shoulders, moving slowly around. The winner of the mock battle will often gallop off with a triumphant bray. Very often it is the lonely stallions who are the noisiest and this was the reason why Misty joined us.

Misty had excellent owners, a kind caring family with children, who spent every spare moment with him. When dad was gardening, there was always a carrot or a biscuit as he finished one chore and went on to the next and Misty would stand in his paddock watching him, quietly and happily waiting.

Unfortunately for Misty his paddock was surrounded by other houses but as long as he could see activity in his house he was content. The problem came when the family wanted to go out. No sooner had the family car driven away than 'eeyore, eeyore', blared forth, and the unfortunate occupiers of the other houses suffered until the family returned and peace was restored.

The family began to receive complaints, at first almost laughingly given, but gradually the atmosphere changed and Misty began to be an embarrassment. Then the family had a bright idea! When they had to go out they moved the television set to the lounge window overlooking the paddock and turned it on at half volume! The change was fantastic. Misty, with his chin propped on the rails, would follow every second of every programme, ears twitching, tail swishing, whether in approval or disapproval no one ever knew, until the family returned and he settled happily for the night.

The problem was solved until the family needed a holiday and, hoping against hope that Misty would be all right in the care of one of the now friendly neighbours, the family left him without the TV set! To Misty the week was a nightmare. No family to talk to or give him titbits. No television to watch. He quickly became frustrated, bored and finally naughty. He leant over the neighbours' fencing pulling out plants by the roots, he pushed at garden fences until they sagged and he trotted round and round the field braying pathetically during the long hours of the night.

A deputation of grim neighbours met the family on their return – there could be no reprieve – Misty must go or the family leave. A tearful call to us explained the situation and it seemed Misty was in need of help. We did point out that we could not offer a stable with TV but we hoped the friendship of other donkeys would prove acceptable and within twenty-four hours Misty had arrived. There was no doubt the neighbours had a point. His bray was loud and a deafened unhappy family left him with us. After a few hours to get over the journey, he was introduced to Maxi with whom he became friends.

No donkey can remain a stallion at the sanctuary, for obvious reasons, so five weeks after his arrival he was castrated. Misty recovered from his operation very quickly and, as so often happens, his temperament began to change from rampant stallion to quieter gelding. He began to take a great interest in his surroundings and loved the frequent visitors to the sanctuary. His recovery box had high beams and it was amusing to see him let the hens and cockerels use his back as a half-way house to the rafters on their way up to safe perching at night.

Now Misty has grown from the young fifteen month-old stallion on arrival to a handsome gelding. He is still with his friend on Brookfield Farm where he has many other companions and acres to play in. He doesn't need to bray anymore, he is never lonely and has quietened down and become a normal donkey. When his family visit him they hardly recognise the quiet, happy, gentle donkey he has become. There is a far away look in his eyes when they pet him, perhaps he is thinking of the TV programmes he is now missing?

They Shall Eat Cake

One group of donkeys arrived at the sanctuary in a terrible state. One of them, Bilko, was suffering from severe rickets and malnutrition. The driver having unloaded them said, 'The owner has sent them in with a large load of cake for you, Mrs Svendsen.' We refer to cake normally as pony nuts or feed of this kind and, on opening the two large crates, it was shattering to be faced with loads of chocolate cake, Battenburg, ginger cake and to suddenly realise that, in all good faith, this person had been feeding Bilko and her friends on nothing but cake for the last year, thus their terrible state.

Ridicule

In England, bankrupts in the sixteenth century were placed on donkeys face to tail and apparently, at a later date, so were henpecked husbands.

Your donkey may not always be quite as co-operative as you might wish . . .

GEORGE

We first heard about George in July 1980. He had been rescued by a vicar living near Windsor, who, to put it mildly, had been sadly misled over the needs of the donkey. When he bought the donkey, to save him from slaughter, he was told that he only needed the feet trimmed twice a year and two scoops of pony nuts a day was all the donkey required. No mention was made of the amount of land needed to keep the donkey, worming or the need for shelter, adequate fencing, nor the fact that single donkeys do tend to get very lonely and therefore it is best to keep two.

Despite great care from the vicar and his family, George became difficult and a call for help was made to the sanctuary. It was our field inspector who made the first inspection. She immediately realised that George was very lonely and this was the reason for the problems his owners were experiencing. Unfortunately, as they didn't have sufficient acreage, it was impossible to suggest that he had a friend to live with him, which would have solved the problem. She had no option but to recommend that he came to the sanctuary. The family were very concerned as they felt they had failed George in some way and they were genuinely sad and unhappy to see him go. However, the fact that he was coming to the sanctuary where he could possibly be trained to work with the disabled children at the Slade Centre was some consolation.

George arrived with the usual characteristics of donkeys who have been on their own – he was aggressive, difficult to handle and brayed frequently – but in a very short time he had settled down. George's owners thought he was about eleven years old but he was in fact correctly aged at almost twenty-two. This made him too old to be suitable for training at the Slade Centre and for two years he joined the group of donkeys known as 'Boys' Group' at Brookfield Farm.

After two years George was completely settled at Brookfield: a good strong donkey but one who obviously liked individual attention and he was always following the manager around. Because of this and his excellent condition, as well as the fact that he had made no particular friend and seemed to prefer humans, George was put up for consideration when a very good home was offered at Chiselborough in Somerset. There were already two horses, called Breeze and Rocky, and in view of the fact that before George had been rescued by the vicar he had been in a group with five horses, we decided he could possibly be tried in this new home. Mrs Cade, who offered the home, had been in contact with us for some time and was obviously a very knowledgeable person and had been a contributor to the Donkey Sanctuary for several years. Having received a most enthusiastic report from our inspector, Mr Judge, we sent George to Chiselborough, where he caused great changes for everybody.

Mrs Cade thoroughly enjoyed taking George out for walks and they soon became a regular sight walking together through the lanes of Somerset. Mrs Cade, being well under 50kg (112lb) decided she would like to ride George and wrote to the vicar to enquire if George had previously been ridden or driven. The vicar was delighted to hear from the new owner and see that George was doing so well. He replied: 'By very tortuous investigations (via the pub!) I find George has been ridden – quite a long time ago – but not driven.' The earlier walks and commands he had learnt, such as 'walk on', 'whoa', 'stand' and 'trot on' stood him in good stead. A donkey does not need to be 'broken' and will usually allow rides to anyone of a suitable weight without fuss.

The riding skills required by the rider are exactly those for a pony. Many donkeys join riding classes in local shows and can even complete hurdle races with great credit. Young members of hunts occasionally join on well-trained donkeys and once the horses are used to the strange participant, they take little notice. Mrs Cade and George developed the most wonderful relationship as described in her letter:

George had his greatest success so far on 10 July at Chiselborough Fete, when he entered the pet show and fancy hat competition. With regard to the latter, we tried on the hat unadorned first (ear holes cut out) to see if it would worry George at all. He appeared to love it, and so it was trimmed. It was an imitation straw, black, with floppy brim. When George moved his ears the brim fell foward and although this looked rather rakish it no doubt partially obstructed his vision. We folded back the brim and white lace was sewn all round with a lace rose on top of the crown and a beige rose in front. George wore it all afternoon, and when my husband, Eric, took him back to the paddock, he said George was reluctant to have the hat removed!

As I was in the tea tent all afternoon washing up, Clare, aged 13, took George in the pet show and Eric took him in to the fancy hat competition. George won first prize – a lovely red rosette – for being the best-behaved animal in the show. As he was competing with dogs, cats, rabbits, guinea pigs, gerbils and tortoises we are wondering how the behaviour of the tortoises was judged! Apparently the pet show was next to the coconut shy and George stood by this with sounds like cannon balls exploding around him, without turning a hair. For the fancy hat competition Eric had to lead George round and round with the Stoke Silver Band in full blast. Here George was given 50p and instructions not to fritter it away on ginger biscuits!

The very generous paddock in which George was kept was almost his undoing, however, as donkeys do tend to eat more than they require and George began to get fatter and fatter and his stomach began to sag and sag until a comment of 'When is she due to foal?' persuaded Mrs Cade that the time had come to slim him down again. George was put on stricter rations. The apples in the orchard did cause one or two problems. Mrs Cade used to pick the apples by climbing up onto the loose-box roof via a ladder and one day while she was rather perilously picking, she heard a terrible clatter and, looking down, saw George had knocked away the metal ladder. He was standing looking at her in some amazement sitting on top of the roof and as she knew the baker was due in forty minutes, Mrs Cade felt the situation was rather embarrassing. Luckily for her, a friend called round in the nick of time, the ladder was replaced and dignity restored.

Eventually it was decided that George should be trained to pull a small cart. The many walks on the roads had provided good background training and a beautiful little float with side seats and a door at the back with a step up was purchased. Six months later the basic training was over and they were both able to set off with a reasonable chance of a relaxing drive. To help the Slade Centre, an impressive open day, named Fiesta, is held every second year. Over 6,000 people attend and generally at least £3,000 net profit is made. Large colourful Fiesta posters are printed and Mrs Cade pinned one of these on the back of the cart and made a practice of going out on the B3165 every Saturday morning. As she said, this gave George some practice with heavy traffic and, as they had to stay behind for some time, drivers had plenty of opportunity to read the Fiesta poster.

By this time Mrs Cade had joined the Donkey Breed Society and so she went to the Bath and West Show to watch the donkeys and the driving. She was interested to compare the brays heard here with those of George because by now she was getting complaints from the villagers that they hadn't heard George braying, as apparently the

George in his special fancy hat

whole village used to enjoy this. Mrs Cade wrote regularly and we were most amused to hear that one day, proceeding sedately along the B3165, they rounded a corner to find a combine harvester advancing towards them. The driver sensibly stopped and turned off his engine; George apparently also stopped and turned off his engine and totally refused to move either forwards or back, which caused an immediate traffic jam. Mrs Cade, realising an impasse had been reached, gave George a flick with the whip on his shoulder, and – whether from outrage or astonishment – George moved forward immediately. As Mrs Cade says, she admits there wasn't much room to pass but didn't think George really needed to attempt to scale the bank. However, eventually everything was straightened out again and, as they passed the cavalcade behind the combine, one man put his head out of the window and said: 'That was well worth waiting for.' Apparently George and owner drove on with heads held high.

This road seemed to be their *bête noire*, as, on a further occasion, just when Mrs Cade thought she had met all road hazards possible, she found she had overlooked pneumatic drills. Rounding a corner, they came across a team of men repairing the road with a pneumatic drill going full blast. George came to a sudden halt and the operator very kindly stopped too. However, just after the float had passed, the pneumatic drill started again and, according to Mrs Cade: 'George shot forward like a kangaroo and this activitity continued most of the way up to Norton High Street.'

Frequent letters from Mrs Cade, all amusing, go to show us how many people are helping the donkeys. Regular visits and reports from our inspectors show that George is not alone among the one thousand rehomed donkeys to be thoroughly enjoying his new life. Not only does he have everything he needs but he also has a permanent future guaranteed should he ever find himself in problems with his current owner.

The Donkey Sanctuary

In August 1969 an advertisement appeared in the Exeter *Express and Echo* 'Pedigree donkey mare for sale. Kennetbury Martha. Apply Mr Mogar.' The purchase of this donkey marked the beginning of the present day charity which has to date taken in over 4,000 donkeys and, according to the Charities Aid Foundation, has become the sixty-fourth largest charity out of the top 200 charities in the United Kingdom and there are now over 158,000.

THE EARLY YEARS

Kennetbury Martha (affectionately known as Naughty Face) immediately made herself at home in her 6 acre paddock of our large hotel. It soon became apparent that she was extremely lonely and in urgent need of a friend. For this reason a second donkey, Angelina, shortly joined her.

Learning about donkeys very quickly became a way of life and I became a member of the Donkey Breed Society and was eventually appointed as their area representative for the south-west. A property was purchased adjoining our hotel which had adequate stabling facilities and a breeding programme was started to improve the breed of the donkey in general. All went well until December 1970 when out of curiosity a visit was made to Exeter market on horse sale day. Past the pens of horses, some of whom looked superb and others frightened and in poor condition, right at the fringe of the covered pens where the waggons were unloading, were seven, small terrified donkeys crammed so tightly into a two-pony sized pen that they could hardly move. This sight not only was to change my life but also the lives of my family.

The condition of the donkeys was almost indescribable; their coats were long and full of lice, their feet overgrown and twisted and they were all, obviously, in a state of shock. Several rough-looking men were hanging over the rails. The price of the worst looking donkey was £45. The donkey looked as if it had only a few days to live and the price was obviously exorbitant. The donkeys rapidly changed hands and the new owner said '£55, sorry, but take it or leave it.' I walked away from the pen for a few minutes to try and collect my thoughts, before turning back just in time to see the last donkey driven out of the pen and into a lorry, tail twisted cruelly behind him to speed his departure. I had thought too long.

By chance, contact was made with the same donkeys once more but again help could not be given. We visited a skewbald

A new donkey arriving at the Salston Hotel

donkey mare after seeing an advertisement in the paper. She was in a small stable and not in very good condition. There were donkeys in the next stable but the man announced that the other donkeys were sold and he wasn't authorised to show us any more. After walking away, curiosity overcame us and we slipped into the next shed. In the dim light, packed in tightly, were about forty donkeys, all in appalling condition. They had no food and after breaking open four or five bales of hay lying nearby they started to munch with desperate eagerness. Absolutely sure that these were the donkeys from the market, we enquired the next day by telephone if it was possible to purchase any of these donkeys. We were told they were all sold to a donkey sanctuary.

Four months later a member of the Donkey Breed Society asked for help to obtain a family donkey, a grey mare of about five years old. As none of our members had one for sale, arrangements were made for a dealer to deliver a donkey to the Salston Hotel to ensure she was a sound purchase. She duly arrived and became terrified when approached. Deciding not to press my attentions, thinking it would be better for her to join the others for a feed at teatime, she was left. However, at feed time still she would not come and we went to bed without having touched her.

The donkeys were noisy in the early morning and they were standing by an inert grey form in the middle of the field. The donkey was lying stretched out, breathing shallowly and unable to get up. We carried her to the stable easily – she was virtually a living skeleton. We lay her on a deep layer of straw and covered her with a blanket. She was no longer frightened, she was too ill. She was fed watered-down milk with glucose from a spoon and an infra-red light was fixed up above her. The vet arrived in due course and shook his head sadly giving little hope. He

Goodnight Bray

There is nothing more satisfying at the end of a long, hard day than to do final rounds in the evening and to be greeted by a bray of welcome from every stall. Every donkey needs to be touched for a second and will then happily retire for a good night's sleep.

Naughty Face, who was responsible for starting everything

gave her a vitamin injection and promised to call the next day. After shaking out some fresh hay by the head of the donkey, we telephoned the dealer. He expressed great surprise, she was 'the best of the lot that arrived'. We wondered what the others were like!

Back in the shed, the donkey had her head up and to my great joy had a mouthful of hay! Kneeling beside her and brushing her gently, great handfuls of lice-infested hair came away and sore after sore became evident. By lunch-time, and winning on one side at least, the lice powder was surely taking effect. I wished I'd put some on myself! By evening she was standing up, shakily, but up, and the bran soaked in warm water and black treacle fed to her vanished quickly. My younger son, Clive, came in and said: 'She looks quite different now she's brushed out. Why don't we call her Smartie?' It was a long battle but we won and Smartie joined our herd.

The hotel proved a great advantage for the welfare of donkeys. Visitors seeing them in the field made enquiries and were almost always interested, contributing funds, too. Information began to come in as to where donkeys were in distress and an urgent call came on a boiling hot August day from a guest at the hotel who was visiting a local resort. I jumped into the car and arrived at the beach to find the hotel guest waiting anxiously. 'They've got her in the waggon just leaving', she said. After following the waggon for a few miles, it arrived at a rough field. The waggon was met by a man, obviously the owner, who started talking to the driver. He was large and rough. Together they climbed into the back of the lorry. On peering and asking 'Excuse me, is that your donkey?' a stream of bad language emerged to

A Nasty End

Many of you know that the fate of some of our long-eared friends is to be turned into salami and our attention has been brought to a brand on sale in this country. It was purchased in Thame and the brand name is 'Grand Saint Antoine Saucisson d'Arles'. Most salami is from other animals but unfortunately parts of the continent find horse and donkey very edible and donkey is listed as one of the ingredients of this brand.

the effect that she was a lazy bag and had ruined his day's trade. He struck her several times.

'If you strike her again, I'll kill you.' It stopped him, he laughed. It was an idle threat perhaps but I have never been able to accept violence towards defenceless creatures.

'I'll sell her for £40,' he said.

'I'll give you £35 delivered to the Salston Hotel.'

He lifted his stick again. 'All right, £40 but delivered.' My heart was making thumping noises but the donkey had lifted her head and was looking at me.

After making out a cheque and scribbling a receipt for him to sign, the driver set off for Ottery St Mary and with the truck safely gone I turned to the owner and said: 'I'll tell the RSPCA of this and if ever there's a repeat of this ill-treatment again I shall be back.'

After gently unloading the donkey, she was inspected by the vet. He shook his head: 'She's about forty-five years old and she's had a heart attack – I'll do my best but . . . ' In the same stable that Smartie had been nursed, the old lady fought for her life, and she *did* fight. She was spoon fed, had injections twice a day and, of course, hot bran mash with black treacle which she was able to enjoy! Three days later she was standing up in the yard. The guest who had rescued her came to have a look. 'She really is a lucky lady now,' she said, and Lucky Lady she became. She improved steadily but was not really able to hold her own with the other donkeys. My father-in-law was living on his own in Exeter and had a beautiful orchard, he offered to give Lucky Lady a home until she was able to fend for herself.

Herb with the donkeys

HOUSING PROBLEMS!

An elderly lady rang one night to say that she and her two spinster sisters were prepared to give a home to three donkeys with the assurance that they would be well looked after for the rest of their lives.

Their enormous house stood in beautiful grounds with fenced paddocks, walled gardens and a complete stable block built for ten racehorses. The original grooms, who kept the stables spotless, were still employed despite the fact that there had been no horses kept since their father had died fifteen years before! From the stable boy up (and he was in his mid-seventies) they would all love the donkeys and they would want for nothing. A better home couldn't be found for them!

Three geldings, Bill, Ben and Boots, were firm friends and these were selected for the three elderly ladies. They were duly delivered and received with all the love and attention they could wish for. Their first report was absolutely marvellous, each sister had her own favourite and the donkeys were as good as gold. It was a great relief to know they were settled, so a desperate telephone call in December came as a great surprise.

'I'm sorry, Mrs Svendsen, but you will have to take Bill and Ben back; they've got to be such naughty boys. Boots can stay, he's such a good little boy,' the voice continued, 'but we just cannot cope any longer with the other two.'

'I am sorry,' I said. 'What are they doing?'

'They have become so disobedient, Boots goes straight up the stairs when we tell him, but no matter how we push and pull, Bill and Ben refuse to go up. You know we are elderly ladies, Mrs Svendsen, we can't be expected to do such heavy work.'

'Did you say up the stairs?,' I asked.

'But of course . . . you don't think that we can lie upstairs in our warm beds at night and leave those three little pets in their stables, do you?' The slightly irate voice answered, 'It gets cold, you know – they use the guest bedroom.'

And so, regretfully, back came Bill and Ben, followed one month later by Boots, who ceased to be angelic when his little friends departed!

Note: In the very early days of the sanctuary the vital importance of donkeys staying together was not always recognised. Now donkeys only go out in pairs, even when accompanying a single horse or pony.

Where people have not tried to make the donkeys go upstairs to the bedroom, both man and beast have been happy!

THE DONKEY SANCTUARY GROWS

Becoming known locally as the 'Donkey Lady' and gaining an overnight reputation of being eccentric was not quite what one would desire! By now we seemed to have a sanctuary and information from the Donkey Breed Society and the press indicated there were two similar projects running: Miss Philpin's donkey sanctuary near Reading, a registered charity and Mr Lockwood at Godalming who was not registered.

We made an application to become a registered charity in October 1972 with me and my husband as trustees and with the approval of the Donkey Breed Society. John Lovell, a great friend and also a lawyer, coped with all the paperwork required and in March 1973 the South Western Donkey Sanctuary became registered.

We were still short of space and approached Mrs Judith Forbes the owner of a countryside park which had opened within a few miles of the hotel. If fencing and some buildings were put up she would be prepared to let 5ha (12 acres) of land for the fitter donkeys to roam on.

On returning to the hotel my husband was staring miserably at a set of figures for the year's turnover. It was quite obvious what was happening: any profit made from the hotel was quite literally being eaten by the donkeys. There were not sufficient funds to do the necessary fencing at the countryside park in Farway and unless finances were organised for the donkeys no more could be taken in. Three more stables were desperately needed at Salston Close and the first fencing quotation amounted to £600. Suddenly help appeared. Rosalind de Wesselow a fellow member of the Donkey Breed Society had a good friend, Colonel Gerald Critchley of the Home of Rest for Horses. They also had a great interest in donkeys and thanks to Rosalind's help, the home very kindly agreed to pay the fencing costs! That gave us the encouragement so badly needed to keep going.

At this time the *Down Your Way* team from the long-established radio programme arrived in Ottery. They did an interview which focussed the attention of donkey lovers throughout the country on the work we were struggling to do on our own. One result of the programme was that five more donkeys arrived, their owners having taken note of our address! One donkey was a walking skeleton, she became Twiggy, naturally! She arrived as the new isolation block of stables was being built. Each new arrival seemed to spread a different ailment around our population and it seemed new families of lice were ready and willing to change owners at a minute's notice. A system was developed so that each arrival was put in the isolation block for a period of three weeks.

In the early seventies contact was made with Violet Philpin who ran the donkey sanctuary called the Helping Hand Animal Welfare League Donkey Sanctuary near Reading. She was a very elderly lady caring for some 200 to 250 donkeys which she bought from dealers all over the country. Following a visit to her, help was offered as she was obviously in deep distress and very short of funds. Shortly after arriving home from Reading, Violet Philpin telephoned to ask if we would take six donkeys in very bad condition that had just been delivered from Reading

---

Winter is Over

The funniest part of my job, and indeed the most pleasurable, is to watch a group of donkeys cavorting round a field when first turned out to spring grass. This marks the end of their winter as they tear round the field, heads held high, braying with delight and even the geriatrics run and buck like spring lambs. During this moment of great entertainment some groups of donkeys play their own games of tag while others run wildly about, sometimes colliding with each other and not caring a jot for anything, just like children being let out into the playground on a sunny day.

After a while the initial hysteria dies down and the donkeys get down to the serious business of feeding on the sweet spring grass and once more peace reigns over Brookfield and the valley below.

Charles Courtney,
manager of Brookfield Farm

market. She would send the waggon straight on to us, plus £50 to help cover our costs. The waggon arrived and on board were the donkeys we were to name Biddy, Black Beauty, Bill and Ben, So Shy and Tiny Titch. Their condition was indescribable. My husband and eldest children, Lise and Paul, helped them into the biggest stable which had been emptied in readiness and we all stood quietly in the early morning light in shocked silence. None of the donkeys could move alone and their spirits seemed completely broken.

Early the next morning I met Herb who helped with the donkeys. From being a young boy he had always worked on farms and been with animals. To him farm animals had a simple purpose in life. They were bred carefully, reared properly and when their time came, killed for human consumption. This was the way of the farmer and Herb fully approved.

In the light of the morning we stood looking at the donkeys. 'Tin't right,' he said. 'Look at that poor little beggar's back.' The smallest donkey was shivering in the corner, his back was bent from cowering at the frequent beatings that had been his lot and the hair looked solid and peculiar. The solid lumps on

Tiny Titch were in fact pieces of sacking embedded in his back with small broken pieces of spine showing through. He was only about eight months old. I cried and so did Herb. Could Tiny Titch stand the anaesthetic the vet would need to give him to remove the sacking and could his splintered spine be mended? With the vet we decided to let him recover a little first and put him in one of the smaller stables with the poor little terrified mare, So Shy.

With the help of the vet and Herb So Shy could be touched gently and her teeth looked at to estimate her age. *All* her front teeth were broken, congealed blood still on the gums. She had been beaten as badly as Tiny Titch. The vet gave her an anaesthetic straight away, as she could not possibly eat with her mouth in that condition, and five chipped and broken teeth were removed and lacerated gums sewn. The only good thing was that they were her milk teeth and, with luck, new ones should replace them. Poor So Shy, what a start!

The two stallions, Bill and Ben, were huddled together. They would have to be gelded when strong enough. The other two mares consisted of a tiny middle-aged brown one we had named

Slade House Farm

A DONKEY'S DREAM

A long time ago, an old and weary donkey stood in the corner of a field.

His head was bowed and his eyes were closed. He was too tired even to graze, not that there was much for him to eat because the grass, such as there was, had been dried by the hot sun and lack of water.

The donkey had travelled all day from sunrise to nearly sunset carrying a heavy load over rough stony tracks and parched roads. When he slowed a little, the youth at his side beat him and shouted harsh words of abuse at him to drive him on.

Harsh words and beatings were more numerous in his life than good meals, a donkey was about the lowest form of animal life in existence, truly a beast of burden and as such not worthy of even a kind thought.

As he stood dozing the poor donkey remembered the day when, as a young animal, little more than a foal, he had been taken from a field to a certain place. Someone had laid a hand on his head and in a quiet kindly voice had spoken to him.

Kindness was rare in his life and he had felt pleased and there was a lightness in his step as he had walked briskly, carrying the man on his back. Crowds of people had sung and shouted and waved and strewn palm branches in his path and just for once in his life the donkey had felt important as if he were carrying a king.

He often remembered that kind face and the gentle voice, but he had never seen his passenger again.

The cold night air caused him to shiver, he was thin and weak and so terribly tired, but there was not very much that was pleasant in his life so the next day and the next and all the days after would be just as miserable for him as those that had gone before and sleep was his only consolation.

His head nodded slowly, slowly, and soon he was asleep and dreaming as animals do.

He was suddenly surprised to see, standing beside him, a tall shining figure and the light which shone from him was so bright the poor donkey had to blink many times until he was used to the brightness and could keep his eyes open.

A voice that was so beautiful it sounded like the murmur of a gentle breeze, the kiss of the sun and the bubbling laughter of a cool sparkling stream spoke to him and a hand was laid tenderly on his neck.

'My friend you are tired now but I will lift your burden from your shoulders and carry it for you as you once carried me and from now on you shall walk beside me in the celestial garden.'

The donkey looked up into the eyes of his friend and saw in them all the cares, all the joys and all the kind thoughts of all the people in the whole world, and he too smiled a happy donkey smile.

'There, you are smiling now and you are no longer tired, come, my dear friend, we will go together to the evergreen pastures,' and lifting his hand the Holy One made the sign of the cross over the back of his little donkey friend and they walked side by side.

Next morning, when the man who owned the donkey came to the field to fetch him ready for another day's hard work, he found the little animal lying on the ground still and lifeless, but with a smile on his grey whiskered old face that made it look strangely young for a very old animal.

If you look at the back of any donkey now you will see that he carries the sign of the cross down his back and across his shoulders.

Biddy, and a jet-black mare we named Black Beauty. There is a happy ending to this story. So Shy and Tiny Titch recovered fully and fell quietly in love! When they were better, a wonderful home was found for them in Devon and it was arranged with the new owners that Tiny Titch be gelded when he was really strong, the sanctuary paying. They did this when he was two but just a little too late! So Shy produced a beautiful little foal one year later.

FUNDS

Funds became a real problem. An ever-increasing number of donkeys arriving at the door strained our limited finances and an advertisement was put in the *Sunday Telegraph* which read:

> Help a Little Donkey in Distress . . .
> Recently started Donkey Sanctuary in desperate need of funds to help with the rescue and rehabilitation of not only the old and sick but unfortunately also the young and ill-treated donkey. Donations, please, to the South Western Donkey Sanctuary, Ottery St Mary, Devon.

The response to this was quite amazing and it was a terrible job trying to reply to the many enquiries and letters.

A LEGACY

On 20 June, 1974, events took a dramatic turn. Miss Philpin had died and left me 204 donkeys and all her debts and assets. The debts proved quite substantial; the Helping Hand Animal Welfare League Donkey Sanctuary owed some £8,400 and creditors were already demanding money.

Only eighty or ninety donkeys were at the sanctuary. The rest had been boarded out in various parts of the country at a rate of between £2 and £3 per donkey, per week for their care. This meant weekly bills coming into the sanctuary and no funds available to meet them. I had to agree to pay the staff wages myself to ensure that the donkeys were cared for until I could get them back home. With the help of the Charity Commissioners Miss Philpin's charity was amalgamated with ours and we were then able to begin the task of paying off her bills and ensuring the donkeys' future. Judith Forbes, from the Farway Countryside Park, stepped in with a marvellous offer of help and we were able to rent a large barn from her and some land which enabled us to bring all the donkeys back to Devon.

A NEW FARM

The donkey work began in earnest and the charity began to take on a new secure shape. Slade House Farm was purchased by myself and my husband and this included large traditional barns which, although in poor order, could obviously be put right without too much cost. The large house with outbuildings would be suitable for conversion into offices and beautiful meadows sloping down towards the sea were ideal. Finance again became a nightmare as we struggled to find sufficient funds to purchase the property having to sell our delightful house near the hotel in order to subsidise the charity.

Visiting Time

As the Donkey Sanctuary is a registered charity we have always felt strongly that the public should be allowed to visit at any time without prior appointment so that they can see for themselves the way in which we are using their money. For this reason every day of the year, including Christmas, the sanctuary is open from dawn to dusk. If we happen to be receiving a load of very sick donkeys then people standing near are warned in case this causes them distress and they can then make their own choice as to whether or not they wish to observe the proceedings. We have always been adamant that no charge of any sort is made for any visitor to come into the sanctuary either by way of car parking fees or any pressure for donations. Although many people criticise us for this, saying we could make a large income from the visitors, we feel that they should have the right to see what is happening without having to pay.

Every field needed a shelter for the donkeys and finance was already at a critical level when we found we had to erect fencing which was going to cost £6,500. A small miracle occurred at exactly that time: we were left a legacy of £6,000, the first we had received and one of the biggest. It came from a man in Pontypool. This particular gentleman had always been teased and called a donkey by his friends and to the absolute horror of his relatives, on his death his will quite clearly stated that donkeys should get all his money – everything he possessed was to go to the Donkey Sanctuary in Devon.

ADMINISTRATION AND FUND RAISING

Setting up office procedures for the sanctuary in the early days had presented little problem. Meticulous records were kept of every donation made and every expense incurred and a careful balance maintained between the two. At no time has the sanctuary ever put itself into debt, preferring to wait until a new stable block could be afforded before embarking on the project. Many of the office systems laid down in the very first days are still in operation and proving as sound today as they were in 1972.

Donations are, of course, vital to the sanctuary's existence as are legacies and covenants. Without sufficient donations the essential work would have to stop and the future could be very grim for the 4,000 donkeys in our care. Ensuring that donations continue arriving at the sanctuary is a mammoth task, contributors are continually informed of the work being carried out. Administration costs are kept to a minimum and recent figures produced by the Charities Aid Foundation show that the sanctuary's administration overheads account for only 3.8p in every pound received.

Selected advertisements are placed in the national press with regard to recent intake donkeys giving a brief history of their problems, how we are coping with them and a request is made for the funds required for this donkey and all the others in care. As letters are received they are very carefully sorted by trained staff. Some donations are quite simple to process coming as a straightforward cheque, postal order or indeed cash, clearly marked to show which of the three charities it is for and with the sender's name and address legible. In other cases, however, anonymous donations may arrive with no accompanying letter and to avoid any future problems the postmark is always kept so that if at a later date, a query is made regarding the safe receipt of the contribution we can at least trace it back. The donor's name, when known, goes on to our computer and a letter is sent out thanking them for their donation, clearly stating the amount and the charity to which the contribution has been credited. Our computer has over 70,000 subscriber names and addresses on it and records faithfully every contribution made and from this list a newsletter is sent twice a year to keep those involved aware of the recent happenings at the sanctuary and up-to-date with our progress. These newsletters are extremely well received and their circulation results in more funds for the charity.

The office is managed by Julie Courtney who has been with us for fifteen years and her department is quite large. She is

Buffalo. This painting, by Donna Crawshaw, was used for the Donkey Sanctuary Christmas card in 1987

responsible for all the printing that has to be done: to save costs we print our own newsletter, take our own photographs which we develop and publish small notelets which are one of the very few items that are on sale to the public. Over sixteen books have been written, many directed at children and the sale of these brings a large amount of revenue into the charity. Included with the newsletter is a price list giving details of the books and postage and packing costs.

Visitors to the sanctuary can be shown around by our staff if they wish and during the summer we can have anything up to 40,000 visitors during the three months peak period. Videos are shown in the information room on the work of the three charities and all the items which we are able to produce ourselves are on sale. We have steadfastly refused to start a shop, as such, as we feel strongly that the holding of stocks of manufactured goods awaiting sale ties up capital which could much better be used for the donkeys' day-to-day well-being. Our general rule is if we do not make it or write it, then we do not sell it.

Many supporters raise funds on our behalf by arranging sponsored walks, holding coffee mornings, donkey days, etc. Schools support us in various ways holding fetes and even having sponsored silences. In order, hopefully, to reduce the work of the Donkey Sanctuary in future years, great efforts are made in the

Many of the new intake donkeys have terrible foot problems: Jack

education of children. A lesson has been designed by the Donkey Sanctuary which is available free to every school in the United Kingdom and this goes out along with one of the children's books to form the basis of a lesson to be given by teachers. Quite often one of our inspectors will be invited to the school to give a talk to the children.

STAFF

The sanctuary employs 110 full-time staff throughout its farms, veterinary, inspectorate and office departments, all of whom, of course, come under the administration of the sanctuary.

The veterinary department is headed by John Fowler BVet Med, MRCVS and he is backed up by a very experienced team. In addition this department has its own laboratory assistant (who carries out non-intrusive research and does regular tests on the parasites found in the donkey), a secretary, and staff especially trained to take care of the new intake donkeys.

THE NEW INTAKE

Every animal is isolated on its arrival to prevent the spread of contagious diseases. Blue collars are put on all the donkeys coming in and these are left on during the six weeks the animal spends in the main area of the sanctuary. All animals are weighed on arrival, a blood sample is taken and analysed, equine flu and tetanus injections are given, the donkey is wormed and a full dung count is taken both for lungworm larvae and for gut para-

AN INSPECTOR CALLS . . .

Our journeys to find donkeys – reported to the sanctuary by all kinds of people – have taken us into many previously unknown parts of our own county and we have driven down many hidden narrow lanes wondering what we would find at the end of our travels. We have climbed mountains in Wales, usually in the pouring rain and we have found donkeys in all kinds of situations, from beautiful parkland to the grounds of a city garage. The problem, however, has nearly always been the same – the donkeys' feet – usually caused by neglect or more often plain ignorance. I don't know how many times an owner has said to us: 'I thought donkeys' feet were always like that.' Patiently we try to explain and always leave the leaflet *How to Look After and Care for your Donkey.* I have to say that most people – sadly not all – do listen and so far on our return visits we have found the feet being cared for and in good condition.

We have had help from all kinds of people: the public giving endless directions; farriers going quickly to an emergency case; council officials searching records for information needed. Another side of the work deals with operators who have teams of donkeys giving rides at various functions, or the donkey derby. Few organisers of these events seem to know that the operator must have a licence under the Riding Establishment Act. This means that the operator's premises and animals have to be regularly inspected and approved.

Having been in teaching most of our lives, the work that holds special interest is the work in schools. We usually speak about the history of the donkeys, how they came to this country and how they live and work here. We tell stories and legends about the donkey and deal simply with care and management and some of the problems. We display picture books and posters, saddlery and samples of food and the children are invariably lively and interested and ask many questions. We hope these children will look at donkeys with kindness and attention in the future and some things that have happened have fulfilled this hope. For example, the thirteen year old who said: 'I saw a donkey in a carnival after you talked to us, I stroked him but I was looking at his feet and feeling if he was thin.'

Marjorie Monkhouse and Jay Duckworth, Donkey Sanctuary voluntary inspectors
Donkey Breed Society Magazine

sites. A full medical history of the donkey is started to include age, heart and lung condition, etc. Stallions are placed in individual isolation boxes, unless they come in as a pair, until they are completely fit for the castration operation. After this, with other geldings and mares they are paired up and allowed to make friends during their period of isolation. For a further two weeks after this period the donkeys are kept in one of the outside shelters with a run-out area where we can spend a further time watching them closely.

Many of the new intake donkeys have severe foot problems and this is corrected as soon as possible by the farrier. From then on the donkeys receive the farrier's attention every eight weeks.

The sanctuary is run over five farms and the donkeys are sent to their various quarters depending on their health, age and any other companions they may have had who have already come into the sanctuary. All geriatric donkeys go to the two nearest farms or are kept at Slade House Farm.

There comes a time when the quality of the donkey's life has gone. This is generally with the very old or extremely sick when the animal has lost all interest in his surroundings. All decisions are taken jointly by a member of the veterinary staff and one of the executives of the charity and each donkey is shot in his own stable which, we feel, is the most humane and immediate method and one where the donkey has no prior knowledge at all.

RESEARCH

Very little work has been devoted to the subject of the donkeys' physiology or pathology during the past thousands of years that the donkey has been of help to man and it is for this reason that we have built a specialised laboratory to try to establish reliable 'bench-marks' for the donkeys' physiology. It will be some years yet before statistically reliable conclusions can be drawn but if our veterinary department are satisfied that they have reliable

MBE

To my utmost joy in the 1981 New Year's Honours List I was awarded the MBE. This I feel was in recognition firstly of the donkey himself and secondly of my wonderful team of loyal staff and supporters and my only regret on that wonderful day, when I had the honour of meeting The Queen, was that the donkeys could not be with me!

A new arrival, with a badly dipped back

information to impart to the veterinary profession, then this is done immediately. A book published by the sanctuary, *The Professional Handbook of the Donkey*, has now become teaching material in many veterinary universities throughout the world.

The veterinary department also boasts one of the most up-to-date operating facilities available specifically for donkeys anywhere in the world. Its large modern theatre with overhead gantries allows the donkeys to be moved from the place of anaesthesia to the operating table and from there to the recovery stables without them having to be manhandled. Donkeys are very prone to stress and to provide the very minimum stress during an operation, the donkey's friend stays with the patient until the anaesthetic is administered and is there waiting once the operation is over.

Great attention is placed on reducing stress for all new intake donkeys and great care is taken to see that donkeys who come in with friends remain together and that donkeys who come in on their own are paired up with another suitable donkey as soon as possible.

Donkeys in the yard at the sanctuary

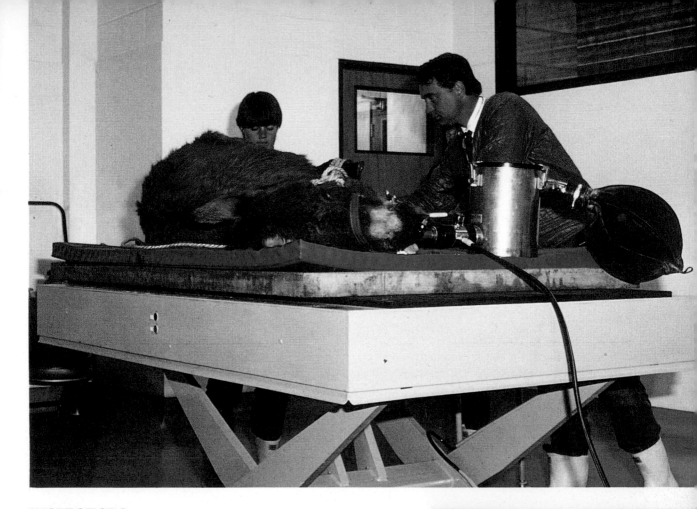

INSPECTORS

The chief superintendent of the inspectorate department is Roy Harrington, who organises six full-time inspectors and fifty-eight voluntary inspectors throughout the United Kingdom. All inspectors receive training from the sanctuary and many applicants are members of the Donkey Breed Society and knowledgeable with regard to the needs of the donkeys. This team is responsible for following up all complaints of cruelty and abuse and also checks homes for our young, fit donkeys who go out on rehabilitation usually in pairs.

The complaints of cruelty are very wide-ranging indeed. Where cases require prosecution the chief inspector is always called in and very often we co-operate with other charities to save litigation costs. The Donkey Sanctuary does not bring many prosecutions, the main concern being to get the donkey away from the situation he is in and placed safely in our care, rather than spend a great deal of time and money on litigation.

The sanctuary's well equipped operating theatre (top); and Trixie in the recovery box at the hospital

Another important side of the inspectors' duties is to oversee conditions for donkeys working on beaches and at donkey derbys. In association with the British Horse Society Riding Establishments Acts Committee Section we have taken over the liaison with local councils where donkeys are being used for gain. This means that through the inspectorate we can keep a tight control on those operators who do not provide suitable working conditions and we can, in fact, advise councils to refuse to grant licences where the donkeys have not received fair treatment.

A DAY IN THE LIFE OF A DONKEY

It's strange to be in a warm airy stable and to hear other donkeys all around! Many lonely years have made me perceptive to any strange sounds and the shock of leaving the only home I can remember in my thirty-seven years of life still makes me tremble. How I miss the humans who looked after me for so long and how pleased I was to see *anyone* at my stable door after five days without food. They tell me my owner died and now, after a long, long frightening journey, I am in this place called the Donkey Sanctuary.

My breakfast has been satisfying. Not what I have been used to, I'll give you that, but wholesome and adequate. I've felt warmth and kindness since my arrival, no harsh words and now I am to be examined by the vet.

I noticed many other donkeys watching with some sympathy and I appreciated the gentle stroking hands of the nurse who held me. I have had two collars put round my neck, one blue and one yellow, but they cause me no concern. I did feel a small pain in my shoulder at one stage and heard them saying I would now be protected from flu and tetanus, whatever those are.

There has been a lot of noise in the last few moments and it was a shock to hear my door being opened and a small grey donkey appear in my doorway. It's strange that it so quickly appears to be 'mine'. I must be feeling more secure, any-how, I have to face another challenge now.

We're both very wary of each other but neither wants to be the first to make a move. A helper came in and led the other donkey over to me, I suppose she can share my hay.

It is very cold out now but we are both listening to some new sounds and are rather wary of a large man in a brown leather apron with a clattering bag in his hands, who is looking at us over the door. My friend's feet were terribly long and had been giving her a lot of pain, but she certainly looks better now, and I feel easier about letting him pick my feet up after watching what happened to her, but we will be glad when he has gone.

Jenny and I have just returned from a walk 'up the drive' for exercise. I feel to be walking on springs and Jenny says she has not felt so good for years. We have had a number of human visitors looking over the door – all seem kindly but none of them has touched us, we are, apparently, in isolation.

Tea was excellent, the bran and oats had molasses in, a sweet, satisfying taste, and it's nice to know as my good friend Jenny and I watch the night fall that the warm light over us will stay on all night and we won't be alone and scared because someone will visit us every hour until the dawn breaks again and we face the routine of the second day in our new life.

DONKEYS OVERSEAS

Many requests were received at the Donkey Sanctuary to help donkeys. It was felt that these pleas for help, concerning the appalling conditions, could not be ignored so a third charity was formed and called the International Donkey Protection Trust. People with knowledge in this field had to be approached to form a good basis for a board of trustees. The charity first met and was registered in 1976. The aim was to help donkeys in other parts of the world, whenever possible, by visits, setting up small clinics, making contact with the local veterinary surgeons and educating local people as to the basic needs and requirements of the donkey.

From this very small beginning the International Donkey Protection Trust has now spread to most parts of the world where donkeys are used, or indeed abused, by their frequently poverty stricken owners. Initial visits were made to Turkey, Greece, North Africa and Egypt and from these trips it soon became apparent that setting up a small clinic in the corner of a large market was not going to help the majority of donkeys and mules in the world but it was very obvious that help was needed. The charity has developed through frequent trips abroad, surveying the problems faced by most countries, some being localised but many being common to donkeys and mules everywhere. The most general cause of the misery and suffering found turned out to be the effect of parasites. Travelling with a small microscope and studying samples throughout the world it soon became apparent that these parasites were absorbing much of the nourishment intended for the donkey. By burrowing through the wall of the stomach, embolisms were being caused making the average life span of the donkey abroad as short as nine to eleven years compared to that of thirty-five years in the United Kingdom. The charity has spent many years working abroad and is gradually coming to terms with some of the problems faced.

THE DONKEY SANCTUARY FARMS

BROOKFIELD FARM

This farm has 55ha (140 acres) and is run by Charles Courtney. The majority of donkeys kept here consist of what is known as 'boys' group'. Most of these are very active geldings, many of whom have been castrated on their arrival at the sanctuary when their stallion tendencies have already been well established. These tendencies can remain some two to three years after castration so the groups of donkeys have to be very well watched to ensure that no bullying takes place.

The donkeys are grouped in units and during the summer all the donkeys are able to graze peacefully in the large acreage assigned to their unit. In the winter all the donkeys come in and have large warm airy stables with extensive run-out yards so that they are not subjected to the adverse weather conditions and their sharp hoofs do not damage the pasture, so vital to them later on in the year. Brookfield is a very exposed farm and good shelter is essential to the donkeys both in summer and winter.

PACCOMBE FARM

Paccombe lies in a sheltered Devonshire valley only 2 miles from the main sanctuary and has 76ha (188 acres) with much woodland. Derek Battison is the manager and he cares for, what are known as, 'grannies' group'. These are geriatric donkeys who still have some years in front of them and who enjoy the peace and warmth found on this particular farm.

Derek also caters for the family groups which consist of mares who have come into the sanctuary already in foal. The gestation period for a donkey can be up to fourteen and a half months and this means that frequently animals coming in to us, sent from markets, have been served by a stallion before their arrival. In this case the foal is granted the same security as his mother. The donkeys are in fairly large groups and one of these groups uses a large barn known as the 'elephant house'.

THREE GATES FARM

After the purchase of Paccombe the sanctuary found itself the centre of some adverse criticism from the local farming community. They began to feel that the Donkey Sanctuary was taking over agricultural farms that could be used for milk production and we began to meet with some resentment. For this reason the next farm to be purchased was bought some 35 miles away. A good grazing area of 77ha (192 acres) was chosen near Sherborne in Dorset and John Fry, who had been working as manager at Slade House Farm, was selected to take this, the largest farm. Special stabling had to be built, miles of fencing erected to protect the vital hedgerows and large barns built for wintering the donkeys. The farm looks after over 500 donkeys and yet each one is known individually by name and each one receives personal attention by the devoted staff.

TOWN BARTON FARM

The fifth farm to be purchased, once again in view of local criticism, was on the edge of Dartmoor. The 62ha (152 acres) of Town Barton stands on the outskirts of the village of Tedburn St Mary and houses over 400 donkeys. John Pile, the manager, has the most recent intake donkeys to make up his large unit. Being the new arrivals, these donkeys need extra special care and more time to settle in their surroundings. Town Barton is almost self-supporting as regards feed for the donkeys as a method of making haylage has been introduced using a silo tower and the system allows the grass to dry a little longer than normal silage. The donkeys thoroughly enjoy this feed, which our veterinary surgeons consider to be healthier than hay in that there is no dust content which can so often cause problems for the donkeys' lungs.

Twiggy, who arrived looking like a walking skeleton

Care of the Donkey

Looks tasty!

The first thing that every prospective donkey owner must accept is that each donkey is an individual. They need company, preferably of their own kind, and also appreciate human company and kind firm handling.

Always approach a donkey from the side as the donkeys' eyes are set in the side of the head. If you approach from the front, he cannot easily see you and is likely to be startled. Always speak before approaching your donkey and as soon as possible place your hand on his shoulder or under his chin but never on his ears as these are very sensitive.

A donkey's ears show the most important signs. When the ears are forward, looking at something, he is paying a lot of attention. One ear forward and one ear back usually means that he is very content and he is probably listening to you. Ears flat back is usually a danger signal so take care as the donkey may be about to attack, run or bite. You can also tell his mood by his mouth. If his mouth is relaxed then he is content but if it is tight then the animal is usually under stress of some sort or is frightened. If the head is carried high then he is not sure of his surroundings. If his neck is stretched out, his ears back and his mouth tight, then he is ready to bolt or swing around. If content his tail will swish from side to side but if it swishes violently then you, or other animals, are too close to his rear end!

PASTURE MANAGEMENT

If your donkeys are going to live out all the year round, you will need at least .2ha (½ acre) of grazing per animal, preferably divided into three. The ideal arrangement would be to rotate the grazing area and allow one area for grazing your donkeys, one area for grazing sheep or cattle, one area for making hay. If the paddock is too small there is the danger of it becoming 'horse sick'. Apart from being bare in patches where the grass has been eaten down and rank where they have fouled, it is also infected with the worms from the donkeys' droppings. It is often worthwhile to rent a paddock at certain times of the year while your paddock grows or while it is fertilised or lime is applied. But be careful, rich and over-fertilised grass can in fact produce laminitis in your donkey.

The ideal pasture must provide not only food but also a cushioning surface for exercise for as long a period as possible during the year. Naturally it must be safely fenced keeping poisonous plants and treasured shrubs or trees well out of the reach of stretched necks. You should also take precautions to protect any

young trees growing within the paddock by covering the trunks with wire netting.

Electric fencing is an effective way of dividing up the available grazing

Donkeys are renowned for being proficient escapologists! Sturdy fencing is essential around the perimeter of the paddock, wooden post and rail being ideal but expensive. The lowest rail should be about 30cm (12in) from the ground and the highest a good 105cm (3ft 6in), as donkeys can become quite proficient jumpers. Old metal stakes and railings are certainly not suitable and could cause damage. It is advisable to paint the wooden posts and rails with Presomet as donkeys like to chew wood. It is a good idea to provide a tree branch in the paddock when possible, with the bark on, for the donkeys to chew. Tethering is a possibility for a few hours but you should be close at hand in case your donkey gets into any trouble.

The aim is to provide conditions which encourage the most productive grasses – ryegrass and timothy – and to discourage weeds and non-productive grasses. Unfortunately productive grasses are not always the most tasty! However, palatability is often a reflection of the way the pasture is managed rather than the type of grass originally sown.

Always place water troughs tight against the fence or well away from it, thus avoiding the chance of an animal getting stuck between the fence and the trough.

Weed Control The most effective way to control weeds is to do everything possible to encourage grass growth. Check the following factors: correct stocking rate; avoid poaching and panning; correct drainage and ditching; alternate hay and grazing if pos-

Sight Restored

One of the donkeys that came into the sanctuary was, supposedly, blind in one eye and going blind in the other. On examination by our vet it was found that she had nothing basically more serious than ingrowing eyelashes. An immediate operation saved the sight of the 'blind' eye by removing the irritation and once the irritation was removed from the other eye she regained her sight totally.

sible: practise rotational grazing if possible; chemical control; reseed as a last resort. If a hormone weed-killer is used, always remember that it works best when the weeds are actively growing; more of the weed-killer will be absorbed into young fresh growth. Spraying old and established growth, especially just after seeding, will not be effective. Do not forget that poisonous weeds are more likely to be eaten after spraying: ragwort is a good example because in the growing state it has a sharp smell not apparent in the dying plant.

Thistles are probably overrated as a favourite food of donkeys. They tend to eat only the top out of the plant which then seems to spread outwards and a sizeable thistle patch can quickly form. It is possible to keep thistles and docks under control by digging them up.

Over-grazing tends to encourage low-growing weeds, whereas under-grazing produces low quality, coarse and rank grasses that taste unpleasant. Because grass growth is uneven throughout the year and donkey numbers are constant, it is very beneficial to have an arrangement with a local farmer to bring cattle or sheep into the fields at times of grass surplus, in return for hay, if your acreage allows this. The sheep and cattle will ingest

A GENEROUS GIFT

A telephone call was received from a Mrs Bourne saying that she and her family were very fond of donkeys and she would like to donate a bracelet to the Donkey Sanctuary and asked if we would accept this. Obviously we are pleased for any donation, of any sort, and agreed happily, suggesting that she sent it and every effort would be made to sell it for a good price. However, Mrs Bourne thought it better that the bracelet went through one of the London auction houses and suggested Bonhams, as her son knew somebody there.

She wished specifically to confirm that we were a registered charity and that if she gave us this gift in total then it could be put to a special use. At that time a new intensive care unit for the isolation facilities was just being built and any money towards the project would be a great help.

We heard no more for many weeks and then received a phone call to say the auction was the following Friday at Bonhams and could a brief description, around one hundred words, of the Donkey Sanctuary, be written to include the story of Islander, Blackie in Spain and Timothy, the poor donkey whose ears had been vandalised. This was so that the auctioneer could specifically mention that the money raised from the sale of the bracelet was going to the Donkey Sanctuary. A hundred words seemed rather a tall order to give so much information so, being in London during that week, I decided to call in. Bonhams were very pleasant and after explaining the work of the sanctuary they offered a catalogue so I could

see a picture of the bracelet. To my amazement this turned out to be a Cartier diamond bracelet and was featured on the front cover with a suggested price of £14,000 to £18,000!

Having recovered from the shock I decided to attend the auction personally to see what the bracelet made. After an extremely nail-biting two and a half hours, lot 243 was announced and was eventually purchased at £19,000 by a very quiet gentleman seated in front of me who only joined the bidding at the very last moment. Overcome at the price and the knowledge that this amount would pay for the complete unit, I bent forward to thank the gentleman on behalf of all the donkeys. He immediately asked if I was Mrs Svendsen and he said, 'I am Mr Bourne'.

It transpired that this was Mrs Bourne's son who had always loved and admired his mother's bracelet which had been a present to her from his father and he felt sad that it was going out of the family although he fully appreciated his mother's desire to put the proceeds towards the funds of the sanctuary. Rather than try to strike a deal with his mother to buy the bracelet, which he felt could never have been very satisfactory because whatever price they reached would not have been an independent one, he decided to let it go through the auction and repurchase it, the purpose being to give it to his wife on her birthday. This delightful story shows how much kindness there is in the world and has an almost fairy tale ending for all concerned.

donkey worms and reduce the worm population. Ideally the sheep or cattle should be grazed after donkeys rather than at the same time, as this has a slightly improved worm control benefit. However there is one type of worm, Trichostrongylus, which is capable of infecting equines, sheep and cattle alike. Sheep and cattle will graze much of the grass rejected by donkeys in the 'camp' area and donkeys will graze right up to the dung pats of cattle.

Harrowing in late February/March when the land is dry enough is useful for dragging out dead grass and moss and to encourage young fresh growth. *But* unless it is done with a heavy spiked or pitch-pole type harrow, it is worthless – others merely make pretty pictures. Harrowing to spread dung patches only increases the area unacceptable for grazing therefore picking up droppings is preferable. Unless droppings are removed in less than twenty-four hours the area will still be rejected by the donkeys. Removal after this period will, of course, still help to reduce worm burden. Harrowing will help to dessicate the remaining manure.

Rolling should be used only as part of the procedure for improving poached or other damaged pasture. It can often do more harm than good and damage soil structure.

Soil Structure Soil should be kept fertile and it is essential to have it analysed every four to five years. Beware of expensive 'trace element' fertilisers. If donkeys are found to be deficient in trace elements, it is usually more effective to feed or inject the animal, rather than try and make up the deficiency in the soil. Unbiased specialist advice is required before this is attempted.

Nitrogen is undoubtedly the key to grass growth but it will not respond unless the quantities of lime, phosphate and potash are also correct. Nitrogen should be applied as and when required, and generally three to six weeks before growth is needed to a maximum of 15 units/acre application. Farmyard manure dressings can be useful to maintain the humus level in the soil and will add some useful phosphate and potash. However, it should ideally be stored for at least twelve months before application and grazing should not take place for a further six weeks after spreading. Be especially careful with poultry manure.

Drainage is probably the most important single factor in the provision and maintenance of grass fields for donkeys. Signs of poor drainage are usually obvious in the form of surface water or water-loving weeds (for example, rushes, tussock grass and buttercups). Before undertaking expensive drainage schemes, make sure that the boundary ditches and existing drainage outlets are clean and not blocked. Advice should be taken from local drainage engineers, or ADAS, on the spacing of drains and the correct infilling material above the drains suitable for the soil type.

Always aim to maintain a good soil structure. Grass growth is often reduced due to structural problems. These result in waterlogging, poor root development and poor growth. Some soils are more likely to suffer structural damage, which is usually caused by grazing too many animals per acre during wet weather or by the use of heavy agricultural machinery. The identification

---

A. A. Milne's Eeyore

No book on donkeys would be complete without reference to A.A. Milne's Eeyore in the wonderful *Pooh* books.

Eeyore is portrayed as a slow, sad little animal and his woebegone face indicates his troubled life. Children remember vividly the picture of poor Eeyore floating down under the bridge upon which Pooh, Piglet, Rabbit and Roo play Poohsticks. Also remembered is Eeyore's touchingly sad birthday with him standing alone in his field when Pooh arrives with an empty honey jar, having eaten the honey on the way and Piglet arrives with a small fragment of a balloon which had burst on the way and Eeyore, with simple dignity, accepts his gifts and spends the next hour happily putting the burst balloon into the empty honey jar.

Eeyore certainly makes a lasting impression on both adult and young and perhaps it is this melancholic dignity which endears donkeys to us all.

of a damaged soil structure is a specialised job and advice should be sought from a drainage contractor or other consultant. Soil structure can often be improved cheaply by sub-soiling and pan busting so long as a suitable under-drainage system is present.

Poisonous Plants Weeds which may be ignored in lush pastures may be eaten in 'starvation' paddocks as will overhanging hedges and trees. Even if the fresh weeds are not grazed, donkeys galloping about may cut them off with their hoofs and then eat them once they have wilted and are no longer unpalatable. Poisonous hedge plants may also be eaten in snow when grazing is not available.

   Poisonous pasture and hedgerow weeds include ragwort and bracken, which are the most serious causes of loss in stock, followed by yew, laurel, box, laburnum and privet. Mare's tail is also highly poisonous and most common on poorly drained land. Even the ubiquitous buttercup is poisonous if eaten in sufficient quantities (eg if eaten in hay). Discarded hedge trimmings or clippings of these plants are also dangerous. Lawn clippings should not be fed as these can ferment and cause colic. Additional plants that should be eradicated are autumn crocus, monkshood, hemlock, bryony, lords and ladies, lupin, bittersweet, foxglove and rhododendron.

STABLING

A shelter is an absolute essential, not only for the cold wet winter months but also for the summer months to enable your donkey to escape from flies. It is possible to have a stable where your donkey can be put at night and a shelter for use in the day. Or with careful planning and incorporating a concrete area your stable can be designed so that your donkey can get access from all of your paddocks.

An ideal arrangement: a small shelter with a concrete yard adjacent

The stable can be in the form of a small shed giving a minimum of 3.3sq m (4sq yd) covered accommodation per donkey with an open door so that he can go in and out freely. The construction can be of wood or brick and should have adequate light and plenty of ventilation without draughts.

If you are going to take over an old shed that has been used by cattle, remember that such things as lice can be picked up by donkeys from the wooden doorposts on which previous occupants have rubbed. A coat of Stockholm tar or something similar, applied preferably a little before the donkey moves in (because of the smell), should eliminate any trouble.

The best site for a stable is on south facing, well-drained land where there is a natural, yet gentle, fall away from the building. The stable should be as protected as possible from cold and biting northerly and easterly winds, with the door and window facing south or west. When this is not possible, a second best is to protect the stables by trees or other buildings. Avoid low-lying, damp and over-protected locations where conditions can become extremely unhealthy in the damp weather of the autumn or the still, hot days of high summer. Low-lying hollows can also be dangerous frost pockets in winter.

Traditionally constructed stables are usually built of brick, double thickness and uninsulated but are not as warm or dry as the modern stable which is usually insulated and built of one of a number of different available materials. If brick is used, then it should be used with a cavity construction, preferably with the cavity filled with insulation such as a polyurethane foam. Alternatively, the wall may be constructed of concrete blocks, which may be cement rendered, using load-bearing insulated construction or of concrete panels or reinforced concrete poured in-situ.

Release Knot

The correct release knot for tying up your donkey is as below. Figs A and B how to tie the knot; Fig C the rope tied to a loop of binder twine for greater safety, particularly with young donkeys, and Fig D the end of the rope slipped through the loop so that the donkey cannot free himself.

The correct way to tie up your donkey

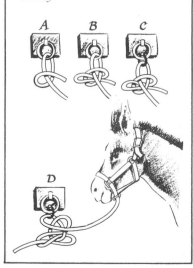

It is also possible to use various forms of timber or concrete prefabricated structures as traditional materials are often very expensive. When using these, it is best to have double linings, the interior lining being of stronger construction than the outer, as these will receive the full impact of the donkeys.

The roof of the stable may be of any suitable modern type but it is desirable to incorporate some thermal insulation. There are two ways of achieving this. The insulation can form an underlining to the exterior roof cladding or a flat false ceiling may be installed. There is no great preference for either construction, but ventilation does tend to be better if there is a pitch on the ceiling. Ventilation air exits in the highest part of the roof should not be obstructed by insulation. The outer cladding of the roof is usually corrugated asbestos or metal and should be sloped. Older traditional stable roofs are usually constructed of tile or slates with an inner lining of timber. This is perfectly satisfactory, but is generally too expensive.

Windows are most important in the modern stable. They need to be fitted at high level in order to prevent damage and to maximise light penetration. It is helpful if windows can serve as part of the ventilation system. This is most satisfactorily achieved if the windows are inward opening and have the bottom hinged with gussets to prevent draught blowing down on the donkeys' backs. The windows must allow maximum variation in ventilation.

The floor must be dry, reasonably smooth, non-slippery, non-absorbent and hard wearing. It must also have sufficient fall to take away the urine and any other fluids but not so much slope to increase the danger of slipping or encourage scuffing of the bedding to one side. A fall of not more than one in eighty is recommended. The ideal flooring is Adamantine clinkers or blue Staffordshire checkered paving but these are expensive and concrete can be satisfactory if care is taken in its use. It should always be laid with a damp-proof membrane incorporated and there is much to be said for the addition of an insulated layer on particularly damp and cold sites.

Thus the total floor construction from the ground upwards should consist of the following:

1 Ground, with all vegetation and top soil removed and well consolidated.
2 Hardcore or firmly compacted material 150mm (6in) thick.
3 Concrete 100–150mm (4–6in) thick.

The surface layer will wear much better if a good granolithic topping is laid.

It is both unnecessary and undesirable to have complicated drainage systems in stables. The first essential is to have a good fall on the floor of the stable to take as much fluid as possible to the outside. The main drainage system will be outside with gulleys to trap straw and other solid matter. Shallow and safe open channelling is much better than underground drains.

Doors should not be less than 1m (3ft 3in) wide or 2m (6ft 6in) high. The door openings should have rounded external edges as sharp edges can cause injury. The doors themselves

Sand-patch

Your donkeys will greatly appreciate a small area spread with sand which they can roll in but put this in an area you do not mind seeing bare and ensure it is stone free. When the donkey stands up after rolling, he will not, like the horse, shake his whole body. He will only shake his head and ears to remove excess dust. In his desert home this dust was needed. It is retained in the coat to protect the animal from both heat and cold and provides very good insulation. It is this characteristic which makes donkeys almost always send up a huge cloud of dust when patted by the human hand.

should be side-hung to open outwards – an animal may prevent the door from being opened while lying down or when ill. These can be the original 'stable door', formed in two halves.

Mangers for the feed are usually placed at about 0.7m (2ft 3in) above the floor. They can be made from vitreous enamel, galvanised steel, stainless steel or timber with salt-glazed channels and can be fitted either along the face of a wall or in the corner. There is no doubt that in spite of its expense, stainless steel is the perfect choice as it has a long life and is easy to clean. A manger may be combined with a hay rack or it is possible to feed your donkey from a bowl. The manger is usually fitted on the wall of the box opposite the door or diagonally opposite the door so that the donkey will be out of a draught when tied up.

Hay racks can either be combined with the manger or be entirely separate. The hay rack must be securely fixed to the wall. Hay nets can be used secured to a ring placed at the side of the manger. Every stable requires fittings for clean, fresh water. The water can be provided in a bucket or an automatic water trough may be fitted. If buckets are used, then there should be a proper bucket holder secured to the wall and water must be replaced daily. Rings are required for tying up donkeys at about 1.5m (5ft) from the floor and another at about 1m (3ft 3in) from the floor for tying the donkey to the manger.

Bedding Straw makes the best bedding and you must clean out daily, removing soiled bedding and all droppings, sweeping the floor and relaying fresh bedding. A good mucking-out means shaking the straw, starting at the door and throwing the clean straw back on to one side; the soiled straw will fall through the fork. The stables should be swept and disinfected regularly. Bedding needs to be deeper round the walls of the stable, and needs to be at least 10–15cm (4–6in) deep.

The bedding is necessary to prevent injury and encourage your donkey to lie down in comfort, to prevent draughts and provide warmth around his lower legs and as an absorbent or drainage material. You will also need a pitch fork, stable broom, shovel and wheelbarrow.

Storage A hay and straw store will be needed near to where you intend to feed your donkey and this should be a totally dry separate building with hard, dry floors and free ventilation throughout. Wet, damp or dusty bedding must be avoided at all costs in order to keep the risk of respiratory disease and allergies at a minimum.

The siting of a good manure store is important. If it is too close to the stable it may create a smell nuisance and increase the fly menace. Ideally the manure store should consist of a concrete base with a fairly steep fall for drainage at the back to ensure that water and effluent do not run back on to the access area. The rear and sides are usually sturdily constructed of blocks, bricks or reinforced concrete. Size will depend entirely on the period of storage envisaged. The more frequent the collection of the manure the better both to avoid smell and fly nuisance and to reduce the size of the store. Do not allow effluent to contaminate water courses.

Preparing for the Farrier's Visit

1 Have the animal at hand.
2 Be sure legs and feet are dry and free of mud (legs are difficult to hold if they are slippery).
3 Fit a safe head collar or halter.
4 Provide a clean, well-lit area which is protected from the elements (a farrier will need to be wearing minimal clothing to do his work).
5 Stay with your animal and show interest in what your farrier is doing; he will in turn do his work with much more enthusiasm.
6 Seek and follow any advice your farrier can give you regarding your donkey's feet, particularly as to when the feet should be trimmed or shod again.

If this advice is followed, you can be sure your donkey has received the best possible attention from your farrier, who in his turn will be quite happy to visit you again.

Tom F. Williams

'Is it feeding time yet?'

Feeding

Donkeys do not thrive on too rich a diet. Lush grass by itself is not a perfect, or natural, feed for donkeys. They require, and will actively seek out, a high-fibre diet. You can make this easy for them by providing good clean oat or barley feeding straw at all times. During the summer months, even though there will be new spring grass, your donkey will probably eat about 1.3kg (3lb) of straw a day. (This will also help to protect trees and fences that may get chewed instead.)

Do keep in mind the outline of a perfect donkey (never fatter than a show donkey but not much thinner either). If you can weigh your donkey remember 9.2 to 11 hands should correspond to about 160 to 175kg (350 to 385lb) respectively, for adults. Don't allow your donkey to eat his head off. Try to prevent unnecessary fatness by subdividing his grass with temporary fencing, by restricting his time at grass and then returning him to some sort of 'playpen', or by sharing abundant grass with some extra animals. It is better to conserve unused grass as hay rather than allow an ever fatter donkey free access to it. A balanced multi-mineral lick should be available at all times.

Access to drinking water is most important, and donkeys drink more than you might probably suppose. A proper cattle trough, properly installed more than makes up for the money spent. If you are unable to provide this, make sure that the container used is suitable, eg not made of lead or plastic, which is so easily knocked over. At least provide yourself with a hosepipe that can run from an appropriate tap to the container and leave it ready for use outside the fence. Do not site the trough or container under trees or it will become full of fallen leaves in autumn.

During the summer months only donkeys working in excess of one and a half hours every day need 'hard' feed in addition to grass and donkeys who do not work regularly should not get pony nuts, even as titbits. If you wish to tempt your donkey when catching-up, or reward him for co-operation, use pieces of carrot.

During the winter months donkeys kept in a well-sheltered stable in air temperatures above 0°C will require 2–2.75kg (4–6lb) of good quality hay per day for the average-sized donkey (9.2–11 hands), and 2.75–3.5kg (6–8lb) of best feeding straw per day. Additionally a small handful of damp bran or chaff including a teaspoonful of a balanced vitamin supplement such as Equivite can be given three times a week. That is all that is required to keep an average young to middle-aged donkey (four to twenty years) healthy, providing he is well wormed and his teeth are checked regularly. Small adjustments can, of course, be made according to size, height and type.

Donkeys under four years old, elderly ones over thirty, those convalescing from operations or disease and pregnant donkeys will need extra increments. Also if your donkey is not kept permanently stabled during the winter or has to withstand low

Please Don't Feed the Donkeys

If your field is easily accessible to the public it is a good idea to display a notice asking people not to feed the animals and explaining why. Some picnic leftovers, such as things containing meat or dairy products, not to speak of the wrappers, can be lethal to an equine. Make no mistake, people do love donkeys and derive great pleasure from stroking and petting them; most donkeys have a fan club beyond the immediate family who owns them.

Hay should not be spread about on the ground: it is extremely wasteful

ambient temperatures, then extra feed should be given. This extra feed could be as much as 50 per cent more than the quantities quoted. Very old donkeys of thirty-five plus do better on flaked cooked barley or maize in a bran mash or chaff.

If your donkey is worked regularly then do give him additional rations according to his average work-load. A simple way of working out how much extra feed to give him is as follows: ADWL (average daily work-load) = total time worked per week ÷ 7. The average donkey in medium work will require .22kg (½lb) of horse and pony nuts per day per half hour of ADWL. This should be bulked-out with a small quantity of chaff. Such nuts from reputable manufacturers have extra minerals and vitamins added, so no further additives are necessary. Soaked sugar beet, and molassined chopped hay can replace up to one third of the nuts, on a weight for weight basis.

Some confusion has arisen over the feeding of bran; some authorities appear to advocate its use whilst others condemn it as a feedstuff. Bran has a low calcium and high phosphorus content. Fed by itself, or as a high proportion of a diet, these relative proportions would eventually be reflected in low-calcium/high phosphorus blood levels. This in turn would stimulate the parathyroid gland into excessive activity. However, if the donkey receives a hay- and straw-based diet, with access to a mineral lick and only receives small quantities of bran then it is unlikely that the overall effect on dietary calcium/phosphorus levels will upset the blood calcium/phosphorus levels. There are alternatives to bran: chaff, chopped straw, chopped hay, mol-

DON QUIXOTE DE LA MANCHA

As they were going on in such discourse as this, they saw at a distance a person riding up to them on an ass, who, as he came near enough to be distinguished, seemed to be a gipsy by his habit. But Sancho Panza, who, whenever he got sight of any asses, followed them with his eyes and his heart, as one whose thoughts were ever fixed on his own, had scarce given him half an eye, but he knew him to be Gines de Passamonte, and by the looks of the gipsy found out the visage of his ass; as really it was the very same which Gines had got under him; who, to conceal himself from the knowledge of the public, and have the better opportunity of making a good market of his beast, had clothed himself like a gipsy; the cant of that sort of people, as well as the languages of other countries, being as natural and familiar to them as their own. Sancho saw him, and knew him; and, scarce had he seen and taken notice of him, when he cried out as loud as his tongue would permit him: 'Ah thou thief Genesillo, leave my goods and chattels behind thee; get off from the back of my own dear life; thou hast nothing to do with my poor beast, without whom I cannot enjoy a moment's ease: away from my Dapple, away from my comfort; take to thy heels thou villain; hence the hedge-bird, leave what is none of thine!' He had no occasion to use so many words; for Gines dismounted as soon as he heard him speak, and taking to his heels, got from them, and was out of sight in an instant. Sancho ran immediately to his ass, and embraced him: 'How hast thou done?' cried he, 'since I saw thee, my darling and treasure, my dear Dapple, the delight of my eyes, and my dearest companion!' And then he stroked and slabbered him with kisses, as if the beast had been a rational creature. The ass, for his part, was as silent as could be, and gave Sancho the liberty of as many kisses as he pleased, without the return of so much as one word to the many questions he had put to him. At sight of this the rest of the company came up with him, and paid their compliments of congratulation to Sancho, for the recovery of his ass, especially Don Quixote, who told him, that though he had found his ass again, yet would not he revoke the warrant he had given him for the three asses, for which favour Sancho returned him a multitude of thanks.

Cervantes

lichaff, chopped grass. In most cases one of these will be as, or more, suitable than bran.

Hansel and Gretel

If your donkey is overweight then his diet should be reduced very gently indeed, so that he loses weight slowly. Crash diets can be lethal (literally) to fat donkeys. On the other hand if your donkey is lighter than 150kg (330lb) then you should consult your veterinary surgeon.

Always try to feed your donkey at regular times as apart from helping to prevent digestive upsets donkeys are creatures of habit. If possible halve his daily needs and feed your donkey night and morning. Try to spend a few minutes each day watching your donkey eat as you might be able to spot any changes in his habits which announce impending illness.

Feed and water containers should, of course, be kept clean at all times. A clean food container will decrease waste and help prevent diseases and upsets. Botulism has been known to develop in wet grain left in the corners of feed containers. Mouldy feed including hay should be strictly avoided at all times.

If the weather is dry and fine it is not necessary to feed your donkey in the stable. However, indoors or out, hay should not be spread about on the ground as this leads to much wastage; inevitably it gets walked on and it will not then be accepted as food. Hay nets, hung high enough to stop a donkey getting a foot caught in the mesh or simple homemade hay racks are appropriate, outdoors as well as in. They should not be positioned too high either as a donkey should not always have to reach up for his food.

If the donkey's field is away from your house and he is not visible unless you actually go off to see him, do ensure that he is checked daily by somebody who knows how to recognise trouble, otherwise he could have an accident and remain in pain or even die without you being any the wiser.

Delousing

The best time to delouse a donkey is at midday in the sunshine. All the lice seem to crawl around to that part of the donkey's body which is in direct sunlight.

FARRIERY

The structure of the foot consists of three parts: the wall, the sole and the frog. All three are horny structures and are non-sensitive with neither nerve nor blood supply. This explains why shoeing nails can be driven through the wall and why the frog and sole can be cut with a knife without causing pain or bleeding.

The structure of the foot

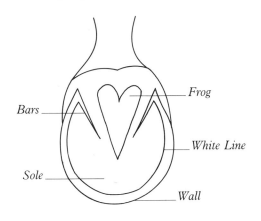

WALL
This is the part of the hoof visible when the foot is on the ground. It grows downwards from the coronet just like a fingernail and in the natural unshod state the rate of growth equals the rate of wear. The wall encircles the foot and is inclined inwards at the heels to form the bars. The outer surface of the wall has a glossy varnish-like finish which prevents undue evaporation from the horn so that it does not degenerate and become hard and brittle. The toe, the quarters and the heel all form part of the wall of the foot.

SOLE
This protects the foot from injury from the ground but it is not very thick and is easily damaged. In a healthy state it is concave, ie like a saucer turned upside down and therefore helps to give a better foothold.

FROG
This is an anti-slipping and anti-concussion device. It is the first part of the foot to make contact with the ground and therefore is important in

GROOMING

Your donkey will love being groomed and daily attention will give him great pleasure. It gets rid of sweat, helps circulation, gets rid of parasites, massages the body and tones up the skin, keeping the pores open and clean, and prevents girth galls if your donkey is used for riding. You will need the following equipment: body brush, dandy brush, metal curry comb, rubber curry comb, bucket, water brush, two sponges, hoof pick and hoof oil and brush.

Begin by picking out the feet with the hoof pick. Pick up each foot in turn, remove whatever may be lodged in it with the point of the hoof pick, working downwards from the heel to the toe. Clear the cleft of the frog and look for any signs of thrush.

Take the dandy brush and start at the poll on the near side. The object is to shift all caked dirt, sweat marks, etc. Certain parts of the body come in for special attention: points of hocks, fetlocks and pasterns. The dandy brush may be held in either hand, and it is used with short strokes or a to-and-fro motion. It may be helpful to grasp the tail with your free hand when working on the hind limbs. The use of the dandy brush on tender parts of the body is best avoided, a rubber curry comb used in the same way is an excellent alternative.

Next take the body brush. The short, close-set hairs of the body brush are designed to reach right through the coat to the skin beneath. Begin with the mane and thoroughly brush the crest beginning near the head. Then working on the body, begin at the poll region on the near side. Take the body brush in your left hand and the metal curry comb in your right, stand well back, work with a slightly bent arm and a supple wrist and lean the weight of your body behind the brush. Use short circular strokes in the direction of the lay of the coat. After every four or five strokes, draw the brush smartly across the teeth of the curry comb to dislodge the dirt. The curry comb in its turn is cleaned by tapping it out on the floor. When the near side has been completed, pass to the off side, change hands and repeat the process.

Now do the head. Untie the donkey, remove the head collar, and fasten the head-strap temporarily around the neck. Use one hand to steady the head and use the body brush carefully to avoid injuring tender parts or knocking bony projections.

ensuring a good foothold. Its peculiar wedge shape, irregular surface and central cleft help its anti-slipping function. Its effectiveness as a shock-absorber stems from its size and india-rubber-like consistency, its upward flexibility and the cushion within the foot upon which it rests. The importance of a healthy frog cannot be over-stressed – much lameness is directly attributable to slipping or to concussion in the leg.

INTERIOR OF THE FOOT

The inner foot is made up of bones, joints and sensitive structures, any or all of which are liable to injury should the wall, sole or frog be penetrated.

Hoofs are subject to wear, not only when the donkey is working, but with every step he takes. This wear will vary according to the weight of the animal, his conformation and gait, the degree of the donkey's exuberance, ground conditions, quality of diet, state of health and previous foot care.

Continued overleaf/

The Donkey Sanctuary vet attending to a patient's feet

Now take the sponge and a bucket of water. Wring out the sponge so that it is soft, clean and damp. Start with the eyes, sponge away from the corner and around the eyelids. Wash and wring out the sponge again and deal with the muzzle region, including lips and the inside and outside of the nostrils, in that order. The sponge should be rinsed and squeezed out after wiping each eye and nostril. Take the second sponge, rinse and wring out, move behind the donkey and attend to the whole dock region including the skin of the underside of the tail. If your donkey has a tendency to kick, or is not reliable, stand to one side to do this.

Once a week when the hoofs are dry, thoroughly oil them with a small brush dipped in hoof oil including the bulbs of the heel as far as the coronet. This not only improves their appearance but it is beneficial to broken or brittle feet.

Finally, the tail. Take only a few strands of hair at a time, do this by holding the tail and shaking a few strands free, brushing the ends clean first with a body brush.

Grooming gives a good opportunity to make a thorough check of your donkey. Make sure that his eyes are clear and bright with no cloudiness or foreign bodies; there is no discharge from his nose; no cuts or sores on his mouth; and no foreign bodies in his ears. Once a week brush out his ears with a soft brush.

Mutual grooming is thoroughly enjoyed

Farriery cont'd

TRIM INTERVALS

No donkey should go more than eight weeks between trims. Most farriers prefer a regular booking to occasional phone calls, so try making a booking for the same day of every second month. Shod animals should be seen every month. Most donkeys do not need shoeing as their feet can cope with even moderate amounts of work on the road. Regular work will stimulate greater foot growth. If your donkey can't wear out a set of shoes in three months, he might be better off without shoes.

FOOT SHAPE

The shape of the foot achieved by trimming should facilitate the donkey's comfort and ease of movement. If the toe is left too long Fig (i) the wear will be thrown on to the heel, creating an even longer toe by the next trim, eventually leading to the classic, but deplorable, 'Arabian slipper' shape Fig (ii). If the toe is too short, Fig (iii) the gait becomes stilted (like a lady in high heels), and the frog may lose contact with the ground. Both extremes will stress either the flexor or extensor tendons respectively and the abnormal load strain through the foot, pastern and fetlock joints will eventually cause joint disease.

These are the suggested parameters for good foot shape: Length Fig (iv); the height of the foot Fig (iv h) should never exceed the fore-aft length Fig (iv l). The angle of the front of the foot to the ground is dictated by the hoof pastern axis Fig (v). A–B should be kept as nearly as possible to the same angle as X–Y. This will normally mean that the lower-most growth ring on the hoof makes a very small angle with the ground Fig (vi). Hind feet are generally about five degrees more angled than front feet.

This should produce a sole with a uniform thickness of wall and white line, with the front one-third of the sole in contact with the ground and with a distinct contact between the frog and the ground.

Pick out your donkey's feet regularly with a hoof pick as thorns, stones, etc can easily become trapped there. This will also accustom him to being handled and he should have no fear of the farrier. Never attempt to trim your donkey's feet yourself unless instructed by the farrier as it is far more difficult than it looks.

Your donkey should not be forced to stand in muddy or fouled ground all day as such conditions can cause infection and deterioration of the hoof with problems such as thrush, seedy toe, etc developing (see A-Z of Donkey Health).

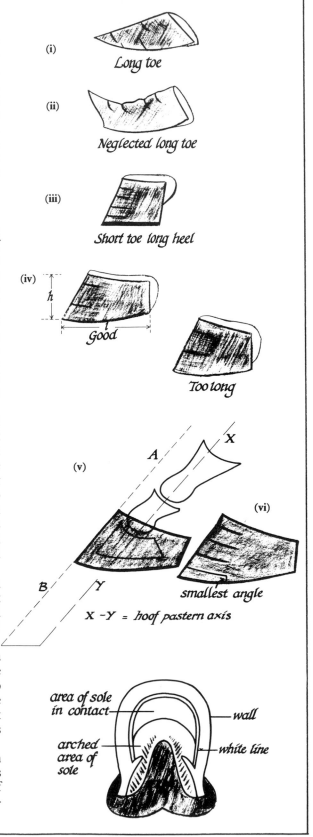

(i) *Long toe*

(ii) *Neglected long toe*

(iii) *Short toe long heel*

(iv) *h* *l* *Good*

Too long

(v) *A* *X* *B* *Y*

(vi) *smallest angle*

X–Y = hoof pastern axis

area of sole in contact — *wall*

arched area of sole — *white line*

GENERAL VETERINARY CARE

This is a guideline on basic veterinary care but it is emphasised that if in doubt the first priority must always be to contact your local veterinary surgeon and get professional help and advice as soon as possible.

WORMING

All donkeys have parasites to a greater or lesser extent and continued control is absolutely essential to the donkey's health and well-being. A basic regime, for a donkey grazing all year round, would be as follows:

Two doses of wormer, one month apart, in late spring, eg one dose end of April, one dose end of May.

Two doses of wormer, one month apart, in late autumn, eg end of October and end of November.

There are many modern wormers available and the following in co-operation with your veterinary surgeon's advice could be used: April – Telmin; May – Eqvalan; October – Eqvalan; November – Astrobot.

Remember when you acquire a new donkey you should isolate and worm him and prove him free of worms by testing, before allowing him access to pasture or before he mixes with existing residents.

If your donkey is stabled for part of the year, worm thoroughly as you bring him in. An additional worming is a good idea if transferring animals from one field to another or time the moves to coincide with your planned worming programme. Remember too, that picking up droppings from the pasture, and hygienic siting of muck heaps, can be as important as routine dosing.

LICE

There are two types of lice: biting and sucking lice, the latter usually infesting the roots of long hair, such as the mane and tail. Both thrive in dirty conditions but may be transferred to clean animals via buildings trees, etc. The animal becomes poor and suffers from itchiness and loss of coat and the insects can be detected when the coat is parted. Cleanliness of the animal and its surroundings is the best preventative but the following methods can also be used.

Insecticidal ear tags give four to six months protection and are best used during the summer as they also repel flies. The tags should never be attached to the ear but stapled to a neck collar or halter to provide a good contact with the coat. Recommended makes are – Stomoxin, Tirade,

Flectron, Stock Guard. 'Spoton' pour-on gives six weeks' protection and must be applied finely over a wide band shoulder to rump.

Eqvalan, an extremely good equine wormer, is used at the Donkey Sanctuary, and apart from eliminating gut lungworms and internal parasites Ivermec, the active ingredient, if given in appropriate dose rate, can also cope with skin parasites such as ticks and lice. Powders are not recommended because of the respiratory side-effects. However, if they are used then the powder should be applied once every two weeks for six applications. Whichever treatment is used all other animals in contact with your donkey will need to be treated too (ie equines, cattle, goats).

FLU AND TETANUS BOOSTERS

All donkeys should be inoculated against flu and tetanus as they can be killers. Once your donkey has been given his initial inoculation then you should arrange for him to receive a booster one year for flu and the next year for tetanus and always follow this procedure.

DENTAL CARE

From the age of five years onwards your donkey's teeth should be checked regularly by the veterinary surgeon and they may need to be rasped occasionally.

STARVATION

If you should acquire a donkey with acute malnutrition this is obviously very easy to spot. The donkey will have no fat reservoir whatsoever down the neck and all bones will be prominent and easily felt. The biggest danger with these animals is to overfeed and the temptation to give ad-lib feed can often be fatal. The first-aid procedures found to be most satisfactory are as follows:

1 Ensure it is in a warm, dry, airy, stable.
2 If at all possible place a small rug on the donkey's back which should be lightly fastened round the chest to prevent it slipping backwards.
3 Give the donkey a very small feed, mainly of bran or chaff with a small quantity of either flaked maize or crushed oats, moistened with molasses. This feed should not be over .5kg (1lb) in weight.
4 Allow the donkey access to approximately one fifth of a bale of hay.
5 Ensure that adequate clean fresh water is available.

Continued overleaf/

General Veterinary Care cont'd

If the donkey is found to be unable to stand unaided, then resist the temptation to sling the donkey (place straps under its body to help it to stand suspended from the rafters) as this can cause pressure sores. It is far better to allow the donkey to lie down, but do not allow him to lie flat out; keep him propped up by carefully placed straw bales. If the donkey is too weak even to attempt the food mentioned above, then glucose and water can be gently administered through the mouth until the veterinary surgeon arrives to fix a drip.

Not every 'starving' donkey will appear as malnourished as that described above. Great care must be taken with any donkey taken from a market as it could be several days since it has eaten and to give the donkey the normal full feed could be extremely dangerous.

Once the amount of feed has been set up by the veterinary surgeon this should be carefully adhered to and a gradual build-up started. Of importance at this time are the psychological needs of the donkey. A companion is a great help during this recovery period and encouragement and attention are needed. The sooner the donkey can be allowed to graze in a pasture the quicker his recovery but the greatest care must be taken that the donkey is not allowed to be exposed to wet and cold weather.

OBESITY

Many obese donkeys are in just as much danger as the malnourished donkey when changing homes. We have found in the sanctuary that the stress situation of perhaps leaving a loving home where the owners have died and the donkeys have been overfed or received too many titbits, can be vastly exacerbated by our trying to impose a slimming routine too early. Very fat donkeys are at risk of a condition known as hyperlipaemia (see page 190). During the possible stress period, which could be two to three months from arrival at a new home, the feed should be kept up and then very gradually a reduction should aim for the ideal weight for that donkey in a two or three year period of time.

LUNG PROBLEMS

These can have been caused by a variety of earlier complaints such as untreated pneumonia or lungworm. With the drugs now available it should

HOW TO AGE YOUR DONKEY

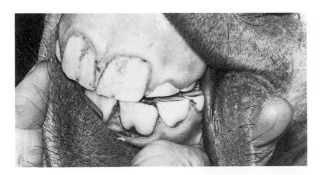

2½ years

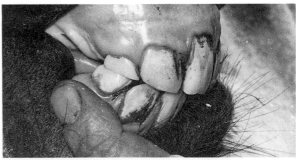

3½ years

8 years

11 years

be possible to control lungworm.

One of the most important things to avoid is dust which irritates the respiratory system and causes great distress to the donkey. The donkey should be bedded on peat rather than straw and fed on a special dampened hay which is sold under several trade marks such as 'Horseage' or 'Haylage'. This is partially dried hay which is then vacuum-packed and contains no dust at all. Donkeys enjoy this diet which during the winter can be interspersed with hard feed ration. Ventilation in the stable is all important.

SWEET ITCH

Skin problems fall into two main categories which can almost be classed as hereditary and environmental. One environmental problem is known as sweet itch. This causes the donkey a great deal of discomfort and distress and in many cases appears year after year. The best treatment is to keep your donkey inside during the hot summer days in a darkened area and only allow him out at night. This helps to a large extent and veterinary treatment with ointments such as 'benzyl benzoate' help to alleviate the situation.

PROTEIN POISONING

This can often be confused with sweet itch and many people telephoning the sanctuary describe this skin complaint. One of our first questions is to ask what the feed regime is for that particular animal and in very many cases we find that far too much protein is being given; the donkey is not able to absorb it and so develops the skin rash. A change of diet can often be the simple solution to this problem. Veterinary advice should always be sought on skin problems.

RINGWORM

The problem with ringworm is not the actual treatment for the donkey, which can be fairly simply carried out by the veterinary surgeon, but the treatment of the surroundings and buildings in which your donkey lives. These must be very extensively disinfected and steam-cleaned to prevent a recurrence of the complaint.

* * * * *

It must be stressed that the veterinary surgeon should always be contacted if you suspect your donkey is ill.

5 years

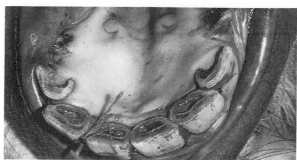

6 years

14 years

15-20 years

Donkeys and Mules at War

Until World War I armies depended almost entirely on animals for transport. Although some mules were bred deliberately for the purpose, many would have been taken from the local farmers in the areas where the war occurred.

Although many mule drivers still speak lovingly of their charges mules and donkeys were often worked to death. Many mules suffered terribly from saddle galls and malnutrition; when men at the front were starving neither time for attention or fodder was available. . .

Henry V is said to have used as many as 25,000 horses and many carts and waggons in his campaign in France. In 1588 a standing British Army of 4,081 horses and 41,380 men was authorised.

In the Peninsular War in Spain and Portugal the Duke of Wellington had 53,000 British troops supported by 10,000 pack mules. Wellington, a fine horseman, disliked wheeled transport, particularly bullock carts, believing it would slow down his columns and preferred pack transport, using mules where available.

The Royal Waggon Train was established in the British Army in 1802 to provide general transport while the Artillery Train was manned by artillery drivers. Due to economies the Royal Waggon Train was disbanded in 1833, resulting in a disastrous situation when the Crimean War broke out, only seventy-five mules and a few carts being landed in the Crimea to maintain 33,000 men. Public outcry resulted in the establishment of the Land Transport Corps with 30,000 horses in the Crimea.

The Military Train replaced the Land Transport Corps in 1856 and was equipped with horses. In the Abyssinian expedition in 1867 British and Indian Army troops on a combined basis made extensive use of pack mules over difficult country. In 1869 the Army Service Corps replaced the Military Train and was equipped with horses, carts and waggons which were used in the South African wars.

By the end of World War I the Army Service Corps had 552 horse transport companies and 605 motor transport companies. The use of horse and animal transport had been almost entirely replaced by motor transport by the outbreak of World War II and reliance placed on the Royal Indian Army Service Corps for pack mules which were used in France in 1940 and in the Abyssinian, Italian, and, above all, the Burma campaigns.

The last troop of mules in the British Army was disbanded in Hong Kong in 1976 and there are now no animal transport units. The Indian and Pakistan armies continue to make major use of animal transport and pack mules and the Spanish, Italian and Turkish armies, among others, still have animal transport units including pack mules.

SADDLERY

The pack saddles used, and the method of fitting, was the same in the British and old Indian armies and remain so in the Indian and Pakistan armies today. The saddles had saddle trees (frames) with front and rear arches of steel in four sizes attached to wooden side bars to fit over the animal's back. Underneath the side bars were strapped large, heavily padded panels of leather and felt which rested on the ribs. The saddle was fastened on to the mule by two strong webbing girths and kept in place longitudinally by a folded leather breast collar and a breeching attached to the saddle by steel chains hooked on to the saddle and also a leather crupper which went under the tail and was fastened to the rear arch of the saddle. These breechings, breast collars and cruppers were the most frequent causes of sores and rubbing of the skin, as it was difficult to keep them always at exactly the right tension.

Correct saddle fitting is even more vital with pack animals than with riding or draught animals. With pack animals the saddle carries the full weight of the load continuously unlike riding or draught animals. Although it is preferable to off-load a pack mule for a short break every two hours, there are times when this is impossible due to the terrain. Prolonged pressure from the load interrupts the blood supply to the load-bearing tissue.

War in Afghanistan

Even today mules are being used in war. In Afghanistan mules are often loaded with missiles and other war material while trekking across mountainous war zones. Due to the high death toll of Afghan mules from landmines and other attacks there is now a mule shortage and Tennessee mules are being brought in from the United States.

Indian Army transport cart, drawn by two mules

A donkey train at Rawalpindi, North-west Frontier Province of India (now in Pakistan) in 1942. The loads of hay were up to 10 feet wide. The donkeys took their work very seriously indeed and travelled at something between a walk and a trot as though there was a prize for the first one home

ACROSS THE CHINDWIN

In November 1944, after being responsible for training animal transport instructors from hundreds of units in South East Asia command, I flew to Burma to join one of the three mule companies which had been allotted to carry 32 Indian Infantry Brigade on an all pack basis to establish the first bridgehead of the 14th Army across the Chindwin in the reconquest of Burma.

My first examination of the mules was a horrifying experience. They were almost all out of condition and many with bad saddle galls which were healing very slowly. Heavy work, shortage of rations and bad weather conditions had taken their toll. I ordered a majority of the animals into the sick-lines to give them a better chance of quick recovery as there was a temporary lull in transport demands.

Within hours I was summoned by Brigadier Mackenzie, Commander of the Brigade, and informed that we would be marching out in three days' time. I warned him that if the mules were used in this condition many would be out of action within a few days and the success of the column would be jeopardised. A quiet giant, a man of great courtesy and leadership, he said we had no option but to comply with the order and that no replacement mules were available. Somebody had blundered with the loading tables and had calculated that every mule would be loaded, instead of providing the required 10 per cent spares to allow for casualties and for sick animals to recover without loads. It was a nightmare situation.

We ruthlessly cut the loading tables. The Brigade Mess had been allotted twelve mules and this was cut to six, which even then I thought extravagant, but it was not so easy cutting the number of mules per battalion which had to carry the men's rations, ammunition and other vital equipment. Additional rations would be supplied by air drops en route. We achieved the 10 per cent cut in the number of load carriers but there was no altering our date of departure and we had just three days to make our final preparations and get our animals as fit as possible within the time available. Our veterinary officers made it plain that they regarded it as a crime even to consider using animals in such a condition.

Three days later we marched out of Palel, east of Imphal, and headed for Mawlaik where our planned crossing of the Chindwin was to be made. Someone had carried out a reconnaissance of the route to Mawlaik which lay through hilly country and which was reported free of enemy. As a trained animal transport man he had paid due attention to watering points. A column of some 3,000 men with 1,400 animals can extend over more than 5 miles in single file as had to be the case most of the time in such difficult country. One of these watering points was located in a position where only eight animals could drink at one time with the result that the column behind was halted for a long period in a place where it was impossible to unload the waiting mules, some of which were stationary for up to two hours. The mistake did not occur again.

The Chindwin at Mawlaik is 550m (600yd) wide, swift flowing and very beautiful. No boats were available to transport the 1,400 animals and they swam in long chains behind a leading mule which was attached to a small inflatable assault boat with an outboard engine. We lost only three animals in the crossing. The mule is a very strong swimmer and despite the strength of the current had no difficulty in coping with the speed or the distance. The danger was that if one mule disengaged himself from the train of mules others would follow and swim downriver with the current. We were very pleased and surprised by the success of the operation and such minimal loss of animals.

Our landing point was some distance downriver on a large, convenient sandbank. Saddles and loads had to be ferried across in the inflatable assault boats. All saddles were numbered and it was a major operation ensuring that all 1,400 animals on arrival on the far bank were reunited with their correct, individual saddles. We were ordered to march out in two hours at first light. It was no good protesting that the men were very tired and that we needed more time to sort ourselves out and ensure each animal had its correct saddle and equipment.

The men managed to struggle in the darkness, without lights, most having three mules each to saddle up and load. There was a look of quiet pride on the faces of the men as we marched off in good order. Our morale could not have been higher. We were heading into virtually uninhabited and unknown country, ideal for mules, impassable for any other form of transport.

The terrain varied considerably. Occasionally we followed the dry bed of a chaung (river) and on one occasion I was actually able to mount my charger, 'Charpoy' ('the bed'), a huge, lazy animal who seemed startled by this sudden burst of high-speed activity as I galloped to the head of the column. Almost all the time it was hard footslogging in single file with much effort at the front cutting or clearing a way through. After much difficulty hacking our way through bamboo to the head of a valley we found it impossible to scale the ridge and the whole column had to be turned round, to some pointed comments from back down the column about the standard of map reading and reconnaissance.

On another occasion we had no option but to traverse a knife-

Travels with a Donkey

His donkey, Modestine, was pronounced unfit for travel and needed two days repose, but eager to reach Alais for his letters and, being in a civilised country of stage-coaches, he sold her.

'It was not until I was fairly seated by the driver, and rattling through a rocky valley with dwarf olives, that I became aware of my bereavement. I had lost Modestine. Up to that moment I had thought I hated her; but now she was gone, 'And oh! The difference to me!' For twelve days we had been fast companions; we had travelled upwards of a hundred and twenty miles, crossed several respectable ridges, and jogged along with our six legs by many a rocky and many a boggy by-road. After the first day, although sometimes I was hurt and distant in manner, I still kept my patience; and as for her, poor soul, she had come to regard me as a god. She loved to eat out of my hand. She was patient, elegant in form, the colour of an ideal mouse, and inimitably small. Her faults were those of her race and sex; her virtues were her own. Farewell, and if for ever . . .

'Father Adam wept when he sold her to me; after I had sold her in my turn, I was tempted to follow his example; and being alone with a stage-driver and four or five agreeable young men, I did not hesitate to yield to my emotion.'

Robert Louis Stevenson

edge ridge. The only way to get the mules on to the ridge without massive hold-ups was to leave them loaded and help them up the very steep approach slope using ropes round their hind-quarters. At the top they had to do an immediate 90 degree turn or drop straight over the other side. It was not possible on the hard rock to fix any restraining ropes and men had to do the best they could to turn the mules instantly as they reached the top. When the first mule went over the top I was lowered down the far side to shoot it if it was still alive. It had fallen about 10m (35ft) in an unbroken fall and was alive with no legs broken and

MULES IN THE FAR EAST

During the siege of Imphal, in which British and Commonwealth forces suffered 12,603 casualties and the Japanese in their greatest defeat 54,879, the humble mule came into his own doing work only he could do. The photograph was taken at Imphal – the valley in the mountain on the Indo-Burma border in April 1944. I am on the left and on the right is Bert Robson of Carlisle, we were both LACs with No 2944 Commando Squadron RAF Regiment. We both had experience with animals; I was brought up with horses and Bert was a slaughterman. The photograph shows a hill-top 1,535m (5,038ft) above sea level which for various reasons was nicknamed 'Nightmare Peak'. This area was the outer defence of 'Kipper Box' protecting the all-weather airstrip of Kangla situated on the valley floor. While the height might not seem that high, to reach the peaks was a very dangerous and hazardous operation, jungle-covered and very steep. To give you some idea, you had to put your head right back when standing on the valley floor to see the tops – it was like looking at a wall. The first stage, although twisting and turning, was fairly easy going, until you came to a very steep rock gulley (this was covered by a machine-gun post). At the top of this the path went round a rocky ledge with just enough room for a cradle-loaded mule – one false move and it would have been a drop of hundreds of feet. Where the photograph was taken was the only part without cover and it must have been taken towards the end of the siege because neither mule nor man lingered here – it was a mad dash to get under cover of the trees on the right. In a period of nine weeks we made 187 round trips with supplies, water, food, ammunition etc. You will see we were armed but not with a stick. We thought the world of those two mules and I am sure they knew it. The only reward we could give them was our hard tack biscuits.

Mules were found to be sure-footed and intelligent animals. Our duo got to know every step of the route. We used to give them their heads and walk behind holding on to their tails, chatting to them, their ears standing up like goal-posts. These mules were the lifeline to some 140 men. They worked under atrocious conditions, the climate just before a monsoon was very hot and humid. You can see the perspiration showing through my shirt. We were surviving on half rations – you can see by our thin appearance. Mules supported the 14th Army when the going was rough – they were its transport backbone without which all would have been lost. Yes, their courage and resilience saw us through, they won the hearts of many Burma veterans and earned their rightful place in the history of that campaign.

Henry Kirk, President, RAF Regiment SEAC Association, *British Mule Society Magazine*

Henry Kirk and Bert Robson with the mules at Imphal on the Indo-Burma border in 1944

lying on its side, still with the loads in position. I took off the top load and to my surprise the mule struggled to stand up. With help from me and relieved of the other load it succeeded and seemed unscathed. Four more mules fell in the same way and miraculously none were hurt.

Each night we had difficulty in finding adequate room to picket the mules inside the battalion box. Sometimes it was a desperate race against time to clear an area before darkness fell. There was almost no available grazing, let alone grazing for 1,400 animals, and we had to rely on feeding grain plus a very limited amount of bhoosa (straw) by air supply, full rations rarely ever being available because of poor flying weather. Water, too, for such numbers was a great problem and on one occasion the animals went some forty-eight hours without water.

At the end of each day's march I inspected all my animals. This often went on long after dark with the aid of a carefully shielded torch. There was little or no foot or leg trouble but the state of the backs was terrifying, with galls and open wounds which would take weeks to heal. We had no option, against all we had been taught and believed in, but to load the less badly galled animals, the most badly galled travelling as spares. We had jettisoned all non-essential loads at the start following my protest to the force commander. Now we were quickly heading into disaster with no hope of the mules recovering their condition under this heavy work.

It had been known in absolute emergencies in the past for the saddle blanket to be cut away to relieve pressure on a gall but this was the last resort used by mule commanders with repugnance. Our situation was much worse and it was a good job that mules could not speak or show pain like humans. From the parachute material and a form of coir stuffing used on the base of other dropped packages I had the saddlers make up tailored panels, like miniature eiderdowns to use on galled animals in place of the blanket, with the area over the gall free from padding, to enable them to continue carrying loads. The other mule commanders viewed the innovation with misgivings as though it remained a crime to use any means to load animals in such condition. The coir filling was harsh and easily compacted but no stuffing wool in the quantities required was available. I thought it seemed to help and that it was the best of a very bad job but we had no option but to press on.

Quite suddenly we emerged into comparatively flat land and our spirits soared. It was marvellous to see the animals grazing again for the first time since we had marched out. We crossed a single railway line, the rails of which were missing and felt we were back in civilisation. We had not seen a single civilian in our 250 mile journey, much less Japanese troops and had achieved total surprise. The Japanese garrison in Budalin fought very bravely almost to the last man before being overcome.

We received a message that the mule commanders were to parade the following day for the Divisional Commander, General Sir Douglas Gracey. I and the others feared we were due to receive at the least a severe reprimand for the state of our mules. Instead, almost with tears in his eyes, Douglas Gracey explained that our capture of Budalin by a given date was crucial to the

Oliver Twist

'Wo-o!' said Mr Gamfield to the donkey.

The donkey was in a state of profound abstraction: wondering, probably, whether he was destined to be regaled with a cabbage stalk or two when he had disposed of the two sacks of soot with which the little cart was laden; so, without noticing the word of command, he jogged onward.

Mr Gamfield growled a fierce imprecation on the donkey generally, but more particularly on his eyes; and, running after him, bestowed a blow on his head, which would inevitably have beaten in any skull but a donkey's. Then, catching hold of the bridle, he gave his jaw a sharp wrench, by way of gentle reminder that he was not his own master; and by these means turned him round. He then gave him another blow on the head, just to stun him till he came back again.

Charles Dickens
From *The Donkey Book* by Phosphor Mallam (Methuen & Co Ltd)

Correct Saddle-fitting for a Pack Mule

1 The withers must not be pinched or pressed, the front arch of the saddle tree is designed to avoid this.
2 There must be no pressure on the spine, the saddle tree is arched to prevent this.
3 There must be free shoulder-blade movement. This is achieved by the rigidity of the sidebar of the saddle tree.
4 The weight must be upon the upper part of the ribs and borne by the muscles covering the ribs. The length of the saddle tree does not extend to the loins.
5 The weight of the load must be evenly distributed over the weight-bearing surface. The position of the hooks on the saddle and design of the stuffing pockets, which are individually stuffed with wool to fit the mule's back, are designed to achieve this if the animal is properly loaded.
6 The saddle should be level on the animal's back. The wool in the stuffing pockets can be adjusted to ensure this.

Major P. G. Malins MBE MC
(ret'd)

whole reconquest of Burma to enable our forces to reach southern Burma before the monsoon set in. We had achieved our objective with a few days to spare against considerable difficulties, not least the condition of the mules. Our men and mules would now have a well-earned rest and recuperate in a gentle march without loads all the 400 miles to Rangoon.

Without loads, with good rations, adequate water and often with good grazing available the mules filled out and after grooming their coats looked a picture. Our three companies reached Hmawbi, 30 miles from Rangoon, the war in Burma having virtually finished.

After Japan's surrender our gallant four-legged comrades in arms were returned to India where it became something of a national scandal when it became known that some had been sold to be ill-treated pulling tongas, the ubiquitous two-wheeled carriage, often hopelessly overloaded with passengers.

TRAINING OF MULES IN THE ROYAL INDIA ARMY SERVICE CORPS

In India in peacetime mules were normally obtained for the army from within the country and an adequate time was available for their training. Indigenous sources were inadequate to meet wartime requirements and had to be augmented with large numbers of mules from the Argentine and other areas.

Facing the Argentine mules for the first time in the paddock was the nearest to bull fighting that an animal transport man was ever likely to encounter. Up to that moment the mules' whole experience of men had been violent – rounding-up and branding in the Argentine, herded on and off transport and ships – and they reacted accordingly, usually kicking and biting furiously. With four weeks' training or less they were transformed into pack or draught animals, highly trained and disciplined.

In 1866 in Australia the German, Lichtwalk, had devised a system to replace the rougher ways of animal training then used. Attempts to use it in the Indian Army had been made on several occasions prior to 1914 but not until after World War I was Colonel Lee of the 15th Lancers successful in having the system recognised in the face of much prejudice and opposition. It was to prove of inestimable value in World War II.

A mule company on the march, Grand Trunk Road, North-west Frontier Province in 1942

The object of the system was to handle Argentine and other obstreperous types of mule quietly to produce, in one month in wartime and three months in peacetime, an animal unafraid of either a dark or fair man, to make him docile and willing to be groomed, saddled and shod, accustomed to gunfire and transport.

In concept the system was similar to that used now for almost all animal training that for a mule 'the way to his heart is through his stomach'. The initially highly strung mule was quietly approached using a blob-stick, a stick about 2.5m (8ft) long covered with padding at one end. Fodder was placed on the padded end of the blob-stick and offered to the mule who would sniff it nervously and after a short hesitation eat it, the blob-stick making contact with the mule's muzzle in the process. After letting him feed in this way a few times and accustoming him to the feel of the blob-stick it was then possible to stroke him round the muzzle with it without putting fodder on it. As the mule's confidence grew the trainer would gradually succeed without risk to himself to get the mule to permit being touched with the blob-stick, until he was able to touch all parts of the mule by hand including the sensitive legs.

As soon as the mule had become used to contact with its legs a 5m (16ft) rope was attached by a padded shackle to a foreleg, and the rope, part covered with felt or a blanket to avoid cutting the spine, was carried over the back of the animal. A blanket apron was attached, suspended by rope from the neck of the animal to prevent chafing by a 6m (20ft) rope which was attached to a hind leg, using a padded shackle and the rope brought up between the forelegs over the apron and through a hole in the top of the apron which contained two leather loops for the rope. This equipment was known as the 'docility training tackle'.

By pulling on the hind leg rope, the leg would be drawn forward, the hoof remaining on the ground and the rope fixed so that the animal could not kick, enabling the trainer safely to play with the shackled foreleg, repeatedly raising it and gradually

Mules crossing the river following the little 'bell' donkey. Mules have been known to refuse to cross a river until a 'bell' donkey went first.

The Friends of Socrates

Socrates: Suppose I persuaded you to buy a horse and go to the wars. Neither of us knew what a horse was like, but I knew that of tame animals you believed a horse to be the one which has the longest ears.

Phaedrus: That would be ridiculous.

Socrates: There is something more ridiculous coming: suppose, further, that in sober earnest I, having persuaded you of this, went and composed a speech in honour of an ass, whom I entitled a horse, beginning: 'A noble animal and a most useful possession, especially in war, and you may get on his back and fight, and he will carry baggage or anything.'

Phaedrus: How ridiculous!

Socrates: Ridiculous! Yes; but is not even a ridiculous friend better than a cunning enemy?

From *The Donkey Book* by Phosphor Mallam (Methuen & Co Ltd)

TRAINING THE MULE HANDLERS

It was necessary during World War II to train men, with no previous experience of mules, to handle them efficiently and fearlessly. Men usually rapidly lost their fear as they became used to grooming and handling their animals, but in the Royal Indian Army Service Corps we tried to give the men additional confidence and enjoyment. Bareback riding without saddles or stirrups was used as a training aid, preferably in a paddock and included jumping and racing.

MULE WRESTLING

Two teams, normally each of six men mounted bareback on mules, would station themselves around a 30yd circle. The teams would advance into the ring and seek to remove the riders of the opposing team from their mules or force them out of the ring. This almost invariably resulted in men hanging upside down with their legs locked round the mule's body or neck before finally parting company. Sometimes men from both teams would be struggling on the same mule. The mules seemed to love it and stood their ground whatever their riders did to each other. The winning team was the one with at least one man on a mule left in the ring.

OFFICER TRAINING

Catching mules in a paddock without halters or any other aids was used for officer training. Each officer would be assigned a mule and all the mules would then be let loose in the paddock, each officer having to catch his mule and take it out of the paddock. When the fun started the paddock would be full of officers and mules, making it comparatively easy for those lucky enough to grab their mules immediately. But as the number of mules and officers was progressively reduced, the remaining mules had more room to run and evade their pursuers who were becoming more and more exhausted and frustrated. The officers who had caught their mules would stand round the outside of the paddock flinging ribald comments at those still struggling. Eventually one poor officer would be left, his mule sensing his dejection and playing up in the most spirited way, apparently trying to prove he, not the officer, was master. It was a point of honour to catch your mule, however long it might take.

MOUNTED TUG OF WAR

Teams each of six men mounted bareback were positioned with the mules at 90 degrees to the rope which passed through the hands of their riders. The mules, probably wondering what it was all about, remained more or less stationary while the riders heaved on the rope as in an ordinary tug of war.

TENT COMPETITION

Competing teams, each of ten men, would be 'asleep' in their tents with their mules picketted. When the whistle blew the men had to strike and pack the tent and other baggage, assemble the saddlery, saddle the mules and load the tent and baggage on to the mules, completing this in about four minutes. Time additions were made for any mistakes, the winning team having the lowest time. This was useful training in case this was suddenly necessary on active service, although animal transport personnel rarely had the luxury of tents on active service, usually sleeping under groundsheets stretched over a piece of rope supported by branches cut from trees.

OTHER TRAINING

Correct saddling-up was critically important and men were trained to assemble the saddlery and saddle-up blindfold so that in enemy territory they could do this noiselessly in complete darkness. Although it was not the responsibility of the mule driver to pack and tie loads, this being done by the infantry or the personnel to whom the baggage belonged, the mule driver had to ensure the loads were properly packed and tied. Each mule driver, therefore, had to be thoroughly trained in packing and loading all types of loads so that he could reject unsatisfactory loads or ensure they were properly repacked and loaded.

Grooming, always vital, was especially important on active service. Each driver normally led three mules which he had to groom daily, often after a long day's march. Great emphasis was, therefore, placed on following a strict sequence of grooming, men usually stripping to the waist to put the maximum effort into the job.

Since mule companies usually operated in rugged country with mountains and often unbridged rivers and streams it was highly desirable that all men should be able to swim and they were trained accordingly. They greatly enjoyed going into the water when necessary and playing around with the strong-swimming mules. Marching and night marching exercises over every available type of country were essential training to accustom trainees to the very exacting conditions normally found on active service. This included river crossings with improvised equipment, entraining, embussing and emplaning animals, and anything else likely to be encountered on active service.

Major P. G. Malins MBE MC (ret'd)

lowering it to the ground. The shackled hind leg was then drawn forward raising it off the ground. The mule thus became accustomed to having its legs raised for grooming and inspection. The trainer next showed he was master by cupping hands over the mule's eyes, to obscure its sight and his nostrils to obstruct his breathing, followed by moving his tail up and down, and pulling the animal off balance.

The mule was then shown the grooming kit with fodder placed on each article. The trainer would pat and stroke the animal before using the kit. Similar methods were used in accustoming the animal to a saddle, the saddle first being shown to the mule with fodder on top of it. While the mule was still eating the fodder, the saddle was passed over his eyes and head and down rubbing his neck and back with it until it was correctly located. This was usually the trickiest moment and it might take several attempts before the mule was successfully saddled and girthed. While the first load was often resented, the mules rapidly became used to carrying loads. Throughout, patience and kindness were essential and were richly rewarded as the most fractious of mules responded to the training.

Noise training was initiated, rattling tins of stones behind handfuls of fodder followed by louder noises and gunfire, culminating in the mules passing repeatedy under a simulated 'dive bomber' in the form of a fairground type swing-boat. The animals were led into a narrow channel in a continuous stream with the 'dive-bomber' with its hand-cranked, blaring siren just skimming backwards and forwards over their backs.

Final training included embussing and debussing, marching under load in column (including passing over bridges, through defiles, over obstacles) and showing them waving flags and other distractions and traffic. With this training the mule settled down with a minimum of trouble with other mules in a company and became almost immediately operational.

Training for draught animals involved putting the mule with a quiet, well-trained mule, padding the parts of the cart on which the trainee mule might injure himself if he kicked out or struggled, lowering the curricle bar of the cart gently on to his saddle and accustoming the mule to reins, being driven on roads, in traffic and over different types of terrain.

No man was allowed to use a twitch on the ears or lips of animals (a common practice among Indian civilian pony and mule operators). The use of twitches was authorised only in the presence of a veterinary officer or a company commander and then only on the lips.

The only permissible restraint which could be used to control a bad kicker was a leather strap called a 'French hobble' which was strapped round both hind legs immediately above the hocks, enabling the animal to walk normally but restricting his ability to kick. The use of this device, if only for a few days, seemed to have a lasting effect in inhibiting an animal from kicking and I never met an animal which needed this restraint for more than a short period.

Hard-worked mules on active service rarely, if ever, played up, perhaps out of commonsense to save their energy, due to well developed habits, good training and handling.

Royal Indian Army Service Corps animal transport officers in training at Garwhal, Himalayas, 1942

Mule wrestling at Jullundur, India, in 1944. Opposing teams of six men on six mules advance from opposite sides of a 30-yard circle. The winning team is the one which has forced all of the other riders' mules out of the ring, or forced the riders off their mules

Helping the Handicapped

For many years, the Riding for Disabled Association has helped children and adults by providing riding facilities using ponies and horses. For various reasons, which included fears that donkeys may upset the horses used or pass on some infection, the donkey was excluded from official activities. However, the Slade Centre, opened in 1978, provides donkey riding or driving for over two hundred handicapped children who come with their hospital or school groups on a regular weekly basis. The project was founded by Elisabeth Svendsen because of her love of both children and donkeys and after a difficult three-year period of negotiating planning permission for the purpose-built centre, it has proved its worth in physical and mental therapy including stimulation of weaker limbs and muscles, extension of vocabulary and experience in learning to care for animals. Most of the children are multiple handicapped and derive much benefit from the space at the centre, after enclosed wards or classrooms, and from the freedom of choice in attractive activities in the form of creative play, toys and games which are provided.

There is no doubt that the *crème de la crème* donkeys selected to work at the Slade Centre really enjoy their job. Each morning they line their rails as the specially adapted ambulance passes with its load of handicapped children arriving for their session at the centre. The children's faces, pressed against the window looking for their first sight of the donkeys, vary tremendously; some are able to fully appreciate what will happen but for others the passive vacant stare can well belie unknown inner feelings. For those 'on duty' the arrival of the bus generally coincides with the final fitting of the tack. The donkeys always like to be ready to greet the children; the more-able ones running from the coach to get their first feel and pet of their donkey for the day.

To the donkey the handicapped child can do no wrong. If an adult were to crawl around the donkey's legs, grasping handfuls of his hair in spasmodic clenched fists, the donkey would soon kick out to remove the offending object. How do they know that this is a child who cannot control movement; how can they stand so patiently with the screams of the mentally disturbed ringing in their ears and how can they so gently with their head nudge away fingers which seem intent on pinching or squeezing? Their reward must be in the very real emotion which spills out from these children.

In the arena itself the donkeys thoroughly enjoy the tasks they are asked to do. Calmly they will wait while their rider attempts to do the exercises or games. For those in wheelchairs driving

Slade Centre children enjoying contact with a new foal

Enjoying the fresh air in the lanes around the centre

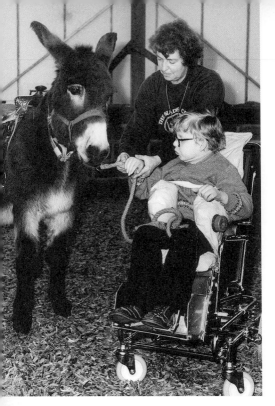

Instruction on leading a donkey from Pat Feather

the traps, the donkeys respond happily to their disabled passenger's requests. No fear here of a donkey bolting startled by the backfiring of a vehicle or the sudden barking of a dog; a donkey's natural reaction is to stand stock-still and survey the situation giving both his driver and himself time to assess the matter.

The donkeys thoroughly enjoy taking the children on the country rides and to the children, for once in their lives sitting higher in the world than any adult, viewing the countryside over hedges and over gates, the feeling of being in charge of a large living animal must be a dream.

Sessions vary in length from one and a half hours to five hours and lunch is a focal point for those staying the day. Each child has a morning and afternoon ride. Teachers, nurses and physiotherapists accompany their groups and find that most of the children, whose ages range from three to twenty years, respond with varying degrees of enthusiasm or emotion to the freedom and happiness of the day.

Facilities consist of a large play area, surrounded by a kitchen, medical room, toilets and office, from which, divided by shatterproof glass sliding doors and surmounted by an eyecatching mural of life-size donkeys, is a viewing gallery overlooking the riding arena. This is floored by a 10cm (4in) layer of sand covered with waterproof sheeting and topped by Dormit bark chippings. There are overhead gas heaters and extractor fans and four adjacent stalls with tack and equipment rooms. A unique feature is the observation room with a one-way glass window through which teachers, medical or riding staff can observe progress with the children unaware of their presence. Dicta-loop head sets are operated from here, with a microphone for instructing those who find concentration difficult and it is remarkable what good results can be obtained when the child hears only his teacher or riding instructor and all other sound is obliterated.

Centre staff consists of Patricia Feather, Principal, a qualified teacher in charge of the centre, a BHSI, a BHSAI, a groom and the ambulance driver who transports the children in the converted minibus and helps with the riding. There are several enthusiastic voluntary helpers, vitally necessary if we are to give adequate support to some of the less-able children.

A great number of the children are brain-damaged which usually means some loss of control over at least one limb and often in all four and lack of co-ordination and balance in consequence, so western saddles are found to be a good means of inducing better posture, while at the same time inspiring confidence and providing a pommel to clutch when reins would be too 'fine' a means of support. Motor impulses are unpredictable and a child can move uncontrollably in and out of spasm.

Small athetoid children are more comfortable and more easily supported in a saddle basket although there is usually the problem of the child's head which needs to be held in a comfortable, forward-looking position, as the motion of the ride causes it to roll or jerk backwards and forwards. The basket is used in only one or two cases and always with enough supporters to ensure safety as the child is securely strapped in. Normal stirrups or alternatively elastic-sided safety irons are used and the children

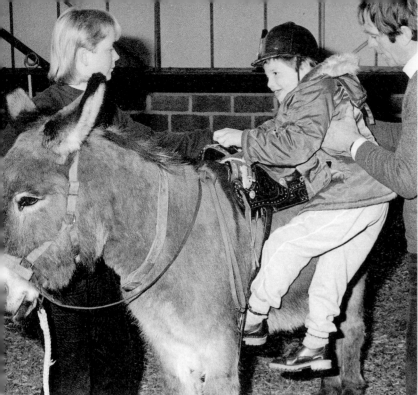

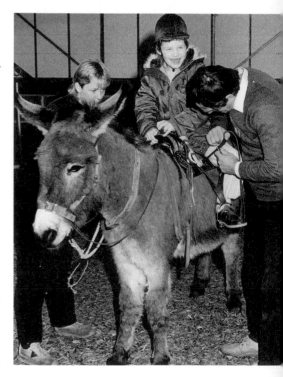

Helping a child to mount (left) and preparing for the off!

are encouraged to use them properly. This is often a matter for constant reminding and habit-forming. Hat wearing is another, for mentally handicapped children frequently dislike the feel of the hard hat and the chin protector and their first, often constant reaction, is to get rid of it. Broad elastic chin straps can be useful. All donkeys are led on head collars, without bits, although for driving a normal harness is used with a bit but the child holds 'false' reins attached to the head collar.

Riding is the important and most therapeutic part of the day at the Slade Centre and where possible it is taught to the best of each individual's ability. For some children this may mean only being lifted onto the donkey, supported throughout, and lifted off after five minutes. With others it involves grooming, tacking-up, mounting unaided, riding with exercises and games executed to a fairly high standard, dismounting, unsaddling and leading donkeys to their stalls or field.

Donkeys and children are matched as far as possible; the 50kg (8st) weight limit eliminates any possible distress to the young and healthy donkeys and heavier children ride in a trap. There is a specially built, lightweight trap with a ramp so that wheelchair children who are too heavy, or for whom discomfort is caused, need not be taken out of the chair. To foster a feeling of involvement and control, there are reins to hold.

To many handicapped children, animals are a cause for alarm, panic and general excitement and much time is spent in persuading the children to approach the donkeys calmly and quietly and to stroke or feel them gently. This has a very beneficial effect on the hyperactive or violently aggressive brain-damaged patients who are usually unable to communicate verbally but who appear to derive satisfaction and happiness from physical contact with such a large shaggy animal, which they cannot pick up, but which will stand patiently whilst being touched.

The Slade Centre

The donkeys used at the Slade Centre in Sidmouth provide handicapped children with healthy exercise, great enjoyment, a challenge they feel they can overcome and, above all, a sense of achievement.

Long may this facility be available. After all, Our Lord rode into Jerusalem on a donkey, and we can all learn something from Him!

Leslie Crowther,
Patron of the Slade Centre

TYPES OF HANDICAP ENCOUNTERED AT THE SLADE CENTRE

Brain-damage, including ESN(S) (Educationally Subnormal)

These children can be the victims of congenital brain damage, pre-natal rubella, accidents or child abuse. Usually there is a lack of speech, little comprehension and often bizarre behaviour – self-mutilation, head banging, rocking and outbursts of violence – most of which becomes less evident when the child is taken to the donkey. We think that there is a therapeutic satisfaction from the warmth of the donkey's hair, into which the child is encouraged to put his or her hands.

One girl, a strong and violent teenager, gained peace by moving her hand over the body of a donkey, smiling in delight, especially at the warm breath on her hand. She was persuaded to lead donkeys, a rare participation for her, in a constructive activity and obviously under careful supervision but nevertheless quite a breakthrough. Another boy, eleven years old at the time, was most alarmed when he first saw a donkey but after weeks of observing his fellows riding, he was persuaded to lead one, which he did quite well and then actually mounted at the mounting block and just sat, getting used to the feeling, until one day, as the donkey was led forward, he gave a roar of laughter and delight and consented to ride every week.

Progress often seems to be non-existent, until records are consulted and it is realised that a child who insisted on lying on his back along the length of the donkey some five years ago, is now actually sitting and occasionally holding the reins.

ESN(M) This term covers a great many facets of subnormality, from the high-grade Down's Syndrome child to the child of intelligent and normal appearance with learning difficulties or speech and nervous disorders.

Donkey riding appeals to them, perhaps more than to any other group, and a particular example is a small boy, able to utter only a few words, whose face lights up with joy and who

PRINCESS ANNE

On 12 September 1985 we had the immense pleasure of receiving Her Royal Highness, the Princess Royal, Mrs Mark Phillips who came to visit both the Slade Centre and the Donkey Sanctuary. It was a marvellous day; we had invited all the schools in the local area to take the opportunity to see and meet the princess and, of course, there were a large number of supporters and local visitors who wanted to be there to enjoy the day with her. Each school was given an allocated position close to the royal walkabout and, as you can imagine, every donkey was given an extra special grooming that day. There was great excitement when the helicopter landed. She was obviously greatly impressed and moved by all the children who were waving and shouting and paid particular attention to over one hundred handicapped children who had come to watch.

Those children selected to ride for the day really enjoyed their moment of glory and the Princess Royal also spent time in the large play area, adjacent to the riding arena, talking to the children and to their teachers. She then made her way through the sanctuary grounds, visiting the hospital in which she was most interested, and spending time with many of our favourite donkeys, including Buffalo. She was very interested in details of the work being done abroad and when she left, over twenty minutes late, she was seen off by a pantomime donkey who had great trouble in giving the necessary curtsy! It really was a day to remember and a great honour for the sanctuary.

Thank You

Dear Mrs Svendsen,

Thank you *ever* so much for allowing us to come to your Slade Centre for such a wonderful camp. I also thank you very much for the inflatable boat (which I won) and the book, it is wonderful to think of all the donkeys able to benefit from your love and care. The sanctuary amazed me, I had no idea there were so many donkeys in Britain! At the camp I cared for Wilma and she behaved perfectly.

I really enjoyed going round the hospital and seeing the soft rooms and transport rail. It was a lovely feeling to be in a yard surrounded by twenty donkeys. I have a collection box and on Friday am going collecting for the sanctuary. I am particularly interested in the International Donkey Protection Trust as I plan to be a doctor missionary. Many thanks, love from Susie Pirie.

PS I have labelled this NOT URGENT as I think you will have more important donkeys to attend to.

laughs out loud the moment he comes through the door of the centre. He makes straight for the donkeys, still laughing, just to feel them and he is always first to demand a ride and has to be forcibly held back each time a group is taken to the riding arena. He has mastered the rudiments of basic riding and it is his greatest achievement so far. While he is in this state of euphoric alertness, we work on his speech which comes so much more readily with his enthusiasm; the knowledge that a second ride comes after lunch keeps the talking going!

A child who is intensely antisocial, who tends to always play alone, looks more relaxed and happy once he is riding: the motion is soothing; an adult is giving him plenty of attention and he will often respond surprisingly with a flow of conversation which may not always be comprehensible but which, for that child, is quite remarkable.

The aim in this group is to fulfil each individual's potential and to work on their difficult areas. If aggressiveness is their Achilles' heel, gentleness with the donkeys is emphasised; if nervousness overwhelms them, they are coaxed and persuaded to make contact with the warm animal; if screaming or shouting is their usual vocal contact, piped music over the loudspeaker system can be the answer. In schools for special children, especially ESN, individuality is the key to treatment. There is a great need for enough staff to cope adequately with each child at the centre, which is why it is important for there to be as many regular staff and helpers as possible.

Down's Syndrome Children Again, there are many variables and degrees of this handicap from those termed 'high grade' with well-developed basic academic skills, to those who will never speak, often suffer from deafness and who lack control over their bodily functions.

The former group do extremely well in developing riding

Posting letters helps to improve co-ordination

Poor Relations?

I'm happy to be included with anything to do with our little friends the donkeys, those passive little animals so loved by the children. Seldom, if ever, do you come across one that is a rogue, or bad tempered and because of their build, they seem to be the poor relation of the equestrian world. . .

Not for them, the sleek classic lines of the racehorse. . . nor the beauty of the Arab stallion . . . nor the classic features of the Lippizaner and denied the power and grandeur of the shire . . . and yet just as willing and lovable.

One has to be thankful that there are homes for retired and ill-treated donkeys such as the Donkey Sanctuary, and they deserve all the support they can get.

After all . . . it was the humble donkey which brought Our Lord to Bethlehem.

Charlie Chester,
Patron of the Slade Centre

proficiency but need much 'good habit' training. They need constant reminding, usually, in all that one takes for granted in the able rider: to put on a hat; to mount from the near side; to hold the reins correctly; to sit up rather than slouch with rounded back, a tendency prevalent in this group. High standards are rightly demanded from them and they derive great joy with development in speech, posture and social training. Occasionally one meets with aggression, this must be tempered by very firm, controlled restraint. Patience and forbearance are vital in the sometimes difficult task of controlling outbursts of temper, violence or abuse from these often volatile children.

Profoundly Deaf Children Deaf children rely on their acute sense of sight and touch. Some little hearing is achieved with modern hearing aids which are left off when riding as the high frequency 'whistle' is distressing to the donkey. Speech must be encouraged in these children and signs disallowed, except in an emergency.

Deaf children do extremely well in riding; they are adept at imitating and need minimal teaching in rein holding, correct position and posture after being initially taught. More adventurous exercises can be attempted and a high degree of control, balance and confidence comparatively easily achieved including riding without leaders. It is essential that deaf children are trained to concentrate on watching what is going on around them; they are not going to hear anything which might result in a sudden donkey jump and must be aware at all times of their surroundings. Riding terms, 'walk on', 'trot on' and 'whoa' are encouraged and deaf children require little explanation of the resulting movements.

Visually Handicapped Children Most children, by using other senses, compensate for any physical lack and in blind children, therefore, touch and hearing are of paramount importance. When a child, on his first visit to the Slade Centre, asked 'What is a donkey?' it was obvious that (a) he was nervously anticipating the unknown and (b) that it was going to be almost impossible to put an image into his mind verbally. After his sensitive hands had been guided over the shape of the donkey with meaningful comments from the instructor – 'feel his long ears', 'he has very hard hoofs', 'he swishes his tail to keep off the flies', 'this is called a saddle and you will sit on it' – the boy was smiling happily and eager to learn how to mount and hold the reins.

Blind children are more aware of their surroundings than sighted people and they keep their place in a line of riders by listening to the number of donkeys in front of and behind them. Usually very intelligent, they learn to control their mounts and respond readily to calls of 'left' and 'right' with retentive memories as to the dimensions of the riding arena after very few sessions.

Spina Bifida and Other Related Physical Disabilities These sometimes grotesquely misshapen wheelchair children, who are often quite intelligent, perhaps gain more than most in the act of riding for they fully appreciate that when mounted, they can at last achieve some degree of physical normalcy. You can fully understand the child who says: 'I like being on a donkey, it makes me feel like you.'

Physical difficulties vary so much in these patients that it is impossible to generalise over the standards and quality of riding which can be achieved. What one can do proficiently with the hands, another can do only by compensating with legs and feet and each must be tutored in accordance with his own needs. We *always* ascertain from teachers or nurses, with their specialist knowledge, which areas should be developed and which left alone.

Spastic or Cerebral Palsied Children In some cases, spasticity is hardly apparent, in others all too obvious. Spastic children can suffer from weak muscles in certain areas and from convulsive spasms. Some spastically paralysed children may have permanent muscle constriction. Obviously the degree of severity must be taken into consideration when riding. Many of these children have no speech or way of showing their emotions or feelings, so much care is needed and it is better to approach the remedial exercise with too much caution than too little.

It is very important for the children to have as much physical contact as possible with the donkeys, and grooming is an excellent way of bringing them together

EXERCISES AND GAMES

These are very simple as most of our children are mentally handicapped and the exercises and games are taught mainly to give confidence, balance, co-ordination and, where necessary, strength to a weaker part of the body or mobility to a spastic muscle. Exercises are done at either the halt or the walk and consist of body twisting, arm raising/lowering, pointing/clapping/waving, touching toes, head, knees, touching parts of the donkey, standing in stirrups and 'round the world' (turning in a complete circle on the saddle).

Games include picking up coloured quoits either at random or specifically requested colours, of varying degrees of thickness, carrying them round two sides of the arena and hanging them

COMMENTS ON THE SLADE CENTRE

'The Slade Centre provides a fun and motivating environment for the children to learn. Riding the donkeys not only enhances their sensory experiences but helps to direct and focus them. In addition dealing one to one with the donkeys aids them in overcoming their fear of animals.

'It gives them a completely different environment from school, thus offering them a wider range of activities and experiences from which to learn.'

Staff of Ellen Tinkham School, Exeter

'The Slade Centre has offered invaluable help to the children of the Partial Hearing Unit. I always feel sorry we didn't take advantage of the facility sooner. I feel we were not aware of what deaf children had to gain and rejected the experience until we had children with balance problems or awkward movement.

'Deaf children relax in the play area, where my assistants and I have a chance to watch and assess them, perhaps the only chance we ever get without the presence of work. The staff at the Slade Centre willingly comment and advise on the children and through their eyes we often see another facet of the children.

'The riding and contact with the donkeys gives so much. It gives a vehicle to extend language. A purpose for offering good speech. Remember donkeys never look shocked if speech and language are not perfect. There is experience to explain at home, something possibly brothers and sisters don't do. It gives great confidence, poise, a chance to excel and even show off. There is encouragement from people who the children count as their closest friends. There is also constant follow-up work and projects we carry on with at school.'

Bridget Roberts, Partial Hearing Unit, Honiton

'The experience gained from the visits to Slade Centre is very valuable for all the children albeit relative to their various levels of ability and awareness. For some it is the thrill of being in contact with a warm, living creature, sitting high off the ground and away from school in a new environment. For others there are the skills developed as they learn to ride and control the donkeys, and this, of course, helps to build up their self-confidence which all too often is so sadly missing.'

Millwater School, Honiton

'The children in the assessment unit have learning difficulties brought about by a variety of physical, mental and emotional problems. All have benefitted from the relaxed, happy atmosphere at the centre and from contact with the patient, gentle donkeys they ride. To give just a few examples – a withdrawn child who had an abnormal fear of all animals now happily rides a donkey and is able to approach and touch the donkeys without fear. Another child who seldom spoke now chats freely to both adults and children. Much of his new-found confidence is due to his earlier encounters with the donkeys and the freedom from pressure that he felt when he was with them. A third child with cerebral palsy can now sit unaided on a donkey, his balance much improved by the riding sessions.

'All our children have gained so much from the Slade Centre. Because of this we are delighted to be given the opportunity to increase our visits from fortnightly to weekly and I am sure that the benefit to the children will increase accordingly.'

Pat Henderson, Newtown First School, Exeter

on a pegboard where peg heights vary from stirrup height to above head height. Posting letters is also a favourite in which a 'letter' or Christmas card is picked up and carried to a mailbox and posted. Games with a competitive element are very rarely played as this distresses many children but a sack race, with a group of fairly able children, is occasionally enjoyed and involves mounting and dismounting. Educational games with numbers are enjoyed, when riders are requested to point to certain single digit numbers and to walk the donkey to them.

RECORDS

It is important to keep individual records not only of each child's actual approach to and achievement in riding but also of his or her activities when not in the riding arena, for these can often affect the actual progress in riding. Obvious habits, such as self-mutilation, rocking, or involuntary habit-formed movements like head rolling, can be impediments to good riding for the child and annoying to the donkey. Very often these movements are not evident from the time the child mounts to the time he is again on the ground or in his wheelchair but a few persist throughout the ride. Recording the need for firm and gentle verbal and sometimes physical, reminders to 'keep still' or 'stop biting your hand' is helpful. Often the condition is helped if the child will hold the reins, or if the donkey is trotted, a motion which pleases the more emotionally distressed child. Play area behaviour is observed and referred to by the staff of the child's school if any particular difficulties are being experienced and may throw interesting light on what has been a dark area. Away from the usual school or hospital environment, reactions are very different, mostly favourable, but occasionally adverse and can be of value in the ongoing treatment or education of the child.

DRIVING

One of the few disadvantages in using donkeys for riding is the necessity for an upper weight limit, after reaching 50kg (8st) the children are given rides in a trap. For some this is as pleasurable as the actual riding mainly because it involves less effort on their part (the mentally handicapped child is often lazy) but it is necessary to create interest and a challenging situation where possible. This is done by teaching driving to varying degrees, which may involve only the use of 'false' reins, giving the child the feel of controlling without this actually occurring and with an instructor in charge, sitting by the child. More able patients can become quite proficient, in particular hemiplegic or paraplegic pupils, the latter often developing strong arm and shoulder muscles to compensate for lack of leg power. They can be strapped into a comfortable position but should be accompanied in case of a sudden emergency.

It is clear that donkeys and handicapped children go very well together. The few disadvantages of weight restriction and the donkey's poor trotting and jumping ability are far outweighed by the good temperament, steadiness, patience and kindness shown to the children by the Slade Centre donkeys.

As a blind child said, on leaving one day: 'This place is ace.'

Driving in the arena at the Slade Centre

Elisabeth Svendsen presenting a prize at a Slade Centre fiesta

THE HISTORY OF THE SLADE CENTRE

The original trustees included David Miller from the social services in Honiton, Pat Feather, June Evers, George Hopkins of Millwater School and Niels and Elisabeth Svendsen and the first meeting was held on 12 August 1975. James Mason kindly agreed to be the main patron, along with Dorian Williams, Leslie Crowther, Charlie Chester, Spike Milligan, Richard Hearne, Bob Forbes, Dr Freddie Brimblecombe and the Bishop of Dunwich, Rev T. H. Cashmore. Brian Drury, the designer of the Diamond Riding Centre for the Disabled in Surrey, was asked to draw up plans to our specified needs.

The idea was for a children's haven, a day away from the rigidity of hospitals and hospital schools, where the luxury of normal living entered these children's days perhaps for the first time. Instead of the bright reds, blues and yellows that the children were used to, it was decided to use subtler, more relaxing shades of paintwork and decoration throughout the centre, the whole atmosphere to be one of enjoyment and pleasure and above all a change of environment that even the most handicapped child could appreciate. So many extremely handicapped children are never able to leave their hospital schools because there are simply no facilities at the places they wish to visit. A special medical room was planned with full changing facilities for children and even a bath for emergencies. A kitchen was included where the helpers could make their much-needed cups of tea and children could be given drinks too.

With George Hopkins' help, a list was made of schools for the handicapped within a 30-mile radius and a simple questionnaire was designed and sent out to see if the schools would like to come to the centre and to gauge the degree of handicap the children suffered from.

The head teachers from all these schools were invited to an informal evening at Slade House Farm. The encouragement they gave was wonderful. Apparently the difficulty was in finding extra activities in the area that provided the proper facilities for the care of their severely physically and mentally handicapped children. A lot of these children had regular epileptic fits so they were thrilled with the promise of beds and even baths for their more difficult cases. The idea of our centre, which could possibly incorporate all these items, was of the greatest interest to them but, to make sure we were working along the right lines, a team of donkeys was taken round to five of the schools for one morning or afternoon each week so that the value of the whole project could be gauged before anything further was spent.

The arrival of the donkeys in their specially adapted horsebox became, to some children, the most important time of the week. The joy on the children's faces as the donkeys came down the ramp was indescribable. It was clear there was an urgent need for a purpose-built centre.

The trustees sat down to work out the best way of introducing the scheme to the planning authorities to produce the quickest results. Time was getting on and it was feared that the progress being made with the children would be lost. The indoor centre was desperately needed so the trustees invited the Chief Planning Officer, Mr Dixon, to advise in the selection of the site. He came on 26 August 1975 and seemed extremely impressed by the idea of the whole project, although he did say there could well be some planning problems as the sanctuary is situated in an area of outstanding natural beauty and within a coastal preservation area.

There is no doubt that the planners were put under the greatest possible pressure. With the architect, a site had been chosen which could not be seen from anywhere and which blended in with the buildings already around the farm. Had the Donkey Sanctuary been of agricultural status a barn, much higher than the proposed building, would have been allowed with no planning permission needed at all and yet the proposal to help local children in desperate need was receiving almost fanatical opposition. After a site inspection the plans were turned down.

A trustees' meeting was called to plan the next course of action. Brookfield Farm had just been purchased by the Donkey Sanctuary and it was decided to put in a new planning application for the centre to be built there. The farm was miles from anywhere and at least the Sid Vale Association (the main opponents so far) would not be able to put their force behind the opposition. Brian Drury had to redraw all the plans.

No sooner had the plans for the centre at Brookfield been submitted to Honiton for consideration when opposition started yet again. A petition was drawn up in a local village and David Miller, one of our trustees who lived in Honiton, began to receive objectionable letters and phone calls despite the fact that many Honiton children were already benefitting from the visits of the donkeys. A hasty trustees' meeting was called when the local parish council turned us down and as the opposition was going to be extremely strong it was decided to withdraw the application from East Devon planning meetings.

Giving up was never considered so battle plans

were drawn up. A petition in support of the centre was organised and the handicapped schools and children were called on for help. Knowing already what the objections would be, the chairman, secretary and treasurer of the Sid Vale Association were invited to a meeting which, although pleasant, did not seem to impress our visitors. All they could say was: 'This is an area of outstanding natural beauty and we don't really think it suitable for you to build a centre and have handicapped children here.'

The official line of the East Devon District Council had been to recommend to the committee that the plans were passed and so they, at least, were on our side but there were many members of both the Sidmouth Town Planning Committee and the East Devon Planning Committee who were totally opposed to the project. The plans were changed as far as possible to meet the planners' recommendations and a desperate appeal for support of readers was placed in the local press, which really proved successful.

The press went to town. Letter after letter and article after article appeared for and against the project. The planning meeting was to be in May 1977 and over 1,328 people supported the petition. A demonstration was arranged outside the planning meeting and every councillor arriving was greeted by donkeys and handicapped children. When the last councillor had arrived the supporters slipped into the public benches, filling them to capacity. On the other side of the public section was the Sid Vale delegation, sitting every bit as tensely as we were. It was wonderful when Councillor Ernest Whitton stood up and supported the project strongly and everyone sat with baited breath while the vote was taken. It was approved by fifteen to three! However, there were conditions, the whole centre would have to be redesigned to meet the planners' requirements. But redesigned it was and again it was submitted to the council before work could actually start. The planning troubles almost solved, finance became the next headache. An enormously encouraging thing happened: the Tiverton Youth Centre organised a sponsored walk and raised over £300, the first substantial sum received. The Charity Commission told us of a special book called *Directory of Grant-making Trusts*, listing many charitable trusts willing to give money to projects like the Slade Centre. Over 200 letters were written appealing for funds but the response was extremely disappointing; why did it seem so much easier to raise money for the donkeys than it was for handicapped children? However, having fought so hard already, we kept on writing and the money began to come in.

The original estimate on the cost of the building had been between £80,000 and £90,000 but with the passage of time this had increased to between £130,000 and £140,000. This figure seemed impossible in view of the great difficulty in raising funds. A firm of architects in Exeter drew up all the plans anew. The centre was made slightly smaller and adapted to the planners' requirements. The cost of the centre was reduced to a more manageable £75,000 and the new plans were passed without too much problem. The foundation stone was laid on 14 June 1978.

The Marquess of Bath offered to help and the Donkey Breed Society agreed to put on a donkey show with all funds going to the Slade Centre. The sanctuary had already agreed that it would be a very special day to show off the donkeys and all the work being done at Slade House Farm. Weeks of preparation and work were put into it and on the great day the enormous marquee was full of donkeys and goods to buy. The Donkey Breed Society had organised a superb show which included fancy-dress classes which were already fully subscribed, a large number of our handicapped children taking part. Sadly, the weather was appalling.

Over 4,000 visitors did, however, turn up to see the work done at the Donkey Sanctuary although the day had not turned out to be a financial success, there was no doubt that many more people knew of the work we were doing and became interested in helping us.

The 5 December 1978 was cold but bright and in a very moving opening ceremony, which was performed by the Marquess of Bath, the Slade Centre was opened and ready to start work. The beautiful big play area had been furnished by the kindness of many companies who had donated toys and furnishings to us. In particular the Relyon group donated play furniture and Piccolo Books supplied a complete children's library. Giving rides to children in wheelchairs had always been a problem and Westland Helicopters were approached to see if they could suggest any way of making a special donkey trap which would take a wheelchair with a child in it. Their second-year engineering students took up the project and built the most magnificent cart where the back came down, ramps came out and the wheelchair was simply pushed up the back and strapped into place, the back ramp being the back of the trap.

Around the centre is the tarmac track for cart-riders and the riding instructors have designed a beautiful set of traffic lights which the children must obey, together with stop and go signs to instil some form of road safety into the lesson.

The Slade Centre operates five days a week and takes children from schools within a 22-mile radius.

Donkey Week and other Social Activities

Maple

Many of our donkey supporters had frequently requested the chance of a visit to the sanctuary but unfortunately we are geographically placed in an isolated position and have no public transport coming within easy reach of the sanctuary. It was decided that the Donkey Sanctuary could possibly do something for these contributors wishing to visit the sanctuary. So, Donkey Week was born.

The basic idea was that people wishing to come and see the donkeys but without transport, or on their own and worried about the problems of baggage and travel connections, could make their way as far as Exeter where they would be met by the Donkey Sanctuary staff and from thereon have no more problems for the week. We approached various hotels in the Sidmouth area and came to a reciprocal agreement whereby they would let rooms to our visitors at the normal rate and would give a 10 per cent donation to the charity. We would arrange to meet everybody arriving at Exeter train or coach station, take care of their luggage and take them to their appointed hotels. We would also have 'get togethers' every evening in the hotels so that people were not lonely and arrange a different trip each day.

In 1983 the project was put into operation and 144 people attended 'Donkey Week'. It turned out to be the most marvellous success, far more so than had ever been envisaged. The original group of people were delighted with the reception they received coupled with the fact that other people staying in the hotel were donkey-lovers and they all had a big interest in common. Every night at each of the hotels, two of us would go down and have dinner with the guests and sit and chat with the group afterwards. Before very long firm friends were being made, not only between ourselves and our visitors but between the visitors themselves and many of these friendships have become long lasting.

The first day was a full day's visit to the Donkey Sanctuary at Slade House Farm and we laid on talks, films, visits to the hospital and the Slade Centre and of course the opportunity to handle and groom and talk to the donkeys. One particular lady from the moment she arrived stripped her coat off and despite her beautiful nails and coiffured hair style, spent the whole day grooming donkeys. Not for her any of the trips round to the other farms; for seven days she spent her whole time round the various barns thoroughly enjoying her close contact with the donkeys and the feeling that she was able to help the donkeys that she so loved. To the others, however, the visits to the other farms proved as successful as the day at Slade House Farm. To get around the farms our tractors had been converted to carry a trailer full of happy visitors piled upon straw and hay bales. The donkeys thoroughly enjoyed the apparitions that appeared in the middle of their fields, particularly when some of the visitors (against our advice!) offered carrots and ginger nuts as the slow journey from field to field around the farm was made.

We had arranged the visits from a Tuesday to Tuesday to avoid people having to travel over the busy weekends and this seemed to fit in well with the hotels, who during that first week of May were not too busy and were very appreciative of the extra custom. By the end of the first week, firm friends had been made and fifty-eight people from that year came back the following year in 1984 when two hundred people turned up. We've held 'Donkey Week' every year since and now this year, in 1988, we already have 305 bookings including 151 repeat visitors. Thirty of those are coming for the sixth year in succession.

Everyone enjoys contact with the donkeys

It is one of the happiest weeks of the year for the staff at the sanctuary; so many visitors write to us on a regular basis and support us in the most marvellous way. It should now be called International Donkey Week, our visitors have included people from as far afield as Australia and Canada.

KEEPING IN TOUCH

Many lonely people are not able to get to Donkey Week but they do write to us and by keeping in contact with them we feel we are able to help them even if only in a small way. When Blackie was due to be brutally killed at the Villanueva de la Vera fiesta in Spain, we were absolutely inundated by telephone calls and letters. Apart from the lonely and the elderly we get many visits and contacts with the young. They hold the future of animal welfare in their hands and we are always pleased to encourage visits from schools. Coaches arrive from all over the country, mainly following interest in the lesson on the donkey which has been received and used by the school.

The children of Dawlish Primary School had taken a great interest in the sanctuary and had visited and met one of our little mares, Chippy, and her foal born that very day. We suggested that the school name the foal and back at school there was a ballot with every child suggesting a name for the new

A DONKEY FAMILY

It is difficult at this point to remember exactly when donkeys decided that we were suitable companions for them, for everyone who has any real experience of life knows that that is the way it happens. It was an accepted fact in our family that as soon as we had the space available we would join the great club of donkey supporters.

In our case we had no justification whatsoever. We had no small children to teach to ride. No problems with disused stables or uneaten paddocks. No interest (at that time!) in learning to drive, or be driven by donkeys. We were also both of an age when we were meant to be mature intelligent people and we were fully in command of our faculties and responsible for our own actions. How, therefore, can one explain our total determination to devote the rest of our lives to being in thrall to various numbers, shapes, sizes and characters of donkeys? We think we know that we have been marked out by that great donkey in the sky, who keeps a benevolent eye on certain other beings besides donkeys, who stand in especial need of sharing the communion and community of the donkey family. We do know for certain that, once selected in this way, there is no escape and what is even worse no desire or even wish to evade the path set out for you.

So no one should be surprised that when my daughter and granddaughter returned to live with us again, and we felt that we had to move to a larger house, we were careful to select one with donkeys in mind. When it came to the acquisition of donkeys we were, originally, thinking in very modest terms. In fact we rather overdid it, since it eventually transpired to our surprise (and possibly to theirs) that we had a grand total of fourteen donkeys in mind. It was only by moving to a house with less grazing and stabling, that we avoided becoming broad providers for forty instead of fourteen.

I am an industrialist and so am fully accustomed to monitoring trends, measuring costs, producing plans and forecasts and watching future developments like a hawk. I can therefore say, without any fear of contradiction, that our donkey acquisition rate was proceeding at a compound growth rate in excess of 12 per cent or, for the benefit of those more interested in inflation adjusted figures, by 7 per cent over the going rise in RPI. In fact we were about to adjust our growth rate to a logarithmic scale of exponential expansion, if fate had not stepped in and ensured that, mercifully, we moved which enforced a break in the continuum.

It all started so innocently! Each one of us scoured the local papers avidly, and independently, without mentioning our quest to the others until at last we all saw, simultaneously, the magic little donkey. Somewhat to our surprise the most popular name chosen by all the children was John. This caused us some problems; we already had a John but we didn't wish to disappoint them. In the past we have had problems as we have four Eeyores and it caused great confusion.

It was decided that the foal should be called Johnny and as they came from Dawlish School it was decided we'd call him Johnny Dawlish. The school arranged a coach trip the following week so that the children could come and visit Johnny. Johnny Dawlish contracted flu, and despite every effort by the veterinary department, died in the second week of his life. Apart from our distress at losing Johnny he died the day before the school children were due to arrive. This left the sanctuary with a tremendous problem. We had other little foals so should we name one of them Johnny Dawlish and hide the sad reality from the children or should they be told the truth, difficult though it may be. The teacher was taken on one side from the excited children, the situation explained to her and we jointly decided that it was better for the children to know the truth. For many of them my little talk was their first experience of death at close hand. However, they joined us in a short little funeral service for Johnny and then all together we went around the sanctuary and chose another donkey that they could adopt.

The boy who never smiles – except when he is with a donkey

words in the small ads, 'One jack and one jenny donkey, for sale to good home.' That was how we met Stephen and Sarah and how the odyssey began. Stephen was an 'entire' jack, of unsurpassed sweetness of disposition, so much so that after we had had him 'done' the only noticeable change was a slight increase in occasional waywardness and grumpiness. We had been warned of the legendary ferocity of entire males and our rapidly acquired reading and the advice that we sought was unequivocally that jacks were bad news – but not our Stephen. A more loving soft touch would be difficult to find!

Sarah was then, and remains, one of those donkeys who knows at heart that she is not a donkey at all, but rather a human in temporary asinine form. As such she is slightly disdainful of the company of her four-legged friends, preferring a cuddle with any available, or passing, human being with or without the benefit of formal introductions. Her main aim in life, however, is to become a fixture in our kitchen and in our previous home she went to limitless trouble to make this wish known to us. Any chance to escape from the paddock or the opportunity afforded by a carelessly adjusted stable door was eagerly seized upon and Sarah's cosy, and to my mind incredibly beautiful, face would appear at our back door, waiting expectantly to be led in close to the Aga.

Sadly, from the point where these two lovable creatures came into our lives it was, so to speak downhill all the way. Sarah and Stephen were the last of our donkeys who had not suffered in some way and in varying degrees, at human hands and yet all of them instantly adopted us, transferring none of the ill will that they were entitled to feel. Not only that, but they speedily overcame their reluctance and suspicions and have become more and more gregarious and loving. They do, it is true, live the life of Donkey Reilly. They are cossetted, vetted, blacksmithed, hoof-picked, bran-mashed and moved about so that they don't get bored. They are beautified, their hooves are polished, teeth checked and they are primped and brushed. Above everything and perhaps most importantly to any donkey, they are loved and cuddled, which is a delight, because they give us back so much more than they receive.

Our donkeys are total members of our family and we feel immensely honoured that they have chosen us to be members of theirs. If more people took the tiny amount of time and trouble that is necessary in order to get to know a donkey and to discover their own, very special, sense of fun and humour, there would be far less cruelty and mistreatment of these patient, lovable, long suffering and intensely rewarding beasts.

Sir John Harvey-Jones

Draft Itinerary for International Donkey Week

Wednesday 4 May Full or half day at Slade House Farm. Collection by coaches from hotels will start at 9.45am. For those who don't want a full day there will be a coach back to Sidmouth at 12.30pm. Another coach will start to pick up afternoon visitors at 1.30pm. Snacks and hot drinks will be available in the main yard. You will be able to groom donkeys all day. Slade Centre will be open to view. The farrier will be working with the donkeys. There will be a fund-raising stall selling goods and Donkey Sanctuary goods and sweat-shirts will also be on sale. Throughout the day in the office videos will be shown of our work. International Donkey Protection Trust and Donkey Sanctuary inspectorate displays will be on show. Coaches will return to Sidmouth at approximately 3.30pm.

Thursday 5 May Choice of a full day at Three Gates Farm in Dorset, leaving Sidmouth at approximately 10am. Snacks and hot drinks will be available. You should be back in Sidmouth at about 4.30pm. OR Full or half day at Paccombe Farm, near Sidmouth. Half day – 10am to 12 noon or 1.30pm to 3.30pm. Snacks and hot drinks will be available. Trailer rides up the track are quite an experience! Walking sticks (if you use them) and wellies are a must.

Friday 6 May Full day at Town Barton Farm, Tedburn St Mary. Pick up at 10am leaving about 3.30pm to return to Sidmouth. Snacks and hot drinks will be available. Trailer rides and donkey grooming.

Saturday 7 May Full or half day at Brookfield Farm, Honiton. 10am to noon or 1.30pm to 3.30pm. Snacks and hot drinks will be available. Grooming, displays and Devon cream teas to be served during the afternoon. Donkey mugs and plates will be on sale.

▶

LIFE-LONG COMPANIONS

Donkeys can be much needed companions. In the early days of the sanctuary we were called out by the RSPCA requesting that a donkey be taken into care who belonged to a blind man who lived in a small village on the edge of Dartmoor. Unfortunately the man had to go into hospital and as he lived on his own there would be no one to care for the donkey. The farmyard appeared deserted when we arrived but eventually a donkey slowly wad-dled her way across to us. She was the fattest donkey ever seen and absolutely enormous.

'Jenny,' came a voice from the house. 'Jenny come here.' She plodded past us up to the back door of the house.

An old blind man was struggling to tip a sack of cow cake into the tub by the door. We made our presence known and offered assistance to the old man. 'Oh, are you here for Jenny?' he asked, and a tear trickled slowly down his old sightless face.

'We'll take the greatest care of her,' I assured him.

'I've no one, you see – it's the end for me – I've lived here nearly eighty years, old Jenny's kept me company since my wife died thirty years ago.' He turned and went into the house.

It was very difficult loading Jenny into the trailer as she was reluctant to go in and only just fitted.

'You'll feed her properly now, won't you,' said the old man. He was standing by the door. 'For the last ten years since I lost my sight, I've just kept her bin full of cow cake and she's helped herself.'

Holding his hand I promised him that Jenny would be cared for all her life and as we drove away the old man stood with tears running uncontrollably down his face.

Very much more recently we took in a donkey called Titus. He was in very good condition except that he was very over-weight and where the donkey's mane would appear down the crest of the neck, Titus had the most enormous fatty crest. The owners who had been very fond of him were unable to explain his obesity but all became very clear to us shortly after his arrival! We received a letter from one of the neighbours saying how much he missed Titus now he had been moved, after becom-ing such a friend of his for at least eighteen years and how he had been feeding him titbits such as biscuits, sugar lumps and cough candy daily, nothing being too good for him. He was pleased Titus had come to us but felt so lonely and asked that we give Titus a sugar lump from him. We are writing to the elderly gentleman regularly informing him how Titus is getting on.

Reading and writing held no interest for James when he was sent to a special school at the age of twelve but the donkey in the field did and skilfully, using his interest in Jenny, the staff found the key to success! Following visits with him to the library, they followed up snippets out of books about donkeys; this persuaded him of the need to read. Then James was given the address of the Donkey Sanctuary and letter writing took on a new meaning as he wrote for information and received replies on donkeys. With the knowledge he gleaned from reading his information sheets from the sanctuary, Jenny became James' first experience in caring. He made sure her drinking water was

Visitors in the yard at the sanctuary

Buffalo in Christmas spirit

▶ Itinerary cont'd

Sunday 8 May Sidmouth College Parents Association will provide a cold buffet lunch for us at Sidmouth College. Coaches will collect from the hotels at 11.30am. Mrs Svendsen will be with you – a chance for all of us to get together. Coaches will return to the hotels at approximately 3pm.

Monday 9 May Full or half day at Slade House Farm. The hospital will be open all day for your inspection and the same events as on Wednesday will be held in case you missed them.

Tuesday 10 May Departure – *Please be on time* – or even early!

not frozen over in the winter and that she had extra food when the frost was on the ground. He moved her from one paddock to the other when he felt the grazing was poor, demanded that they call in the farrier when her hoofs needed attention and was far more fastidious about her sleeping quarters than his own!

Unfortunately, Jenny became very ill-tempered and James agreed that she be sent to the sanctuary for the cause to be investigated. As the head teacher noted, Jenny's final lesson to James had been that of unselfish love in letting her go. We are pleased to add that two rehabilitated donkeys were sent to the school. James already loves them dearly, and Jenny, having done such a wonderful job, has now settled in happily with a group of friends, her ill-temper a thing of the past.

LESSON ON THE DONKEY

The lesson can be adapted for children of all ages. Its aim is to give teaching staff information on donkeys, their origin, needs and care and to make some suggestions regarding activities involving donkeys. The lesson is sent free of charge to any school or group and not only contains seven pages of detailed information on the donkey but also includes a free book, newsletter, posters and leaflets. The following are extracts taken from the lesson.

APPARATUS REQUIRED
1 Picture of a donkey
2 Handful of straw and hay.
3 Curry comb, dandy brush, hoof pick (if possible).

INTRODUCTION
Questions to find out what the children know already.
1 How many have seen a donkey?
2 Is there one near school?
3 What do they know about donkeys?
4 Where did donkeys originally come from?

WHAT THE DONKEY LOOKS LIKE

Eyes Like the horse the eyes are at the side of the head . . . this means he cannot see well to the front, so if you are going up to a donkey you should walk up from the side so that the donkey can see you. He is not as nervous as a horse, but when he was wild his protection was in kicking out when frightened, so take care not to frighten him.

Ears Ask the children why they are so large.

Mouth This is large and soft. The teeth are important and you can tell the age of the donkey by studying the six front teeth. The older he is the shorter and more slanted the teeth.

Back Point out the cross and explain that the long back of the donkey is not really strong until the donkey has reached the age of three years old. If you stroke a young donkey on the back it curves *down* as the bone is not completely formed.

Legs These are very strong and in other countries do tremendous journeys – much longer than horses – but far more slowly.

Feet These are called hoofs and are made of a type of hard horn. If not kept cut by a farrier they grow and twist and can break and make the donkey lame. The donkey feels no pain when the hoofs are trimmed.

Coat Many donkeys grow long, shaggy coats to keep them warm in the winter. Healthy donkeys shed this coat in the summer and become smooth-coated like a horse. The coats are not always waterproof.

Tail This is long and thin and usually has a little tuft at the end, which is useful for swatting flies! It should never be cut as it is the donkey's only protection against flies and insects.

Titus

*Donkeys rehabilitated from the
sanctuary: Basil and Snowy with their
new family*

109

EEYORE MEETS A GIANT!

I'm sure you have all heard of Eeyore. He is well known as the naughtiest donkey in the famous sanctuary in Sidmouth, Devon. His mother, Smartie, had arrived in the most terrible state, so thin that two people could carry her, and covered in sores.

The Donkey Sanctuary is in Devon and looks after any donkey that gets into trouble. To many donkeys, after years of hard work and bad treatment, it is heaven to find lovely big green fields to gallop in, warm airy stables to sleep in and all the favourite food they need! All this plus love and attention should keep any little donkey happy, except perhaps Eeyore!

Shortly after she arrived, Mother (the lady who runs the sanctuary) realised that Smartie was in foal and due to have her baby very soon. The minute he was born Mother cuddled Smartie and said 'You clever girl! What shall we call him?' Smartie threw up her head and gave a great bray 'Eeyore' she said, so the baby was called Eeyore. From the moment he was born, he led everybody a dance.

Poor Smartie would stand by the fence and Eeyore would dodge underneath it and gallop just out of her reach, eating Mother's best roses. He pinched the fire buckets and ran round the field with them. He pinched the bobble cap from a little boy's head, and, even worse, he pinched the handbag of a headmistress who was leaning over the fence telling her class of children how sweet little donkeys were!

Eeyore grew up happily with his firm friends, Ruff, Pancho and Frosty and despite many adventures and being terribly naughty, Mother and all the donkeys loved him.

Every day the sanctuary lorry went out to collect donkeys in trouble and on this particular Tuesday, Perry, the driver, had to go to Derbyshire where he had six donkeys and one mule to collect and

Eeyore up to his usual tricks

bring to safety. Now a mule has a horse for a mother and a donkey for a father. They are usually bigger than donkeys but have some parts like a horse, some like a donkey. Sometimes the mother is a donkey and the father is a horse and although they are still mules, these animals are known as hinnies.

Perry collected his first two little donkeys called Bill and Ben, then went to collect Jubilee, the mule. He just could not believe his eyes. She was enormous!

The man who had bred her had grown to love mules in the army. The soldiers used them to carry heavy goods. They were very strong but rather obstinate. Every time they came to a river, they would refuse to cross until a little female donkey called a 'bell' donkey went across first. Then they would all follow her, her little bell ringing out to tell them it was safe!

Jubilee's owner decided to breed the biggest mule in England. He chose the mother carefully, a sister of a famous racehorse called 'Rubstic' who had won the Grand National. That's the race with the enormous fences the horses have to jump! For the father, he chose a very special donkey, very, very big with long hair, from France called a Poitou. His name was Eclair.

Jubilee was born in 1977, the Queen's Jubilee year and that is how she got her name. Unfortunately, her owner became ill and Jubilee was sent to a horse stable to be trained to pull a cart but Jubilee did not like that. One day she would be very, very good, but the next day, she would gallop away and go so fast that the cart would turn right over and everybody would be thrown out. She was so big and strong that no one could be sure what she would do next and she really became rather naughty. One day her owner decided that she could not manage her any more

Continued overleaf/

Elisabeth Svendsen meets Jubilee

Eeyore Meets a Giant cont'd

and decided that she should go to the Donkey Sanctuary!

When Perry arrived, he and Jubilee stood looking at each other! Perry had collected almost all the 3,000 donkeys to come into the sanctuary but never one like this! He carefully measured her and then went back to the lorry and measured that! She would just fit in but he would have to take her back to the sanctuary with Bill and Ben. There was no room for any more! He rang Mother, who could hardly believe her ears and she rushed off to find John, the vet, so that they could find a big enough stable.

It was a long way home and Jubilee felt very sad to be leaving Derbyshire. She did not know where she was going and she did not particularly like the two little donkeys who kept staring up at her from their partition in the front of the lorry. A big tear ran down her cheek as she wondered what on earth would happen to her next!

It was dark when the lorry arrived and Mother and John stood watching with the big yard lights on as Perry opened the ramp. If Mother and John were surprised, what do you think the donkeys thought! John led Jubilee into the biggest stable the sanctuary had. It had plenty of headroom and Jubilee could look out over the door and see the donkeys.

Bill and Ben were led into the airy barn where the new arrivals went. How fast the news spread. Eeyore was asleep in his shelter at the other end of the sanctuary. He woke up when he first heard the braying and he and his friends decided they just had to see for themselves. 'I'll check the gates,' said naughty Eeyore, 'I've been good so long they may have forgotten to put the chain on.' Although the chain was on, the padlock was not properly shut. Eeyore twisted his neck round and got his little teeth round the hasp. He pulled and pulled and suddenly the padlock fell to the ground. The four friends pushed on the gate together, but it would not move.

'Come on, all together!' brayed Eeyore. 'One, two, three, push!' They all pushed and the gate opened so suddenly that Frosty fell right on top of Eeyore! When they had got back on their hoofs Eeyore led the way importantly along the lane and down the track to the isolation boxes.

'Where is this thing?' he asked Bridget, one of the oldest donkeys.

'Over there, Eeyore, in stable eleven,' she said.

Eeyore went and stared into the stable and then suddenly he saw the most enormous donkey he had ever seen. Jubilee looked down at him. She was feeling even more miserable. Despite the warm box and the lovely hay, she was missing her horse friends and she was beginning to think she didn't like donkeys.

'Go away, you nasty little donkey,' she said, 'leave me alone. I don't want to talk to anyone,' and she turned her back on Eeyore.

'Nasty little donkey?' said Eeyore. 'Me? I'm Eeyore and I'm the most important donkey in the sanctuary, so you'd jolly well better be polite to me!'

Jubilee had had enough. 'You cheeky young donkey,' she said, 'I'll teach you a lesson,' and she ran at the door meaning to stick her head out and give Eeyore a shock but oh dear! The door had been built for donkeys, not the largest mule in England! With a horrible rending crash, the whole door broke and Jubilee plunged into the yard, with the frame around her shoulders and broken wood everywhere!

Eeyore, Frosty, Pancho and Ruff were terrified, they galloped desperately up the track, hearing Jubilee's hoofs pounding behind them.

'Quicker! Quicker! She's catching us!' brayed Frosty. But Eeyore was stopping. He could no longer hear Jubilee's hoofs.

Eeyore looked around. There was Jubilee, standing on the track. The frame was round her neck and she was trembling from head to foot, Eeyore looked closer, surely that wasn't . . . but it was. Great tears were running down Jubilee's beautiful muzzle and splashing to the ground. Eeyore hesitated a moment and then slowly walked towards her. Silently they looked at each other and a strange feeling came over both of them.

'Frosty, Pancho, Ruff, come here please,' said Eeyore quietly. 'Frosty, you push the frame at that side. Pancho, you go to the other side and Ruff and I will pull from the front. Put your head down, Jubilee.'

The four little donkeys pushed and pulled until at last Jubilee put her head back up, the frame no longer round her shoulders.

'Thank you Eeyore,' she said, 'I feel better now.'

For a few moments nobody moved. Then Eeyore made a big decision. 'We will stay with you tonight, Jubilee,' he said. 'Come back with us to our stable. Mother is sure to find you in the morning.'

And Eeyore, rather proudly, led the big mule and the three little donkeys back up the lane and into their own home. All the little donkeys waited outside until Jubilee had found a nice place to lie down in, and then they carefully stepped around

Eeyore, Frosty, Ruff and Pancho

her until they found an empty space. Eeyore lay right next to Jubilee and as they dropped off to sleep Eeyore's head was close to Jubilee's.

What a morning that was in the sanctuary! There was panic when John, going to check the new arrivals, found the box empty and no Jubilee! Everyone rushed off to find her but Mother suddenly shouted 'I bet it's Eeyore!' Everyone stopped looking and all the staff, with Mother in the lead, went to Eeyore's field. First they found the gate open. 'Oh dear, I knew it would be something to do with Eeyore,' wailed Mother, and then she saw John beckoning from the stable. They all looked in. The friends were still fast asleep, tired out after their adventures but Eeyore lifted his head and looked at Mother.

'Oh Eeyore, I should be so cross with you,' she said. 'But thank you for looking after Jubilee. You're not always the naughtiest donkey!'

I wonder what Eeyore will get up to next!

GRATEFULLY RECEIVED

The Donkey Sanctuary has regular subscribers, obviously elderly pensioners and many probably on supplementary benefit who send sums such as 25p every week and many of these prefer to do so anonymously. The spidery writing on the envelopes, the post mark and the issue from the Post Office confirm their regular sacrifice. Every donation, however small, is acknowledged and appreciated. We have had the joy of sharing winnings from Littlewoods Pools, windfalls from Ernie, birthday gifts and are frequently remembered in wills.. When we receive a legacy we are always so very grateful and never fail to ask the solicitors to thank the families concerned who, we know, must sometimes feel that the charity has received money which they could well have done with themselves. We also have a memory wall here at the sanctuary as we feel that no matter how small the legacy or bequest, it's nice to commemorate the name of the person who loved the donkeys so much to think of them in this way and it's also a comfort to relatives visiting and perhaps a source of pride to see their mother's or father's name on our memory wall. Many other people send donations which they would like given to a specific project such as a new barn for the isolation donkeys or a tree on our new beautiful walk or a seat where visitors, as they themselves have been, can sit and enjoy watching the quiet simple life of the donkeys.

Breeding and Showing

In the early days both breeding and showing of donkeys was very much a fun pastime but much of the fun has now gone out of this as professionalism has crept in and breeders' reputations are at stake. The pride of the donkey owner as he walks his donkey around the ring, both looking impeccable, is apparent and the triumphant parade with the winner's rosette on the headband quite possibly makes the donkey's day as well as that of the delighted owner or breeder.

One of the pleasures of donkey ownership throughout the world comes from breeding strong healthy stock and of bringing them on to win at donkey shows. The rules and regulations in the UK are clearly laid down and owners can therefore travel their donkeys to any part of the country, confident that similar conditions will apply. In the USA, however, this is not always the case. The American Donkey and Mule Society has developed no universal show rules, with the exception of their own annual national show. They recognise that shows in different parts of the vast area of the USA differ greatly from area to area, and rules would be difficult to enforce. Many shows include mules: Texas has its Donkey and Mule Show featuring the World Championship Mule Pull, with a $6,000 prize and trophy buckles! Australia and New Zealand both have Donkey Breed Societies, and shows there are run on similar lines to those in the UK.

When thinking of breeding a donkey you should always approach the experts and most of these are members of the Donkey Breed Society. One of the aims of the society is to improve the conformation of the donkey through selective breeding and over the years a Stud Book has been produced to build up a knowledge of available stallions and the quality of their offspring. The Donkey Breed Society (originally called the Donkey Show Society) was formed by the Hon Robin Borwick in 1967 and the majority of the more important agricultural shows started to include donkey classes in their schedule.

BREEDING

For the owner of a pet donkey the decision to breed must be taken very seriously. As in the pony world, many donkeys are bred for the wrong reason and the sad fact that the Donkey Sanctuary cares for over 4,000 unwanted donkeys should be sufficient grounds for caution in the owner's mind. If you do not wish to keep the foal yourself and do not have a home organised for it, then do not breed. Having said that there is nothing so delightful and rewarding as a young donkey.

Handy Tip

Prevent your donkey from getting dried eyelids, especially during the summer, by smearing a little baby oil or Vaseline around his eyelids.

Selecting a Stallion After deciding to increase your donkey family you will need to find a donkey stallion and pay a stud fee. The Donkey Breed Society provides members with lists of studs. You will also be charged livery, ie, the cost of keeping the mare whilst visiting the stud.

Delightful donkey foal grazing amongst the flowers

Both the stallion and the stud at which he stands should be carefully considered. The stallion's and mare's pedigree and conformation faults should be compared. Other members of both families, such as the stallion's dam and his progeny from other mares, are important to show which genetic features are obvious in each generation. By appointment mare owners should visit a stud prior to sending their mares and discuss all aspects of the mare's forthcoming visit.

A young stallion's reputation may well be based on his achievements in the show ring and on his own pedigree. However, after two or three years at stud, such factors, whilst still important,

115

should be considered together with the progeny that the young stallion is now producing. A stallion might produce up to forty foals in one year, so the impact on a breed of a popular stallion can be remarkable. There are many excellent stallions who do not show at all.

A mare is only able to conceive when she is in season, which is approximately every three weeks for about seven days so obviously you should arrange for the mare to be delivered to the stud at this time. It is possible that the stud owner may wish to keep your mare for a further three weeks after she has been covered to ensure she is in foal.

Before sending the mare to stud ensure she is in fit condition, free from parasites, correctly vaccinated and with feet in good order. This will help the mare to get in foal and make her more likely to carry a foal to term. It is most distressing for the mare (and the owner) to lose a foal in the early stages of pregnancy, and therefore every step must be taken to prevent this from happening.

Mares who have to travel to stud are more likely to stay in foal if they are used to travelling. If the mare does not regularly travel it may be wiser to leave her at the stud until she is well in foal, perhaps as much as twelve weeks.

Before visiting the stallion, the stud owner will have given the mare owner a nomination form which will include details

THE POITOU DONKEY

Poitou is the name of the old province of France, which lies between Brittany in the north and the wine-producing country around Bordeaux in the south.

The Poitou is not a pack animal; he does not work in the fields; he provides neither milk nor meat. For hundreds of years he has been bred solely to be used in mule breeding, an activity which made an important contribution to the French agricultural economy and for which the Poitou has a world-wide reputation.

The main points of conformation of the Poitou stallion are: long heavy head; long ears well covered with long hair; thick strong neck; long straight back; slightly prominent hips; short croup; long well-muscled thigh; straight shoulders; large broad feet. The height is 14 to 15 hands, the colour of the thick coat (which is matted and tangled) is brown bay, the belly and inside of the thighs being light grey. The Poitou does not have an eel stripe. The mare stands 13.1 to 14.1 hands; the coat is not as thick and the pelvis and croup are wider than the stallion.

Records that exist indicate that over four hundred years the conformation has not changed, probably because the Poitou has not been used locally to improve other breeds of donkey. The history of the breed itself allegedly dates back to

the tenth century. Customs such as keeping the Poitou stallion stabled, without exercise and ungroomed are regarded as unacceptable by modern management standards in other countries, but these customs – and others – have been traditional in this remote area for hundreds of years.

In the past the Poitou was exported to Russia, Turkey, Egypt, the Belgian Congo and North Africa but from 1950 there was little demand for the Poitou. The mule could not compete with the tractor and the lorry and they were no longer required by the army. Mule-breeding ceased to provide a living for the breeder. The effect on the Poitou was catastrophic and numbers have dropped.

The International Donkey Protection Trust is working with the French authorities, breeders and SABAUD (Association to Safeguard the Poitou) to help the breed survive and is setting up a bloodtyping programme to complement their stud book, and is also hoping that a process can be set up whereby semen can be frozen and stored.

Just recently the first two female Poitou donkeys arrived at the sanctuary and hopefully a breeding programme set up in the UK can act as a back-up to the work being done in France in joint efforts to prevent the breed from becoming extinct.

of pedigree, age, colour, height, whether maiden/barren/or with foal at foot; details of worming and vaccinations and previous breeding record. This is a very important part of the process, as it gives the stallion owner vital information regarding the correct care and handling of the mare and will help to ensure that her visit to the stud is successful.

On collecting the mare from stud, the mare owner should pay the stud owner's account which will include any veterinary bills incurred. This account is due before the mare may be removed. It is usual for the service certificate to be forwarded at a later date.

Care of the In-foal Mare When the mare returns from stud, fitness and health should be maintained throughout pregnancy. Do not feed the mare for two just because she is in foal. However, her feeding habits should be carefully monitored. A vitamin supplement is essential.

Assuming foaling is to take place from about March to May, it should be remembered that the mare will be very heavy in foal at just the time of year when ground conditions are at their worst. During this period ploughing through deep mud or hard, rutted, frosted ground to reach shelter is not ideal. If possible keep the mare on a sound even surface with a sensible amount of steady exercise. The gestation period is variable in the donkey and can range from 10½ to 14½ months.

A

B

Foaling The foaling period begins when the mare starts 'bagging up' (this is when the mare's udder starts swelling some three weeks or so prior to foaling) and includes when the foal is born, up and feeding. During this period careful consideration should be given to where the mare will foal and where she and the foal will be afterwards. If possible have the mare stabled at night and out in a small secure paddock during the day.

The stable should be at least 3.6m (12ft) square, airy with no draughts, well drained and should be disinfected before use. Infra-red heat in the box is useful for winter or spring foals. The bed in the stable should be deep clean straw and should be put down several hours prior to foaling so that any dust from the straw will have settled.

About seventy-two hours before foaling, the mare's teats will become distended and she may run a little milk. Her pelvic muscles slacken and the bones around the top of the tail become movable. When foaling is close, the mare may be restless and will stop eating. Usually the act of foaling is quite quick, about thirty to sixty minutes from the beginning of the contractions and with very few exceptions, donkeys are more than capable of coping on their own. The normal presentation is forelegs followed by the head. If this is not the case or there appears to be too slow progress, then *call a vet immediately*. Inexperienced owners can cause a lot of harm by trying to assist the mare. If present at the birth, keep out of the way, still and quiet. When the foal is born, make sure the nose is clear of the bag. Do not help the foal to break the umbilical cord, as the blood flow between mare and foal is completed after birth. After a few minutes rest, either the mare or the foal will start to move and the cord will break naturally. The foal's navel should then be sprayed with antiseptic spray. Keep the foal's environment as clean as possible.

The mare must still pass the placenta or afterbirth which may take up to an hour. During this period the mare will usually turn round and begin cleaning the foal by licking it all over. This establishes a bond between mare and foal and is very important. Try not to interfere, especially with a young mare. If a mare doesn't attempt to clean the foal up then a quick rub down with a clean towel can stimulate the foal. A sprinkling of salt on the foal's back may encourage the mare to lick.

C

D

E

F

Mother and baby doing well!

G

THE BIRTH OF A FOAL

A *The bag appears*
B *Make sure that the foal's head is freed; the bag is full of amniotic fluid*
C *The foal should be allowed to slide out slowly*
D *Check that the foal is alright, and that there is no mucus blocking any passages*
E *The mare resting before passing the placenta. A vet should be called if this has not appeared after one hour*
F *Close contact and licking the foal helps to start the milk flowing*
G *The natural 'rubber' protection around the sharp hoof protects the mother during the birth, and soon shrivels*

When the foal tries to get up he will fall over several times but each attempt is assisting the natural strengthening of the muscles in the legs. Providing the foal is not in danger of injuring himself, then leave the foal well alone. When the foal has got the hang of walking, he should start to search for the mare's udder. This next hour or so is the hardest for the owner. Most mares and foals get everything sorted out without help.

A few maiden mares may not like the idea of the foal suckling, usually because they are so fascinated by the foal that they keep turning round with it. Often all that is needed is to hold the mare's head for a minute or two and all will be well. Very occasionally a young mare will actually reject a foal, in which case contact a vet immediately.

The mare's first milk or colostrum is most important to the foal. The sooner the foal starts feeding the better, the antibodies in this milk protecting the foal over the first days of life. It is essential that foals should receive the colostrum in the first two hours from birth. If the foal will not feed call the vet immediately.

If the mare foals normally, call the vet to give the foal a multivitamin injection and an anti-tetanus injection the next morning. The foal will then be vaccinated against tetanus when old enough. The vet will also check the mare and foal fully and will also check the afterbirth to be sure it is complete. Once checked this should be burnt or buried. Shortly after birth the foal will pass the meconium, a dark brown substance. If the foal is straining and passing nothing, you should advise your vet.

Bottle-feeding Arctic

Foals very quickly adjust to their new world and after a few hours will be moving quite fast around their box. Weather permitting both mare and foal may go out on their own in a small paddock the next morning. Small donkeys can quickly become ill, and any listlessness in a foal should be immediately checked. If the foal's temperature is raised above 100°F, then call the vet. All mares with foals should be stabled at night and all young stock should be stabled during their first winter.

The next problem will probably coincide with the mare coming into season some seven to fourteen days after birth. The mare's milk changes consistency and the foal has a tendency to scour. If the foal is listless, again check the temperature, and call the vet if necessary.

It is preferable to leave foals on their mothers until natural weaning takes place, between seven to twelve months. However, if the foal is an entire colt, care should be taken. It has been known for a thirty-two-week-old colt foal to get a two-year-old filly in foal.

Early Training During the early months the foal has much to learn. Firstly, that humans are good and that they should be obeyed. It is so simple to ensure a trouble-free future in leading, riding or driving by teaching the young foal to walk over every possible different surface, including 'slow' signs on the road and even the dreaded drain! The foal should learn to be tied up regularly, be groomed, have his feet picked up, rasped and tapped. Within a week or two of birth, the foal will be pushing in to inspect his mother's short feed and soon will enjoy a bucket of his own. A worming programme after advice from your vet should be started at four weeks old.

During the early months a foal can be introduced to the horse box or trailer. Place the box in a small paddock and close the shelter up. The mare will probably go straight in to explore anyway. Hay and straw can be left in the box and the donkeys can use it as a stable for a day or two in the daytime, under careful supervision. Then one day the foal and mare can be shut in, taken for a short drive, returned to the paddock and released again. Time spent in this way pays dividends later on.

If your foal is an entire colt then you must, of course, make arrangements with your veterinary surgeon to have him gelded at the appropriate time.

TRAINING FOR SHOWING

Donkeys are not like the rest of the equine world and should not be broken in by the same methods as a horse or pony. Donkeys think things out, so you must always be careful to keep their confidence. The first step is to start taking them for short walks. This they regard as fun and less boring than being stuck in the field all day.

The best headgear to start him on is either a head collar or showslip. The latter has a slip noseband: when the animal pulls, it slips tightly round his nose, thereby preventing him from pulling too hard. If placed fairly low on the nose for schooling, it should help to get the head in the correct position. The head should be held up with the nose dropped so as to produce the

All legs and head!

effect of a nicely arched neck. Never hit your animal or he may learn to pull to one side.

Your voice is the only weapon your donkey should be taught to understand. Encourage him when everything is going well and be very firm in how you reprimand him if misunderstandings occur. Never shout; the word 'don't' should be enough to check your young donkey if he wishes to break out of the trot. The donkey shows his intelligence if you give him the correct word always and never vary it. A click of the tongue once only should mean 'go forward', a second click means 'go from a walk to a trot' and finally 'whoa' should mean stop.

If things do go wrong, as indeed they can, then take the line that somewhere, somehow, you made the mistake, never your animal. If you really love your donkey, he will never let you down. This is why showing is such enormous fun because donkeys can show the public how super they can look and how clever they are in obeying your wishes.

If purchasing an animal for in-hand shows, go for a standard size, ie 10–10.2 hands. Obviously, riding and driving require larger animals. Your ideal show donkey should have a reasonably small, neat head, good limbs, suitable width of chest, deep heart space and rib-cage. He should not be too long in the back and looked at from behind, he should have good straight hocks. You will find that some faults are easily corrected by a good farrier.

Preparing for the Show Your donkey will need a bath the day before the show providing the weather is suitable. His mane should be trimmed, the grey being taken out of the black mane on a grey donkey and the brown taken out of the black mane on a brown donkey; all rough patches should be trimmed with franking scissors. When the donkey has had his bath, great care should be taken to dry him thoroughly and even in the stable he should be covered by a light cotton sheet. Your show-grooming tray should consist of a dandy brush, body brush, water brush, sponge, hoof pick, hoof oil and hoof brush and a small bottle of Vaseline which should be used around the eyes and on the nostrils before entering the show ring.

Take a second rug to the show with you; you will then have a dry rug for the donkey to travel home in. On returning home from a show, never put your donkey straight out in the field, if it is cold or wet. It is best to put him in the stable until the next morning. Remember that, by bathing your donkey, you have removed all the natural oil from the coat, thereby making him very vulnerable to wet and cold.

In-hand Classes At the show the judge usually watches all the entries come in and walk down one of the long sides of the ring, so you must remember that your own animal is only very briefly in front of the judge's eye before the next exhibit comes along to take its place. Do not imagine that this is the only time the judge will be looking at you, for a good judge is perfectly capable of having a quick look round at any time during the class.

Your donkey should walk freely and well on a fairly long rein and try not to have your hand too close to the bit. Remember your donkey must walk: jigging along at a jog-trot does no good

Dozing in the sun

at all, as the judge will either suspect his walk is so bad that he can't keep up with the handler, or else that there is something physically wrong with the poor animal and he is unable to walk true. It can also spoil the picture if the handler has to drape his arm over the donkey's back so that he can keep his animal moving straight with the helpful aid of a whip on the off side. Equally unfortunate is the animal whose handler carries a long schooling whip in his left hand and just tickles up the donkey's hocks from time to time hoping to make him move faster. Donkeys soon learn to swing their quarters away from the whip and all the judge sees as you go past is a not very attractive view of the animal's back end.

Many judges ask their steward to halt the exhibits in a corner so that, one at a time, they can be trotted down the long side of the ring. This enables the judge to see how they move. If you have done your schooling well at home your donkey will enjoy trotting along beside you as this is something he has done often before. How much more attractive this is going to look compared with the donkeys who just will not co-operate. Once everyone has been pulled in for the first inspection remember that you must not relax, especially if you are lucky enough to be standing at the top, or near the top, of the line. The class is not nearly finished and now is the time to make sure that your donkey is standing square on all four feet and that you are placed beside him at his head. Judges often glance quickly along the line, even when it looks as if they are occupied with watching an exhibit's individual show and a well positioned, alert animal is going to appeal far more than one that has gone to sleep and whose handler is having a good gossip with the person next in line.

Each exhibit will now be carefully examined, the judge sometimes checking the feet and looking in the mouth. Obviously a foot which has seedy toe or sandcrack, or which badly needs trimming, could cost a few marks. You must remember that

No You Don't!

When a mother is trying to discipline a foal she will often give him a sharp nip just above the knees and a useful tip when training young donkeys is to give them a slight tap in this position as the young donkey immediately knows that this is a reprimand and will take more notice of than any other form of warning.

this is a show class and perfection in conformation, type and manners is the aim. While the judge is examining your donkey, be sure to stand him up straight, with the hind leg nearest the judge placed slightly further back. You yourself must now stand in front of his head, so that you do not block the judge's view. The donkey's conformation is now being inspected and all points are being carefully noted.

When you are asked to walk your donkey out on his own, and then turn and trot back, do try to move in a straight line. Go directly away from, and then towards, the judge, so that he can really see the animal's action and check the straightness of its limbs. After everyone has given a show, the final walk round begins. This can be a vital moment and a good alert walk may help a judge to make a decision in your favour. Try not to get too close to the donkey in front of you. When you are called in, wherever your placing may be, accept it with good grace.

Driving Driving is becoming extremely popular. In these classes you will be judged first on 'presentation', which means the general picture you make on driving round the ring. Is your cart the right size and type for your particular donkey? Does it look properly balanced? How well is your donkey moving?

After everyone has been pulled into line, the safety and correct fitting of both harness and vehicle will be checked and your set of 'spares' examined. Many a class has been lost by ill-fitting breast-collars or cruppers, or traces incorrectly adjusted. The condition and soundness of the vehicle will be closely inspected as will the neat and tidy appearance of the 'whip', as the driver is called.

ST PADDY'S MOMENT

In January 1973, Bob Forbes, a well-known interviewer on BBC *Spotlight* rang to say he would like to come down and do an interview and would be arriving in one and a half hours! Sure enough, a minibus arrived laden to the roof with men and cameras.

'Right, we want a good "hee-haw" noise to start with,' said Bob Forbes, and the sound man, the camera man and all the other men stood in silence outside the stable block waiting hopefully. Of course, donkeys *can* be stubborn occasionally, and one hour later we were all still waiting.

'Right,' said Bob, 'get all the donkeys together and I'll do an interview.'

It was explained that some donkeys were rescued mares and never mixed with our pedigree stock who were fit to have foals or with St Paddy who was in the most presentable, easily accessible paddock with his three wives and three children. We decided to feature St Paddy.

The man responsible for sound, Tony Turner, was wearing one of those very long hairy Afghan coats, a sort of motley brown colour, and he set himself up carefully with his gear behind Bob Forbes and facing me. Time was spent arranging 'the set': a large rack of hay was by me and all the mares and foals gathered around to enjoy the action.

A little clapperboard man sprang in front of me and the show was on. It felt most unreal, as Bob Forbes said in his BBC voice: 'Mrs Svendsen, what made you start looking after donkeys?'

Although trying to concentrate and answer clearly, behind Bob and the camera I could see St Paddy, he was pawing the ground and snorting. The camera was running and a microphone and boom were dangling on a long pole one foot above my head.

'But why donkeys?' insisted Bob Forbes. I was just explaining what gentle creatures they were when my eyes became riveted on to St Paddy. My voice faded as he started his charge – he had decided the sound man was a new mare and obviously he had a duty to perform. There was a muffled shriek behind Bob and the sound man collapsed!

Black Jack and Mrs J. F. Hartland, driving champions

You will be asked to give an individual show: a trotted circle on both reins, a halt, a rein-back, and a quiet walk forward again with a salute to the judge is all that is required. Sometimes the judge may ask if he may drive your donkey himself, to help him come to a decision, so be sure your entry is accustomed to someone other than yourself holding the reins. Driving is great fun and the donkeys appear to enjoy it as much as their owners.

Ridden Classes Here the younger generation come into their own. Safety of the child and an enjoyable ride are obviously important. A free-moving donkey giving a smooth trot is what the judge is looking for, especially in leading-rein classes where the rider is often very young and a jolting trot can be most uncomfortable. Older children, riding off the leading rein, should be able to show they are in control of their mount both at the walk and the trot and when asked to give an individual show, it is nice if they can manage to canter as well. They may be asked to dismount and mount again, to demonstrate the good behaviour of their donkey, so make sure that he is taught to stand still and does not move off when the rider has only one foot in the stirrup.

Young Handlers' Classes Young handlers' classes are judged on the way the handler sets about showing his donkey. The donkey is not being examined. Some judges will have devised a short test for the handler to perform and they will be marked on how they carry it out. Other judges will be able to sort out the ability of the competitors by watching them carefully as they go through the routine of an ordinary in-hand showing class. It always helps if the handler is neat and tidy in appearance and has got his donkey well groomed and clean.

In all classes, no matter where you are placed in the line-up, smile and be polite when receiving your rosette. Only one exhibit can win the class and should you be unlucky at one show remember that there will be other days and other shows and other judges as well. Keep a cheerful face and enjoy your showing, and if you have done your training well at home, both you and your donkey will be able to give a pleasing performance and that red rosette may find itself being pinned up on your tack-room wall.

Crofters Cash in on Sporran Fibre Ruminant

Crofters on the Western Isles of Scotland are cashing in on fibre from a new breed of ruminant produced by genetic engineering.

The donkora has been produced by genetic substitution in Highland cattle with selected genes from donkeys and angora goats. This has resulted in a hardy herbivore with a fast-growing coat of exceptionally lustrous dark-grey fibre.

This new fibre-farming animal can be shorn three times a year and high yields of fibre have been harvested.

It is all for sporran-making on the nearby island of Jurna, which in recent years has run into a serious shortage of fibre for the booming market in sporrans and other traditional Scottish dress from visiting tourists.

Farmers Weekly
April Fool!

FROM A JUDGE'S VIEWPOINT

There is something about judging donkeys that is unlike anything else; large sums of money are not involved and exhibitors and breeders do not expect to make their fortunes out of these delightful creatures, hence a great friendliness exists between competitors which infiltrates through to the judge and makes for an enjoyable job and for happy times worth remembering.

Exhibitors travel miles and work hard preparing their donkeys for the show ring and in good faith accept the various opinions of judges. As a judge I am always thankful if I have enough time to give every exhibitor my full attention wherever they stand. In my humble opinion I think it is extremely hurtful to be flipped over if you are placed at the end of the line and manners are expected both from the judge and exhibitors. One meets so many cheerful characters who are more often down the line than up; they still turn up all smiles; I do admire them for their sportsmanship. When the donkeys enter the ring I already know where they will be lined up and where I shall watch them run out. As they go round I stand with my back to where the line up will be and watch them go past at the walk. I do not believe in turning round too much but watch each carefully. I look for the good walker that uses his shoulders and covers the ground well, with a purpose. If I spot one, I run my eye over him and if he pleases me I remember him. I pick out the best in my mind. I do not walk them round too long as I have more chances to look at them later.

TROT ROUND

I ask my steward to stop them at the left-side corner and then ask each exhibitor to trot across in front of me. I look for a good mover with good conformation; the movement should be strong, hind and front legs being well used, not too much knee. The animal should cover the ground well as in the walk. A donkey that uses its shoulder will catch the eye. Having seen the entire class I then tell the steward to ask them to walk on. Here it is permissible to look around a bit as you do not want to take too long lining them up. I pick my donkeys and, when coming to the end of the line in a big class, ask the steward to let them place themselves as I can sort them out when they do their individual show. While the steward is occupied I ask the first to come out of the line and stand broadside on to me. It is now that I make a close inspection of the animal.

INSPECTION

I look at the top line. Well-carried ears, good neck (not ewe-necked or too short or bolster-shaped crest sagging to one side). Back not too long (brown donkeys allowed a little more length). Stallions must have good strong backs, not sway or dipped, but well muscled and strong loins. No sway backs in young stock. If I have a good looking mare with a dippy back I enquire how many foals she has had, and her age, and I make an allowance if justified. Good quarters and tail carriage; nothing mean about them. Passing over the top line I observe the front of the animal; it must not be too narrow-chested or slab-sided; no crooked legs or knock knees. Good strong knees and short cannon bones are desirable. When standing at the side, the top line and bottom line should not be parallel; you want a good deep girth and plenty of heart room.

The shoulder consists of two separate bones, the scapula or upper bone of the shoulder and the humerus or lower bone of the shoulder. The scapula stretches obliquely forward from just below the wither to the point of the shoulder; the bone should be broad and long and lie well back; it is essential that the length lies in the scapula and not the humerus. An over-long and over-horizontal humerus bone will push the forelegs too much under the body, resulting in the animal failing to have the necessary leg at each corner and generally upsetting the balance, making it uncomfortable as a ride.

The head should be in proportion to the animal; not too big. A dishy face with a generous eye is always attractive if accompanied by well-set ears. Coarse lips sometimes spoil the picture. Teeth should be healthy, not overshot or undershot. Sometimes in young stock the irregularity is slight and I allow for it righting itself at maturity but in brood mares or stallions it is a detriment and could be a reason for the donkey being lowered in its placing. Eyes should, of course, be healthy and set well apart.

The limbs should be free from bad blemishes and not light of bone. Joints and limbs should be clean. Knees good and not back of the knee. Forearms should be well developed and not tied at the elbows. Hind legs must be strong; a good second thigh and gaskin is essential; the hock must be strong and flex well. Bent or sickle hocks go against the animal. Hoofs must be a good shape and well tended; not boxy or heavily ringed or deformed. Frogs and soles should be inspected if in doubt as to the state of the feet generally. Pin-toed or splay-footed are bad points.

RUNOUT

Having inspected the donkey for conformation I then ask the exhibitor to walk away from me. This is my chance to look carefully at the donkey's action. As he walks away I look to see whether the animal plaits with his hind feet; a bad thing if he does as it means he could knock himself. I also observe the hind leg to see whether it is weak or wobbly and look for cow hocks (turning inwards) which is not a good thing. When the donkey is trotted towards me I look for plaiting in front, or over-wideness in front. As he goes away I watch for closeness of hocks or too wide; trailing behind or dishing in front; all bad faults. Now I refresh my memory with his action generally.

RESHUFFLE

Unless I mean to leave the exhibits as they are I ask the steward to send the class round in a circle so that I can re-place them and bring them in their new positions. If you are undecided between two animals that are in the ribbons, wherever they stand, you should not be afraid to have them both out again if necessary.

The penalty of judging is that people occasionally get a bit upset. If approached in the right manner, at the right time, I never mind being asked by exhibitors why I did not place their animal. They want to learn; some are new to the game and if I can help I will and, as I have said before, it is only my opinion. Bad losers just upset themselves and other people and can spoil a happy day. If you are a judge people have every right to criticise you but then they soon forget and there is always tomorrow when we all tear out of bed and enjoy the hustle and bustle of getting to the show; the tears, tantrums, tempers and tribulations of a happy family, ending with trophies, or 'I'll try another judge next time!' What fun it all is! And all thanks to those delightful long-eared friends the donkeys, God bless them.

Alison B. Hancock, *Donkey Breed Society Magazine*

Judging the championship at Hickstead

THE DONKEY IN THE UNITED STATES

We have a very large number of donkeys in the United States and they come in great variety. They range from a tiny 74cm (29in) at adulthood to a towering 17 hands.

The American Donkey and Mule Society was founded in 1967 as a National Breed Society. In the beginning it was intended to be a donkey society, but in the United States donkeys and mules are inseparable, so it became the breed society of both. Donkey breeds are recognised by size and it became imperative to establish a single set of terms to define our animals. There had never been a society for all breeds before and the terms used were a mixture of two languages and many regional terms. The breed terms established for donkeys were 91.5 cm (36in) or less at maturity; standard 91.5cm (36in) up to 122cm (48in) at maturity; large standard from 122cm (48in) to 137cm (54in) in the case of the jennet (jenny or female donkey) and 122cm (48in) to 142cm (56in) in the case of the jack (male); mammoth jack stock 142cm (56in) and up for jennets and 147cm (58in) and up for jacks. The terms jennet and jack are used for male and female although jenny is also often used. The terms mare and stallion are never used as we prefer to keep all of our differences from horses alive and accentuated.

One of the chief uses for all donkeys is breeding mules and some hinnies. Mules are increasing in numbers and uses every day in the United States. Our breed designations for mules are based on both usage and the mare the mule is bred from. The basic mule breeds are: miniature mules 127cm (50in) and under; saddle, these are mules of any size above 127cm (50in) but of riding-type conformation and out of riding-type horses; pack and work mules of mid-range size from 14 hands to about 15.2 or 16 hands but strongly and heavily built or suitable for farm or pack work rather than saddle work; draught, the dam should be a pure or part-bred draught horse and the mule should be of a definite draught type. We register all breeds of donkeys and mules. Our donkeys are registered by inspection and pedigree.

HISTORY OF THE DONKEY AND MULE

In the early days of settlement of the Americas, the western and south-western parts of the United States were explored and finally settled by Spanish speaking peoples. Donkeys were mixed with the horses they brought. They used these medium-sized work donkeys called burros for work and for breeding fairly small, very tough mules for work and riding. To this day a standard donkey is a burro west of the Mississippi river and a donkey to the east! If a Westerner sees a large standard donkey with good conformation he tends to call it a Spanish donkey or Spanish jack. Since all of our donkeys, especially the standards, are from Spanish ancestry this term had no real meaning and we have not encouraged its use. The American Donkey and Mule Society has reserved the term burro for the feral animals that are caught in our western states and put out to the public for adoption. These are officially called wild burros by the government and the people working with them and so we use the term formally only for these animals.

In the eighties, as in the past, the vast preponderance of the donkeys in this country are the medium size, Spanish ancestry standard donkeys. They have always been kept as pets even in the past and of course this is their chief function now. In the past they were heavily used for work in the west and south-west but only kept as incidental animals in the rest of the country. In the areas which had been settled by Spanish speakers the burro toiled under the pack saddle, under saddle, in teams pulling freight, in agriculture and in all the other ways that poor countries find to use their donkeys. Today there are more of them than ever. They are widely spread around the country and it is estimated that there are thousands in every state. They are very popular pets and are used as companions for horses, to teach calves and colts to lead, to guard sheep and goat flocks, for riding, driving single and in teams, showing and in many other ways. They come in all sizes and colours and conformation types. Their conformation has improved greatly down the years and many of the standard donkeys we see are very elegant and well-built animals. Their colours are most commonly the grey-dun (grey with cross and dorsal stripe), or some shade of brown or black, but they are quite commonly seen in white, spotted, shades of red roan, blue roan and shades of chestnut ranging from pink to very dark. A few true bays even appear but they are rare as is the very dark chestnut.

The breed that the United States is particularly known for was created in this country. This was done quite deliberately by importation of European stocks and inbreeding. It was created specifically for breeding mules and is known as Ameri-

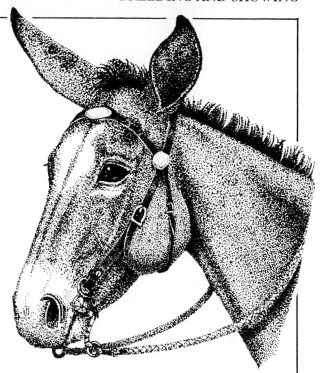

can mammoth jack stock. It is never correct under any circumstances to refer to these animals as donkeys. They may be called asses if a technical description is needed but they are correctly referred to as either jack stock, mammoth jack stock, or mammoth jacks and jennets. These animals have a very interesting background because the founder of the breed was George Washington. Mr Washington was a dedicated agriculturalist and felt that mules were the power source that were ideally suited for the hot and humid, even torrid, regions of the southern United States. Washington asked that the King of Spain send him some jacks and jennets to try to propagate a large breed of asses in this country. At that time export of the fine Spanish asses was forbidden but the King sent some as a gift from one head of state to another and the American mule industry was born. The fashion for importing large jack stock was followed by many prominent Americans such as Henry Clay and soon by anyone who was interested and could afford it. Quite soon after that professional importers got interested and imported what they could find and sold them to the highest bidder. Jack stock from Spain and many other Mediterranean countries was imported and blended in this country to create our own strain. A breed registry was started with certain standards of size and colour which still exists today. It is called the *Standard Jack and Jennet Registry of the United States*. In those days the animals were called standard jacks and jennets because they were bred to a standard; the term mammoth after one of the great sires of the breed and their obvious size.

From the late forties to the early sixties, because of the lack of demand for mules, the breeding of these truly splendid animals was almost wholly neglected and only a few of the faithful kept their stock. By the late sixties the hobby breeders were

Continued overleaf/

beginning to bring the breed back and today there are many, many beautiful individuals to be found. The breed is thriving and continually improving as the breeding of mules for recreational purposes, especially beautiful saddle mules from well-bred registered pure-bred saddle mares, is a booming business and, of course, the large jacks are needed to breed the mares to produce these popular animals. In the past jacks and jennets were used only for producing their own kind and for producing mules but in line with modern recreational uses they are now often seen being ridden on the trail, at ranch work, for harness work and in the show ring. Due to their size they work like mules when properly conformed and trained and are becoming quite popular since they have the kind donkey temperament (when properly handled).

The miniature donkey (full name the miniature Mediterranean donkey) is justly popular. People often refer to them as Sicilian donkeys as these stocky little donkeys were originally imported from the islands of Sicily and Sardinia in the fifties. The registry for the breed is called the *Miniature Donkey Registry of the United States* and was formed by the original importers, the most important of whom were Mr and Mrs Daniel Langfeld of Danby Farm, Omaha, Nebraska and Mr August Busch of St Louis, Missouri. Very small donkeys were imported from the Mediterranean region (one even from Abyssinia!), and inbred to form a truly new American breed. The registry started out with the height limit of 96.5cm (38in) but the breed has progressed so much that it recently was able to lower its limit to 91.5cm (36in)

at maturity. The original animals were all grey with the dorsal stripe and cross but inbreeding has brought out brown, black, chestnut and recently, spotted animals. The *Miniature Donkey Registry* has recently been transferred to the care of the American Donkey and Mule Society but retains its original identity as a separate breed registry for these tiny donkeys. These animals are exceedingly popular and are bred in all states.

To save the feral donkeys from being shot for overgrazing the western public lands, they are rounded up and offered for adoption by the public. Feral donkeys, if properly handled, settle down and soon cannot be told from domestic donkeys in either looks or behaviour. These animals provide a very welcome dose of genes into the domestic donkey gene pool. These animals have very tough bone and feet and an endurance of body brought about by many generations of tough desert living and survival of the fittest. There is a registry for these animals too, although many are registered or double registered with the American Donkey and Mule Society.

The American Council of Spotted Asses is a colour registry and registers all donkeys of any size or type which have spotted coats. It promotes the breeding of this lovely colour pattern.

The donkey is alive, well and thriving in the United States, his admirers are legion and there are several organisations devoted to his welfare.

Paul and Betsy Hutchins,
founders of the
American Donkey and Mule Society, 1967

Competing in a driving class at a show in Arizona

Miniature donkeys

Elmer Zeiss of Valley, Nebraska, with his wagon team of spotted adopted wild burros

The International Donkey Protection Trust

Throughout the world find a working donkey and you will find poverty and people living on, or below, the breadline. In all parts of the globe, donkeys play a vital role in agricultural and family life. Owing to the poverty of their owners, veterinary care and adequate food are the exception rather than the rule and so conditions, at best, are poor for the donkey and little is known from a professional point of view as to the minimum amount of food and water on which they can live and work. Although all Third World donkeys tend to be overworked and undernourished, they are treated very differently from one area to another.

The International Donkey Protection Trust, after its foundation in 1976, has visited and worked in many countries. It was found that the average life expectancy of donkeys and mules in countries visited was eleven years, whereas the average expectancy of 1,600 donkeys at the Donkey Sanctuary was thirty-seven years. To the poor peasant the death of his donkey is a major calamity and to continue his farming and transport of goods he has to dig in to any capital, he may be lucky enough to have, to buy another donkey. Simple research, carried out during working trips abroad and followed up by official trials, has proved parasites to be the major cause of death.

The difference in the condition of animals treated by a simple worming dose bi-annually is significant. The scant food eaten is digested by the donkey rather than the parasite, so the animal is able to increase his body weight. This means a thicker cover of flesh over bone, which reduces the terrible saddle galls and injuries caused through rubbing, so frequently seen in working donkeys. A fitter donkey means he is more capable of doing his job and the fact that his life should be extended dramatically will be of major help to the poor of the Third World.

PROBLEMS ABROAD

Spain A variety of problems have been found by the International Donkey Protection Trust throughout the world. In Spain many donkeys are used as part of the tourist industry and many are abused. A code of practice has been drawn up jointly by the International Donkey Protection Trust and the World Society for the Protection of Animals and presented to the Spanish Government. The code was adopted in Tenerife as a test case and this has now come into force and will help conditions in riding establishments. It is hoped that in due course this will be enforced throughout Spain.

In areas such as Marbella and Mijas, large numbers of donkeys used in tourist excursions had to stand all day without water and shelter but, after pressure, these facilities are now provided. The International Donkey Protection Trust has appointed a Spanish-based veterinary surgeon to make fortnightly visits throughout the summer and monthly visits during the winter to ensure that these donkeys remain in good health. Our charity has objected to photographs taken for postcards where donkeys are clothed and made to sit in unnatural positions as well as the use of donkeys on a merry-go-round, where they are tied and forced to walk a continual circle carrying tourists.

A great deal of concern and attention was focussed, by our charity and the national press, on the annual Lenten fiesta held at Villanueva de la Vera. The carnival lasts for four days and it has been the custom that on Shrove Tuesday the men, called 'calabaceros' (pumpkin sellers), lead their 'boss' through the streets of the village riding a donkey. The 'boss' was usually the fattest man of the village and the oldest donkey in the village was selected. The man was put on the back of this donkey who

> **Earthquake Victim**
>
> A small white donkey was freed after being trapped for sixty-nine days in his stable following the Italian earthquakes. Troops had kept the beast alive by pushing hay and water through a hole in the rubble. The fourteen-year-old donkey had survived in the mountain village of Castelgrande, which is in the region worst hit by earthquakes.
>
> Rescuers were unable to free him earlier because the stable was perched on the edge of a precipice and covered by rubble from a house which had collapsed. There was a risk that the stable and donkey would disappear if bulldozers were used, officials said in Naples.

Safe at last – Blackie and Elisabeth Svendsen

was then dragged through the cobbled streets by a long, thick rope with over fifty knots in it. Youths and men each took a place at a knot in the rope and dragged the terrified animal through the village streets. The donkey fell frequently, partly because of the cobbled streets, partly because of the weight and partly because of the jerky dragging that he was subjected to. Each time the donkey fell he was kicked and poked and forced to stand again until, at last, after over fifty minutes, he was dragged into the market square. Eventually, when the animal was no longer able to stand, the crowd of men surrounding him would throw themselves onto the donkey chanting a song which included the words 'Finally Aunt Vinagre's donkey died . . .' The donkey was crushed by the crowd and, although on first hearing that the donkey was killed we found it difficult to believe, we were given photographic evidence which showed the crowd on top of the donkey with only the donkey's leg protruding underneath.

In 1987, two weeks before the fiesta was to take place, we learned that a donkey was again to be used in the normal custom despite our efforts and those of a Spanish-based welfare organisation. The world press reported the events that were due to take place and we were inundated by pleas to help from the British public. We forwarded three thousand letters of protest to Spanish officials in an attempt to stop this needless slaughter.

Vicky Moore, a committee member of the RSPCA, funded by the International Donkey Protection Trust would represent us and do all she could to save the donkey. She arrived in the village to an antagonistic welcome.

The donkey used in the fiesta was nicknamed 'Blackie' and due to the presence of Vicky Moore, other animal welfare organisations and the press, he was not unduly harmed except for rope burns on his neck and sides and some damage to his fetlocks. After the fiesta the *Star* newspaper purchased Blackie and the Donkey Sanctuary was asked to take ownership of him. It was felt that, if left in the village, it was possible that the villagers might take revenge on Blackie for altering the custom of their fiesta. John Fowler, the sanctuary veterinary surgeon, and Roy Harrington departed for Spain to extricate Blackie from the village into a safe resting place until quarantine regulations allowed him to enter Britain.

During the thirty days of Blackie's quarantine in Spain we had been constantly pestered by the press so arrangements had to be made in secrecy to go over to Spain on the Easter bank holiday. It had been agreed earlier that the *Star* reporters would accompany what was to become known as the 'A-Team', in bringing Blackie back. Our lorry departed by ferry to France and it was agreed that the whole team would meet in Madrid. Accompanied by the *Star* newspapermen I departed by air and set about the difficult and frustrating task of getting the paperwork cleared in Madrid. The agent did not want to be associated with Blackie, in case of reprisals, and so he refused to put the species 'donkey' on any of the veterinary and customs forms required, insisting on classifying Blackie as a horse! This caused innumerable problems, both at the Spanish docks and back in the United Kingdom.

After carefully loading Blackie onto the lorry we set off for the port. Arriving there, we found that the authorities did not have the necessary paperwork! In fact, it was only at the very last minute before the ferry was due to sail, and after hours of waiting, that matters were finally resolved.

We had hoped that our arrival would be a secret. However, our hopes were quickly dashed as, on reaching Plymouth, we were informed that the press were 'all over the docks'. The police and customs men did a marvellous job and had somehow managed to move all the reporters off the dock and behind the wire. Pandemonium broke out when we went through the gates. The reporters were told that the lorry would stop and the ramp would be opened for five minutes, so that they could photograph Blackie, but due to the ensuing melée we closed up the ramp and drove off. Blackie travelled exceptionally well and was unloaded into the stable prepared for him. Nearly all the staff had returned to the sanctuary that evening to see Blackie's safe arrival. Shortly afterwards Blackie was introduced to a little donkey called Lola, who had come from Wales after having had a fairly tough life and they have become firm friends and will spend the rest of their natural days at the sanctuary.

Throughout the remainder of 1987 and the early part of 1988 the International Donkey Protection Trust wrote to Spanish officials and all members of the European Parliament in order to prevent a donkey being used in a future fiesta. Mrs B. Castle, MEP, drafted and tabled a motion in an attempt to prevent a

Searching for food in Lamu

CODES OF PRACTICE FOR DONKEYS/MULES USED FOR COMMERCIAL AND TOURIST EXCURSIONS IN SPAIN

GENERAL WORKING CONDITIONS

1 The maximum work rate of any donkey/mule shall be not more than six consecutive days, followed by one full day rest period. Donkeys/mules shall be used for not more than one and a half hours continuous work and this shall be followed by a minimum of half an hour rest. A donkey/mule shall not be harnessed for more than eight hours in any one day.

2 Any tack that is used shall be in good repair and designed so as not to cause abrasions or injuries and shall be properly fitted so as not to cause any discomfort.

3 Each excursion group shall be led by a responsible and experienced adult. In addition, one assistant shall accompany every ten donkeys/mules in that group.

4 No donkey/mule shall carry excessive weight in consideration of the size, age and physical condition of the animal and the following guidelines of maximum weight limits should be borne in mind:
(a) Small donkeys/mules (under 102cm (40in) in height to shoulder) – only children under 50kg (110lb).
(b) Medium donkeys/mules (between 102–112cm (40–44in) in height to shoulder) – weight limit of 63kg (139lb).
(c) Very large donkeys/mules (over 112cm (44in) in height to shoulder) – weight limit of 76kg (168lb).

5 Lame or sick donkeys/mules, including those with sores, shall not be used for work.

6 The operator shall have a minimum of ten per cent reserve of extra donkeys/mules in sound health and suitable for immediate replacement of sick or lame working animals. A reserve donkey/mule shall be taken on all excursions as a replacement in the event of an animal becoming unsound during a trek.

7 Stallion jack donkeys shall not be used on touristic excursions and shall be kept in a separate area from excursion working donkeys.

8 A donkey in foal shall not be worked after the eighth month of gestation nor before the third month after foaling, or as specifically recommended. The operator shall keep records of all donkeys in foal, or suspected to be in foal, and shall display the same in a conspicuous area.

9 Donkeys/mules shall not be ridden until at least three years old and a weight limit of 38kg (84lb) shall then be imposed until four years old. Working time shall be limited to a maximum of three hours per day until four years old.

10 A hoof pick shall be available during an excursion and where the animals are shod, sufficient tools shall be available at all times to remove twisted or distorted shoes that may occur during the ride.

HEALTH AND FEEDING

11 The feet of all donkeys on the premises should be inspected and cleaned out with a hoof pick at least once daily. Where it is the practice to shoe donkeys for working, these shoes must be correctly fitted by a farrier. The hoofs of shod donkeys shall be trimmed and shoes refitted every three to four weeks or more frequently if necessary. Donkeys with loose shoes shall not be used for working. Where it is expected that a donkey will not be in work for a prolonged period the shoes shall be removed.

12 The minimum feeding cycle for donkeys/mules in work shall be two feedings per twenty-four hours, an adequate wholesome supply, consistent with keeping the animals in adequate condition for work, to be made available.

13 A sufficient feeding area shall be provided to permit all animals to eat simultaneously without aggression. Separate feeding areas shall be provided for slow eating animals and/or timid ones.

14 Donkeys/mules shall have continual access to fresh water when not in work.

15 Adequate protection from the sun, rain and wind shall be provided for all animals whilst not at work.

The donkeys/mules shall be routinely visited by a veterinary surgeon and/or a designated inspector at a minimum of at least six-monthly intervals or as he deems necessary, and his recommendations must be complied with.

donkey being used. However, as Shrove Tuesday approached in 1988 it appeared that action would have to be taken once more.

It was confirmed that the fiesta was to take place and a national appeal was launched requesting people to write letters, expressing their horror, which we would photocopy and send to King Juan Carlos, the mayor of Villanueva de la Vera, the Ministry of Agriculture in Madrid and the Spanish Embassy. The response was amazing and 25,300 letters were forwarded. Even more important the mayor of the village, Senor Felix Perez Gonzalez, invited a special team from the charity to attend the fiesta as official observers.

On the day itself Roy Harrington, Neil Harvey and I arrived in the village square early in the morning. There were still drunken revellers from the night before but we were allowed to stand right beside the town hall where the donkey, nicknamed 'Beauty Thatcher', had been hidden. After four frightening false starts, with gangs of men rushing out of the door with a long rope to which the donkey was supposed to be attached, both doors were suddenly opened and it was almost impossible to see the donkey for the group surrounding it. Guns were fired around the donkey and with the crowd pushing and jostling we were swept through the streets for a period of fifty-four minutes.

The streets were cobbled and uneven and on most of them there was a central open water drain as an additional hazard. Although some of the crowd were antagonistic, the majority were in good humour and the ring of men around the donkey was there to protect it from the drunken revellers and to prevent the donkey slipping.

The man on the donkey's back weighed no more than 57kg (9st) and the donkey was large and well fed. Due to the steps taken by our charity and the world press the only possible danger seemed to be that the donkey might easily have fallen and, if this happened, there is little doubt that she would have been injured and possibly crushed to death in the enormous crowd which was surging backwards and forwards. Immediately the procession returned to the square the donkey was released and with her owner and four or five protectors, driven out of the market square down a side road. At this stage we were alongside the donkey and although she had sweated up slightly and was obviously frightened by the mob of people and the noise, she had suffered no ill-effects. A Spanish-based veterinary surgeon pronounced that he was completely satisfied with the donkey's condition.

We saw the donkey back to her stable and inspected her again two hours later, finding her to be in good condition and eating normally. There was no necessity to even consider moving the donkey from the area this year as we were satisfied that the Spanish authorities took every step they could to protect the animal. On arrival back in England a full report was forwarded to the European Parliament, Intergroup on Animal Welfare and Eurogroup for Animal Welfare.

Although Beauty Thatcher was not harmed and the mayor did his best it was nevertheless horrifying to see the donkey dragged through the streets and a solution would be for a life-like

---

Letter from Adow in Lamu

I would like to inform you that I have presented your medical gifts to 258 donkeys, the remaining doses are just waiting for any donkeys with great luck. And how I would like to inform you that by the time you are telling me you would try to do something about my scholarship I was about to drop with joy, just by the mention of your willingness to try the scholarship for me was as if you removed from my flesh a thorn that has pricked me long ago of which I was unable to operate it. Besides relief and joy has stayed with me since, knowing at least and at long last someone in a far corner of the world could help me have what I longed for, ie having sound veterinary knowledge to help animals and particularly donkeys . . .

donkey to be made and this could be presented to the village for use at future fiestas. The village can then revert to the fattest man riding and the cruel rope with fifty knots can again be used. There should then be no problems and the donkey can be dragged through the streets and the shotguns fired at will. The mayor will be invited to Donkey Week so that he can see Blackie for himself and hopefully he will agree to our new suggestion.

Greece In Greece, from 1982 to 1985, with the support of the Agricultural Bank of Greece and the Ministry of Agriculture, the International Donkey Protection Trust set up worming trials to control the parasites in mules and donkeys. The donkey will always be part of the Greek peasant's working life particularly on the isolated islands and in mountainous regions. The Greek Government has, in fact, taken responsibility for improving conditions and has allocated 150 million drachmas to the worming of animals. The majority of Greek people treat their donkeys well although the custom of adults riding the donkey will take many years to alter. Overloading is the main problem but the situation is improving rapidly. On Santorini, where the donkeys have to carry tourists up some 597 steps, conditions have improved. The government has installed a telpherage and there is talk of a permanent agricultural veterinary surgeon being allocated to Santorini.

Egypt Egypt is perhaps the worst place in the world for equines. The charity is now working closely with the veterinary university in Cairo and a worming trial has been set up here. Veterinary

Working mules in Egypt

surgeons are consistently amazed to see for themselves how willing the local people are to reveal the sores on the donkeys' backs by removing harnesses whilst in the markets. Most countries visited are following up our work by taking groups of students into the markets to carry out first aid and to educate the people on the needs of their animals.

Donkeys in Mexico with terrible hoof problems

Tunisia Frequent visits were made to Tunisia in 1970 and a study on conditions and health was set up in desert areas such as Gafsa and Tozeur. Much direct cruelty was apparent in this area, the donkeys frequently being beaten and heavily overladen. Working with SPANA (Society for the Protection of Animals in North Africa) many injured donkeys were treated and a good working relationship set up. We were able to supply modern drugs and methods of application, which were of tremendous use. The dressers normally had to treat infected hocks and legs by brushing on raw iodine or gentian violet; no easy task with a kicking mule! The introduction by our charity of terramycine sprays were of immense value both to the dressers and the animals.

We were prevented from further work in Tunisia by the government veterinary department who resented our presence but the startling results from the original parasitic trials gave us the necessary determinaton to start again from scratch.

Cyprus Dr G. Papadopoulos of the World Health Organisation invited veterinary surgeons throughout the world to attend training courses arranged in the United Kingdom by the International Donkey Protection Trust. Dr George Evstathiou from Cyprus is one such vet and was most impressed with his visit to the Donkey Sanctuary and invited us to Cyprus to see the conditions of donkeys for ourselves and to help in the setting up of a worming trial. The animals were found to be in a superb condition; very large, sprightly donkeys and mules and much valued by their owners. Most of them lived in the mountainous regions where their main task was to help in the grape harvest. The Department of Veterinary Services immediately took over the task of treating the donkeys with anthelmintic and expressed their gratitude for drawing this need to their attention. Every donkey and mule in Greek Cyprus is now dosed against parasites.

Australia The situation for the feral donkeys in central Australia, the Northern Territory and the Kimberleys is a desperate one. The number of feral donkeys in the Kimberley region of Western Australia was estimated at one million. According to the Australian Government the donkeys poach food and water from the cattle and damage the soil surface with their hoofs. The government has ordered a cull aiming to wipe out the whole feral donkey population. They are shot by high velocity rifles from helicopters and the shooter aims to kill up to one hundred donkeys per hour. It is very difficult to kill the donkey outright in this way and much suffering is caused. In a recent cull in the Kimberleys over 15,000 were shot in a four-week period and after six years of culling it is estimated that the donkey population is down 80 per cent from the original one million.

Self-defence

The donkey in Africa when attacked by a savage lion, tiger or puma, saves himself by lying on his back kicking his legs in the air.

139

South America The donkey plays a vital role in village life in South America. One small village, perched high on a mountainside, had no water, the stream being at the foot of the mountains down 2 miles of tortuous zigzag road. At 6am each morning the donkeys gathered by the village well of their own accord. Their large wooden saddles were fitted on their backs and enormous empty water pitchers were slotted one on each side of the saddle. The village women arrived with armfuls of washing which they piled on the water pitchers and the whole procession set off down the track. On reaching the stream the women filled the water pitchers and with a smack on the rump the donkeys set off completely alone up the track to the village while the women did the washing. As each donkey arrived in the village it waited patiently until one of the men arrived and emptied the pitchers into the well. The donkey then set off down the track and repeated the process. Four trips later, the donkeys waited by the stream, browsing, until the women called and then they did a last trip with water, women and washing. This time the women unloaded the donkeys who then rambled off to graze and rest all night, completely free.

THE DONKEY – FOUR LEG

There is considerable interest in efficient methods of power provision for remote rural areas in the tropics. It is therefore appropriate to review a model that has been available for over 5,000 years and is fully field tested.

The donkey comes in a range of sizes to suit individual requirements. The most popular model normally weighs 150–175kg (330–385lb). It has two alternative seating positions and a carrying capacity of approximately one-third of liveweight according to maintenance level and condition. It can also be used as an independent power unit for cereal threshing, water drawing or haulage. Continuous draught power is 12–15 per cent of liveweight and with the use of a suitable cart the donkey can haul three times its own weight. Where power requirements are particularly high several donkey units can be conveniently combined to meet the needs of the situation.

Particular features of the donkey are illustrated in the accompanying diagram and include low fuel costs, independent four-leg drive and self-repairing road gear. All models can be replaced at conveniently managed intervals from 3–4 years of age when female and male versions are brought into close contact. The process takes approximately twelve months but can normally be repeated up to 10–15 times if desired. This is an economically important feature unavailable with mechanically powered competitors. Furthermore longevity is a particularly important characteristic of the donkey which means that the time required for producing replacements is kept to a minimum.

Maintenance requirements of the donkey are low. Externally, attention is required to prevent insect damage but this can be accomplished by washing with suitable fluids. Internally, there is a risk of parasitic damage which can be avoided by appropriate dosing, normally required only twice per year. Regular lubrication of internal parts with water is an important requirement. Daily lubrication is advisable but intervals of two to three days are acceptable under difficult circumstances of use. A particular feature of the donkey is its ability to take on water lubricant very quickly without damaging the internal mechanisms. The water lubricant is also used for cooling purposes and no other special equipment is required for this purpose.

Fuel for the donkey is widely available in rural areas at very low or zero cost with fuel seeking and self-filling as standard characteristics. Distances travelled per full stomach are routinely 20–30km (12½–18½ miles) per day but can exceed this considerably if necessary. Normal running speeds are 4–5 kmph (2½–3mph) which minimises the risk of accident and injury to other road users.

Further features of the model include a facility for programming to verbal commands and an anti-theft and predator warning system. The latter involves all-round visual and auditory sensors and an ear shattering warning bray which is impossible to overlook or misinterpret.

The donkey has been available to users for thousands of years. The original design has

Mexico We have been working for several years with the superb assistance of Dr Aline de Aluja from the Faculty of Veterinary Medicine of the National University of Mexico. Three young veterinary surgeons have been appointed to her team, two of whom have been to England on our training courses. Trial anthelmintic programmes have been carried out in isolated villages and the general health of the donkey and the knowledge of the local people has improved. It is now proposed to set up a mobile clinic which will visit the many markets in Mexico; in some cases the donkey being the only method of bringing in goods to be sold.

Jamaica Happy-go-lucky attitudes and ignorance seem to cause the problems for donkeys in Jamaica and the Caribbean. The tendency to hobble the donkey tightly by a front and back leg, or two front legs, causes both pain and immobility which makes the donkey an easy target for attack from children, dogs and flies. Raw sores are common and untreated because of the owner's poverty. Saddles, or improvised back packs, using nylon cord are frequently used in tying down large loads of cane or

DRIVE RURAL POWER

changed little and has clearly met the requirements of rural dwellers particularly in the dry tropical areas. There has been some short-sighted suggestion that mechanical transport may be a better future alternative to the donkey. To meet this challenge donkey agents internationally are sponsoring comparative trials on the basis of foreign exchange requirement, initial and recurrent costs, employment creation and lifetime performance. Demanding field comparisons with mechanically powered vehicles in rugged and mountainous terrain are also expected to bring interesting results.

It is thus with considerable pleasure that we re-launch *the donkey* – a successful model from the past with an impressive future as a four-leg drive agricultural and transport power source for tropical rural areas.

Dr D. Fielding, Tropical Equine Project, Edinburgh School of Agriculture, University of Edinburgh

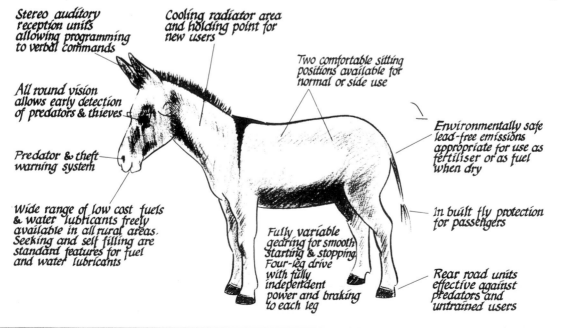

Stereo auditory reception units allowing programming to verbal commands

Cooling radiator area and holding point for new users

Two comfortable sitting positions available for normal or side use

All round vision allows early detection of predators & thieves

Environmentally safe lead-free emissions appropriate for use as fertiliser or as fuel when dry

Predator & theft warning system

Wide range of low cost fuels & water lubricants freely available in all rural areas. Seeking and self filling are standard features for fuel and water lubricants

In built fly protection for passengers

Fully variable gearing for smooth starting & stopping. Four-leg drive with fully independent power and braking to each leg

Rear road units effective against predators and untrained users

Attending to sores on donkeys' backs in an Ethiopian market

bananas; the cord tightens around the girth, becomes wet with sweat and then can cut deeply into the donkey's flesh.

The Gambia In Africa the donkey is experiencing something of a revival. The Gambia has seen an enormous upsurge in the donkey population in the last few years. In 1955 the Department of Agriculture in The Gambia began training both young men and oxen for periods of six to nine months so that they could go to remote areas and demonstrate the ploughing capabilities of the oxen. From 1976 donkeys were also included in the training. Donkeys are slightly more resistant than horses to the tsetse fly, the cause of trypanosomiasis. Unfortunately, the life expectancy is brief; disease and the tsetse taking their toll. One big advantage of the donkey in ploughing is that frequently only one person need be used to control a donkey while several people are needed to work with oxen. The increase in the use of donkeys is also being experienced in other African countries such as Kenya and Ethiopia.

Ethiopia Regular trips to the Ethiopian University and the commencement of a trial involving two hundred donkeys will hopefully speed up the recognition of the donkeys' agricultural value and lead to better treatment. The worst problems in Ethiopia are malnutrition, early death due to parasite infestation and acute back sores due to the total lack of any type of saddle or protection for the donkey's back from the load he is forced to carry. The charity arranged for one thousand 'soggies' (Kenyan-made rush pannier-type baskets) to be delivered to Ethiopia and it will be interesting to see whether the Ethiopian people, having experienced the benefits to their donkeys will find their own local resources to manufacture similar items. Donkey dung is an important fuel being flattened and dried and sold in the markets thus adding yet another benefit to the ownership of a donkey.

Kenya In Kenya the charity has set up its first sanctuary abroad. The KSPCA copes admirably with the work in the Nairobi area and the charity moved down to the coastal regions where severe problems were being experienced. The island of Lamu is part of the archipelago which stretches along the northern coast of Kenya, separated from the mainland by mangrove swamps. This district is served by a divisional veterinary officer and it was to him that the charity first went. It seemed there were almost four thousand donkeys on the islands but it was almost impossible for him to visit or treat these animals in view of the financial restrictions and the amount of work in hand. The town of Lamu is Muslim and is known as the second Mecca. The streets are very narrow and normal vehicle transport will never be possible in the town. Every item brought to the island by boat has to be transported by donkeys and they are, therefore, a major necessity for everyday living.

The state of the donkeys when we arrived was poor. Many were starving and suffering from tetanus, trypanosomiasis and all had a severe parasite problem. The results of the anthelmintic treatment were so dramatic on the island that, on the second

---

The Merrylegs Family

Our inspector was told of the plight of five donkeys kept in appalling conditions by gypsies near Hatfield. They had been found by the Animal Liberation Group in Leighton Buzzard who were desperately trying to effect a rescue. Our inspector went with them to the site, and after much arguing, the owner signed them over to avoid being prosecuted.

It was a very sorry looking little group that arrived – very malnourished, wormy and anaemic and including one emaciated pony whom we named Mrs Merrylegs. She was accompanied by her week-old baby mule (the most enchanting quiet little black foal); there was another mule in poor condition, as well as two poor donkey stallions.

After care and attention at the sanctuary the foal became a very lively little chap that led his mother, the nursery group and us quite a dance! At one time he actually jumped the post and rail fence 1.05m (3ft 6in) high and normally donkey proof!

Donkeys being brought into the refuge at Lamu. Many were in very poor condition when the IDPT first visited

visit, the team were inundated with requests to dose those donkeys that had not received treatment on the earlier visit. The condition of the donkeys that had been treated was obviously superior to the others and the owners were highly delighted with the results.

After visiting regularly for two years it was decided to set up our first sanctuary in the area, in view of the long-term continuing use of the donkey, and it was officially opened on 4 July 1987. Almost every donkey that is used to load and unload cargo walks past the gates and the drinking trough installed there has alleviated the daily suffering of many of the animals.

Sick and ailing animals are taken in and there are four internal stables for those requiring prolonged treatment and the outside exercise yard has plenty of shelter. Any donkey found in trouble wandering around the streets in a starved condition is housed and fed and the whole project has received the most enormous support from the local people. Regular visits are made to Lamu where a local manager, Abdalla Hadi Rifai, has been appointed with a small staff to run the refuge. An extremely close relationship is maintained with the veterinary officer who calls on a daily basis to administer any drugs required (provided by the charity) and to advise on difficult cases. A small laboratory is included in the building and regular routine checks are made on the health of the animals.

One of the young men who helped on the earlier trips around

TUNISIAN MARKET

The souk was smelly and noisy. It was early morning in mid-December, a bright clear Tunisian day with a sharp edge to the air which had the local traders wrapped in hooded cloaks over their flowing national dress of flimsy cotton djelebbas. I'd been in Tunisia for just over a week, enjoying some late winter sunshine and a much needed break after an intense two years with hardly a gap to draw breath.

The trip to a camel market was the last excursion from the hotel before we collected our bags and flew home to Devon. I went out of curiosity, my naturally inquisitive nature telling me this would be yet another experience to add to my catalogue of life. I'm still not sure what I expected to find. Local colour, of course, a carnival atmosphere perhaps, or a pitch of excitement on which to end my holiday. There was none of that. It was a place of sadness and pain. Careless indifference and brutal indulgence.

I can never enjoy the surroundings of a British market place where animals are prodded and kicked from pen to sale ring and manhandled into lorries. What made me think this would be any different I can't imagine. In fact, if I had thought about it I would have known that it could only be worse, far worse. And of course it was.

Camels and donkeys corraled for sale, with most of their owners demonstrating their saleability by proving how docile they remained when severely beaten. There's a hopelessness about penned animals at the best of times. This was a veritable trough of despair, and I could not bring myself to look into their eyes.

I had to leave the market. I couldn't buy them all to put them out of their misery and I couldn't stay to add to the circus. On my way out past the spitting, snorting camels and the bowed heads of the donkeys, one of the traders began calling out to me. He spoke in French, Tunisia's second language, "Achetez, Madame. C'est petit, très petit." The 'très petit' donkey he was referring to was hardly visible as he, all 16 stones of him was sitting bouncing up and down, presumably to show me how comfortable he was. The donkey was indeed very small, and very young. He stood, frail legs almost buckled under his gross weight, head bowed, a pathetic testimony to a country where donkeys are the equivalent of a second-hand car and often treated with less respect. I don't have a brilliant command of French, but found words I hadn't used for years, scouring the

the islands dosing donkeys has now, with the sponsorship of the charity, been educated to the point of entering veterinary school. He will, hopefully, become one of the first that the charity has been able to help to take up a position as a fully trained veterinary surgeon in their own country.

THE WORK GOES ON

In almost all countries, donkeys suffer by being worked too young and damaged legs, feet and dipped backs clearly illustrate this. Constant overweight loads affect the older donkey too. Lack of nourishment is common and although many owners grow alfalfa grass to feed the donkeys, or allow them to graze on long hobble chains, others hobble their donkeys too tightly and they are unable to forage a wide enough area to maintain health. It is rare to find hard feed being given to donkeys. It is fair, however, to say that in some countries care of the donkeys equals that of the children. The unnecessary use of bits in Arab countries prevents the donkey from supplementing his poor diet by browsing. Some extremely cruel and sharp bits are used, frequently crudely wired together, which can actually grow into the wounds they cause in the donkey's mouth.

Wherever possible the International Donkey Protection Trust aims to work with charities already established in other countries. This reduces duplication and ensures the maximum co-operation and benefit to the donkeys.

Body Condition Scores (for working donkeys and mules)

Grade 1
Very Poor – Emaciated. Ribs, spine and tubercoxae very prominent. Coat dull.
Grade 2
Below Average – Spine prominent, coat dull.
Grade 3
Average, Good – Spinous processes palpable but not prominent. Coat and skin generally in good condition.
Grade 4
Above Average, Very Good – Spinous processes not easily palpated. Well muscled. Coat shiny, skin intact. Overfat donkeys given this score.
Grade 5
Excellent – Body well rounded with generous muscle and fat cover. Spinous processes palpable. Coat shiny, skin intact.

---

very depths of my gutter knowledge of the language to tell him what he could do with his offer of a sale. He laughed, bounced some more, and I left. Furious but impotent.

Back at the hotel, when people asked what the market had been like, I advised them not to go unless they wanted to be upset, and back in England I wrote to one of the international animal leagues naming the market and adding my support to their work. It all seemed so futile, but what else was there to do? If you are really concerned I suppose what you do is give up your life to animals. Travelling the world, prodding governments, educating those prepared to listen and, gradually, inch by inch, succeed in turning the great wheel of apathy into one of positive momentum. Which is precisely what Elisabeth Svendsen has done. And it's because I can't do that that I admire her for the gutsy lady that she is.

And while Elisabeth, and others like her, roam the world campaigning for change, I lend my support, like millions more, to try and improve the lot of animals in general – though the donkey seems to evoke such special feelings with his gentle, sad expression. There are times when I burst with pride at the way mankind has shown compassion and understanding towards those creatures who share this planet with us. But others (and they are sadly frequent) when my heart sinks and I despair at the arrogant indifference of one species on this planet to the needs, and rights, of the rest.

The film I made at the Donkey Sanctuary, so many years ago, was a double-edged sword. There was great pleasure for me in seeing so many animals happy and secure after lives often spent in misery. But equally great sadness at knowing that there are still many more who will be abused and neglected.

Although we are a Christian nation, I believe we could learn a lot from Buddha. Not only from his respect of animals and the environment, but also from his teachings. There is a saying of his I believe, which says that even the longest journey must begin with the first small step. At the sanctuary in Sidmouth they have certainly made the first small step to greater understanding and compassion towards donkeys. I just hope that it doesn't turn out to be an epic voyage.

Angela Rippon

DONKEY WORK IN KENYA

This is an extract from an article written by Alex Thiemann, a fifth-year student at Cambridge veterinary school. Alex was one of four recipients of a BVA overseas travel grant in 1987 and she joined our team on a working trip to Lamu, Kenya. Alex's article was published in the *Veterinary Record*.

Every morning, and some afternoons, we would hold clinics. Owners would bring their donkeys in to be wormed and treated, if necessary. We noted the age, sex and body condition of each donkey, then marked it. Each day we saw a variety of ailments and prescribed treatments with Abdalla acting as translator. Common conditions included tick and lice infestations, sores and abscesses, laminitis and wounds, including hyaena bites on the belly and vulva of pregnant females, some of which needed stitching. Many donkeys were pyrexic and appeared depressed. . .

It was extremely sad to see cases of tetanus. The donkey's ears go rigid first, then the nostrils

appear squared, and gradually all the limbs become rigid and paralytic. Local treatment for paralysis is to apply red hot irons to the shoulder and thigh. Consequently, we treated paralytic donkeys with suppurating wounds. In one case vigorous antitoxin therapy did appear to be successful.

The following week we visited the other islands by motorboat to hold clinics. These trips turned out to be mini-adventures in themselves. We would walk some miles through mangrove swamps, receding tide and small villages to reach our destination. On arrival the number of donkeys varied from three to several hundred. I think we provided everyone with great amusement, they would watch as we tried to catch and hold semi-wild donkeys by a flimsy coconut rope.

Each island had different problems. On one only stallions were kept so there were several deep neck bites to treat, on another the ticks were particularly bad, while on Pate island the inhabitants seemed unprepared for our visit so we ended up walking round the farms to treat individual donkeys. Often villagers would present us with other ailing livestock – dogs, goats, hens . . . One old gentleman proffered a somewhat scabby foot to be purple sprayed, he seemed quite satisfied!

One day we were called to the mainland to treat a sick donkey. This may have been suffering from trypanosomiasis and was in a terminal condition when we arrived. In such cases it would have been humane to be able to perform euthanasia, but this is not allowed under the Islamic religion. I was made very conscious of how fortunate veterinarians are in the United Kingdom to have this option open to them.

Part of the time was spent in performing faecal worm egg counts using a modified sugar flotation technique, on dung samples pre- and after seventy-two hours post treatment with different anthelmintic pastes. We took species of worms and ticks for subsequent identification in the United Kingdom. With any work like this, part of the time is taken up with meeting local veterinarians and government officials to maintain good working relationships and build up enthusiasm for working with donkeys . . .

A plot of land has been found to keep a Somali pony stallion at stud. The farmers feel that mules (strictly hinnies) can work harder than donkeys and a breeding programme will soon be started. There is also hope of improving the laboratory facilities in Lamu.

In the fifteenth century a Portuguese visitor to Lamu commented of the donkeys that 'they had larger ears and were even more useless than their brethren elsewhere'. Donkeys have always received an unjustifiably bad press! I certainly feel privileged to have been able to help these hard-working animals through the International Donkey Protection Trust . . .

Alex Thiemann

Hard work in Lamu

DONKEYS IN AUSTRALIA

Along with the distinctive call of the kookaburra bird (laughing jackass!), the resounding bray of the donkey would have been a familiar sound to the population clustered around Sydney Cove in the infant colony of New South Wales. According to records, at least ten donkeys had been shipped to Australia from India in the period 1792–95, all no doubt very much sought after.

Today, almost 200 years later, there are hundreds of thousands of feral donkeys in Australia, but unfortunately very few of these beautiful animals are wanted. But in earlier times demand was such that donkeys continued to be shipped from India and Asia at intervals, while large draught donkeys important for infusing size and strength into the developing Australian donkey and for mule breeding, were brought from Spain and Mexico. Even as late as the thirties very large jacks were imported into Queensland from the United States for the breeding of working donkeys and mules.

No doubt the first settlers used the available donkeys in traditional ways such as pulling light farm implements and vehicles and carrying wood and produce. But in the vast Australian continent with its extremes of terrain and climate, the heyday of the donkey arrived with the development of outback settlements, mining towns and huge pastoral runs. And many farms were shaped out of virgin scrub with the aid of donkey power, rolling logs, pulling stumps, ploughing, cultivating, seeding, drawing and carting well water and delivering produce to the railway sidings. And the adventurous lone prospector found the donkey ideal in size and temperament as pack bearer and companion.

In the harsh and isolated outback donkeys were ideally suited to the rugged conditions of heat, scant brackish water and sparse native vegetation. His efficient cooling system, strong and pliable feet (which did not usually require shoeing), the strength of his hindquarters, combined with a generally amiable and adaptable nature, made the donkey good value for money. He was also relatively easy to outfit, quick to harness and did not wander far at night on long inland treks.

Particular donkeys showed considerable intelligence and were effective as team leaders or in other important positions. Some donkeys were real characters that liked to hang around camp, sampling damper and johnny-cakes (a scone mixture baked in hot ashes) while rummaging around the tents. They came when called by name, very helpful when travelling and made wonderful companions for lonely children.

The native herbage, shrubs and berries, though sparse in places, kept the donkeys in good health. Some species, such as the saltbush, were considered to be medicinal. Horses quickly lost condition on such a diet, hence the importance of donkeys. In the Kimberley district in the north of Western Australia, horses were virtually useless because they succumbed to 'Kimberley disease' from eating a poisonous bush which the donkeys either did not eat or were unaffected by. Sores caused by the rubbing collars or harness were one of the few health problems suffered, even routine gelding operations were carried out by teamsters with very few complications.

Jacks and jennies were used for team work, but preference was given to 13–14 hand geldings because of their strength and stability. Young donkeys were broken in simply by being placed in a team between experienced animals. Pregnant jennies were lightly worked until about one month before foaling and again a few days after the birth. Though unwelcome arrivals on long treks, donkey foals were often placed in chaff bags with holes cut for their legs and carried on the load until old enough to walk alongside their mothers.

The average team comprised about thirty donkeys, but this number could be doubled up in difficult terrain such as over sandhills or creekbeds that had become bogs after soaking rains, or for pulling very heavy loads of mining plant, transportable buildings, etc.

The basic harness consisted of leather-covered straw-filled collars with metal hames fitted and trace chains held up by back bands. Bridles and bits were not needed as the team was driven by verbal commands from the teamster, who walked or rode alongside the donkeys. He used the whip sparingly, to liven up the team if it got a little dozy, or to smarten up a slacker. Huge flat-top or box waggons of 8–9 ton capacity were used for carting wool bales and ore from the mines, while drays and carts were used for lighter work.

Often whole families accompanied donkey teams as they travelled hundreds of miles for months on end, carting foodstuffs, clothing, fencing materials and so on from railhead to isolated homesteads, later making the return trip loaded with the station's woolclip.

While awaiting completion of shearing, the teamsters would sometimes be employed on fencing jobs, cutting wood, scooping dams and channels, even carting local stone for station buildings, or moving water tanks on site using small teams of donkeys.

The donkeys earned the respect and affection

THE FIRST 200 YEARS

of their handlers for their patience and endurance and for some teamsters it was a sad day when they had to disband their teams. Often waggons and harness were left where they lay, the donkeys never again to come when called and stand in their correct positions as they had done each morning. The choice was to destroy or turn loose and many a teamster chose the latter, not realising what the aftermath would be.

Their era did not end suddenly with the first mechanised transport, for those vehicles were quite unsuited to outback conditions but, as reliable and tough motor trucks were developed and better roads constructed, donkey power was phased out.

Donkeys that had escaped their owners over the years, and later those that had been turned loose, formed herds and bred up in a climate and landscape that suited them well. With some exceptions they are a fine lot of animals, sleek, well developed, long eared and long legged, with bright, keen eyes, and standing from 10–14 hands high, the average being about 11–12 hands.

There is a range of colours with the many shades of grey/dun and dark brown/ black predominating, then perhaps comes cream/white, but tones of pink, apricot, chestnut and various roans are seen, but I have yet to see or hear of a broken coloured Australian donkey. Many of these bush donkeys (often transported long distances under dreadful conditions), or their offspring, can be seen and heard in paddocks right around the country.

It seems, however, that the seventies' fashion of keeping a donkey on an acre just to look at or to eat the weeds has thankfully passed. Due in large part to dedicated work by donkey society members and other enthusiasts, the majority of donkeys are at least given basic education and adequate care. Many are used for riding by children and adults, or harnessed to sleds, sulkies, carts and cultivators, for carrying packs on picnics or safaris, as calming companions to spirited young horses, and suitable donkeys are even used in helping train young cattle to lead! Some are hitched to small covered waggons touring outback roads, while others with especially gentle and calm temperaments give much delight to disabled persons. And as Australia celebrates the 200th anniversary of European settlement, there are at least two donkey teams of fourteen animals pulling waggons, showing South Australians that while times have changed the kindly and willing donkey has not.

Nevertheless it is a depressing fact that these loved animals are just a tiny minority compared to the hundreds of thousands of feral donkeys being shot from helicopters every few years in Australia's north-west, where they compete with cattle for grazing and water. Bush donkeys are periodically destroyed in other remote areas also where they wage a desperate fight for survival among sheep, cattle and native animals. It is a continuing problem for which no one has found a more humane, or acceptable, solution.

The Australian donkey deserves better. He is remembered by the daughter of an outback teamster as 'a lovely, faithful little animal that worked so hard for our early settlers'.

Kath Burbidge, Australia

Donkey team about to leave Moolooloo woolshed with a load of wool for Parachilna. Taken by A. R. Riddle in 1908

Riding and Driving

RIDING

When choosing a donkey for riding, temperament is of the utmost importance. A mare or a gelding, over four years of age, is suitable but never a stallion. Size is a personal choice as some people like a small compact donkey but 10 hands or more makes for a good all-round donkey. The weight of the child should not exceed 50kg (8st). The donkey should have a good conformation but don't be put off as no one has the perfect donkey!

If you obtain a donkey that has not been ridden, it is a good idea to long rein him to start with. Usually he will accept the saddle very quickly. To start with put a light child up, just to get the donkey used to someone on his back.

Tack The most suitable saddle for the very young rider is the numnah pad saddle with a leather handle. Check that the stirrup bars on the saddle are open, so that the stirrup leathers can slip through if the child should fall off. A crupper is usually necessary to keep the saddle in place, particularly on a fat donkey! Stirrup leathers should be of good quality and kept supple and the stitching checked regularly. There are two types of stirrup irons, standard and safety. The latter have a leather or rubber release catch. Stirrups must always be made of stainless steel, never nickel and they should be wide enough to allow the foot easy movement.

The bridle, if possible, should be made to fit the donkey, but this can prove to be expensive. The next best thing is a Shetland pony bridle. Donkey's heads vary enormously and their brows are usually wider than a pony's, so check to make sure that the browband is not too tight. Check the length of reins, if too long they may become tangled with the child's legs. There are two types of bit, a jointed snaffle or a half-moon nylon snaffle. Sometimes it is necessary to use rubbers to stop the bit slipping through the mouth of the donkey if he has a hardish mouth. The half-moon nylon bit is probably the most comfortable. When in place the bit should not pinch the mouth at the sides nor should too much of the bit show at the sides.

Donkeys are fun to ride for the very young and for the more mature child. They are gentle, intelligent, move sedately and seem to have an understanding of the child's needs. They also have a sense of humour! When teaching, at the beginning an unhurried start certainly bears fruit later on and a nervous child will gain confidence more quickly. To start with, let the child watch while the donkey is made ready to ride and the bridle

---

Cleaning Tack

From the start it is a good idea to teach children how to clean tack. Take the bridle and saddle apart, wash and dry the bit. See that all stitching is sound and that the bit has no rough edges which could rub the donkey's mouth. Watch nickel bits for wear and tear, as these can bend out of shape and can wear thin at the joints. The bit should be washed after use and the leather of the bridle wiped over with a slightly dampened sponge and saddle soap and then dried with a clean cloth. At least once a week take the bridle to pieces; clean the individual parts with special care and use a nail, matchstick or other suitable implement to clear dirt, grease or saddle soap from the holes in the straps. It is better not to put the bridle together after cleaning; just hang the pieces on a ring. Do not hang from a nail or you may end up with a nasty crease in the headpiece.

The felt saddle should be lightly brushed and the pieces of leather on the saddle sponged with saddle soap and dried. For the tack you will require a bar of glycerine soap, sponge, tin of Ko-Cho-Line or other leather preparation, pieces of soft towelling and Brasso for the buckles.

Young cowboys!

Smartly turned out for the show: Carol Jermyn and Miss Madam

Basket saddle, ideal for young children

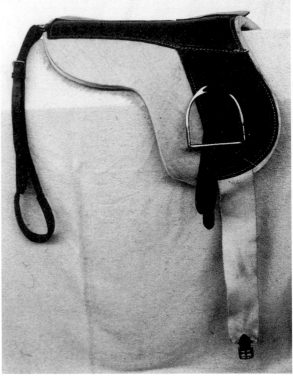

Felt-pad saddle with crupper

ANIMALS IN ROMAN LIFE AND ART

The whole purpose of breeding mules in the Roman period, as in earlier and later times, was to exact from them services of the most laborious kind.

Pairs of mules, rather than horses, were regularly used for drawing vehicles on the highways of the Roman world. The numismatic evidence suggests that they also served on some ceremonial state occasions to draw the 'carpentum' or two-wheeled covered carriage in which Roman matrons in early times and later state priestesses had the privilege of driving through the city on a feast-day.

We know from literary sources that in Claudius' British triumph his wife Messalina followed his chariot in a 'carpentum'; and that Nero's mother, Agrippina II, drove in a 'carpentum' to the Capitol. The carriages used by the officials of the state post ('cursus publicus') were also drawn by mules.

In the Langres Museum is a piece put together from a number of fragments which shows a four-wheeled chaise carrying a driver and two passengers and drawn rightwards by two pairs of mules, one behind the other. All four animals wear collars and are stepping out briskly. The two next to the carriage are clearly yoked together, the driver's reins being fastened to the yoke. The pole that must have passed between these mules is not visible in the carving; but the reins of the leading pair, attached at one end to the creatures' collars, must have been fastened at the other end to the pole's termination, just below the heads of the beasts behind. This pair, immediately controlled by the driver, would, when checked or urged on, automatically have caused the two in front to stop or press forward. This quartet seems to accept its task quite lightheartedly. But on another relief from Langres two mules plod laboriously along towards the right with lowered heads, straining under the weight of a vast wine-barrel on the four-wheeled cart that they are forced to draw. These two must have been equipped with yoke and pole, although the details are far from clear. In the background is a third mule attached to the cart by long reins and serving as a kind of trace-horse. It tosses its head and appears to be taking only a minor share of the burden.

From *Animals in Roman Life and Art* by Jocelyn Toynbee (Thames & Hudson)

and saddle are put on. First place a head collar on the donkey. Brush him and pick out his hoofs.

Approaching from the near side, slip the reins over the donkey's head and remove the head collar. Put the bit into the mouth, holding the top part of the bridle in the right hand; using the left hand and gentle pressure with fingers at the corner of the mouth, open the mouth and slip the head piece over the ears. Adjust the cheek pieces. It should be possible to fit two fingers inside the cheek piece and three fingers inside the throat lash when fastened. The noseband should be comfortable. Again it should be possible to insert two fingers inside the noseband. All parts of the bridle should be put into keepers for neatness and safety. The bit should be high enough to prevent the tongue getting over it.

The saddle is placed on the donkey's back slightly behind the withers. The crupper strap is inserted through the ring on the saddle and adjusted. Make sure the hair under the crupper lies flat. If a leather saddle is used, it is sometimes necessary to have a breast strap. Do up the girth, not too tightly, again laying the hair flat under the girth. Pull down the stirrups and, if safety stirrups are used, the rubber part should be on the outside of the foot.

Mounting The child stands close to the donkey on the near side facing the tail, takes the reins in the left hand and throws the loose rein over the neck. It is advisable to have the right rein slightly shorter in case the donkey moves off. Holding the front of the saddle, put the left foot into the stirrup, taking care not to dig the animal. Gently put the right leg over the saddle

Western saddle, with the traditional high pommel and cantle

> **Riding Clothes**
>
> Clothes for riding, other than at shows, can be of a more casual nature. A pair of jodhpurs is not necessary. Jeans or long trousers will do just as well. Riding boots, jodhpur boots or laced shoes with a heel are suitable, but not wellington boots, gym shoes or sandals, as these can be slippery and wellington boots are positively dangerous.
>
> An anorak or short jacket should be worn. Hard caps are expensive, but the cap is the most important part of the outfit. It should be a good fit and with a chin strap, which must always be fastened.

Donkey beach-type saddle with safety irons. The rubber band on the outside of the iron will give way should a child's foot get caught up

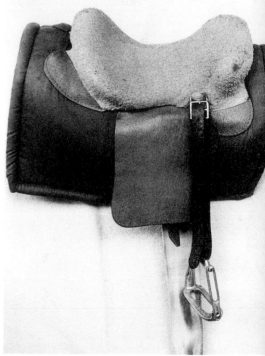

into the right stirrup, being careful not to touch the donkey's croup. The stirrup leathers are adjusted to a length which feels comfortable. As a guide to length, the ankle bone should be level with the tread of the stirrup iron when removed from the stirrup. Standing up in the stirrups is helpful to see if the leathers are equal. The ball of the foot should be on the stirrup with the heel slightly down. The girth should be tightened as animals blow themselves out when a girth is first done up. The more advanced pupils can adjust their own stirrup leathers and tighten the girth. The reins are held with the rein running through the hand between the little and third finger and are secured by the thumb, the hands level with the pommel of the saddle, wrists bent, thumbs up with hands a few inches apart.

Check the position of the child in the saddle. The seat should be in the centre of the saddle, head up, shoulders back, but not tensed and legs in line with hips and shoulders. Most children who ride donkeys are beginners and should really enjoy themselves and have lots of fun.

Moving Off Having put on a well-adjusted neck strap and lead rein you are ready to go. The handler should lead from the near side, level with the donkey's shoulder, the lead rein held slack in the left hand and the right hand on the lead not too near the donkey's head. Commands should be brief and spoken clearly. 'Walk on', 'trot on', 'whoa', 'stand' being the main ones. It is well worth the expense of taking some lessons if both you and the child are inexperienced.

To dismount, take both feet out of the stirrups, press both hands down on the front of the saddle and swing the right leg over the back of the donkey, all the time holding the reins firmly until both feet are on the ground. Slide the stirrups to the top of the leathers and put the leathers through the stirrup irons. Undo the crupper strap and the girth, putting the latter over the saddle and remove. Put the lead rein from the head collar round the donkey's neck before removing the bridle. Undo the throat lash and slip the head piece and reins gently over the ears. Put the head collar on, brush the donkey and remove his head collar before turning him out in his field.

Driving four-in-hand has always been popular. Note that the wheeler pair are wearing blinkers

DRIVING

Most donkeys are physically capable of being driven, but to drive well the following qualities are needed.

Have fun with your donkey!

The Physical Aspect Initial training should ideally start at six to twelve months but it is possible to start at any age but more time and patience may be required as an older animal is often less receptive. This initial training includes general handling and basic word commands and acceptance of control on head collar or cavesson from either side. Geldings are often preferable to mares who can become unpredictable when in season.

Donkeys are remarkably strong for their size but overloading can cause distress to them as well as souring their enthusiasm for work. The average donkey can easily pull a vehicle weighing up to 125kg (275lb) plus a medium-sized adult or two lightweight people on a fairly level road at trotting speed which can be maintained for 2–3 miles at a time and for a total of 6–10 miles. At walking speeds loads of up to 152kg (336lb) can be pulled.

Donkeys are unlike their larger equine relations when it comes to feed for work. Feeding should be related to the amount of work done, not that to be done. Increase rations sensibly.

When donkeys are worked regularly on roads, shoeing is advisable to help prevent flints and small stones working up

> **Road Sense**
>
> Saint Thomas in the US Virgin Islands was occupied by the Danes but sold to the USA in 1917. It was then decided to change to driving on the right-hand side of the road. However, the donkeys refused to abide by the new ruling and it was therefore agreed that all transport should revert to driving on the left.

into the laminae and to protect the horn from rapid and uneven wear. However, on a reasonable road surface, up to 6 miles per week should be possible without shoes. Regular attention with a hoof pick is essential for a harness donkey.

Exercise should be started gently. Walking exercise for 2–3 weeks should precede trotting and helps to increase fitness without producing boredom. Lungeing is unsuitable for donkeys; long reining can be kept more interesting. In the later stages, donkeys can be ridden by people under about 50kg (8st).

THE ORDER FOR HARNESSING AND 'PUTTING TO'

HARNESSING

1 Collar
2 Pad
3 Back strap, crupper and breeching
4 Traces
5 Bridle and curb chain
6 Reins

PUTTING TO

1 Tie the animal up or have someone hold him.
2 Bring the vehicle to the donkey with the shafts well above his back.
3 Slide the shafts through the tug loops.
4 Attach the traces to the vehicle, passing them inside the bellyband.
5 Attach the breeching straps to the shafts, making sure that the traces lie above or through them, not under.
6 Adjust the height of the tug loops to make the floor of the vehicle level. If this is not possible, the vehicle is the wrong size for the donkey. If the floor slopes back the vehicle is too small for the animal, if forward, then it is too large.
7 Adjust the traces so that when they are tight, the back band and tug loop hang straight down the centre of the pad when the tug loops are against the tug stops.
8 Adjust the breeching so that there is a hand's width between it and the rump when the traces are tight. In height it should lie half way from the tail head to the hocks.
9 A full collar should allow comfortable room for a hand between it and the windpipe. A breast collar should be 5cm (2in) above the points of the shoulder; most breast collars are fitted too low.
10 The bit should be fitted high enough to cause a small wrinkle at the corner of the mouth. The eyes should be in the centre of the blinkers which should not gape when the reins are tightened. There should be room for two fingers between the curb chain and the jaw.
11 The reins should be fitted either rough cheek or first bar as plain cheek gives no curb action in an emergency.

An unusual eight-in-hand, seen in South Africa: a pair of hackneys; a pair of mules; a pair of donkeys and finally a pair of young oxen

The Mental Aspect The donkey is a highly intelligent animal, far more so than many people will admit. This intelligence tends to make training more complex than in the case of a horse or pony. The average donkey learns quickly so repetitive daily work or lessons soon bore and frustrate him. Therefore, to keep the animal alert, happy and co-operative, training times have to be varied and of short duration. Most donkeys can be trained to drive at quite an advanced age, often well into their 'teens', but we will consider the training of the young animal as this will cover all the points needed to train an older donkey.

From Foal to Two Years This is the most important age for training and lessons learned at this stage will be remembered for life. The donkey should learn to trust the handler who will try to give him confidence, training him to be led from either side and to obey basic verbal commands. The physical contact of grooming is helpful with these lessons in soothing the animal and gaining his confidence. It also helps the person doing the training to build up a relationship with the donkey and teaches the donkey to stand still. The basic word commands needed are 'walk on', 'trot on', 'whoa' and 'get back'. The lessons should be restricted to twenty to thirty minutes in duration, about three to four lessons per week. This is to maintain the donkey's interest and is quite different from the regular training of a horse or pony where each lesson is repeated many times and daily. New items should be introduced during the lesson and not at the end when it is best to finish on a successful note with something previously learned. The animal is then likely to return to his stable in a peaceful and relaxed frame of mind.

From Two to Three Years The initial training to long rein is best done with an assistant who leads the animal on a lead rope on a head collar. At this stage it is best to long rein and continue training with the reins attached to the noseband to preserve the softness of the mouth of the young animal. Even after the animal has been introduced to the bit, long reining is continued from the noseband. The very first bit used can be a curb chain inside a tube of chamois leather. Smear this with honey and the donkey will play with the bit. When the donkey has accepted the control of the long reins and is obedient, a Liverpool bit can be introduced with the reins attached in the soft cheek position. Long rein work is always useful.

At three years of age the donkey may be lightly shafted. Immediately before shafting, the donkey should be taught to pull a motor tyre or similar weight to accustom him to pressure on the collar. Before fitting the vehicle to the donkey for the first time, he should be faced to a wall or confined to a yard to discourage him from walking away from it. Once the vehicle is attached, it should be gently rocked backwards and forwards to give him the feel of it. The donkey should then be led forward by the assistant whilst the trainer long reins him from behind the vehicle. Once the donkey is relaxed, the trainer can sit in the vehicle but the assistant should retain emergency control by the lead rope until it seems safe to dispense with it.

Anyone for Mints?

A very special tip from Neil Harvey, our driver, who to everyone's surprise always appears able to approach and talk to the most difficult donkey. With a rather sheepish grin he explained the secret of his success! He always chews a mouthful of Polo mints before going near the donkey. The donkeys are so attracted to the strong smell of his breath, as they have a very soft spot for Polo mints, that his trick works miracles especially in front of owners who are reluctant to send their donkeys in and are overcome to see the obvious immediate bond struck between donkey and sanctuary staff.

An incredible ten-in-hand consisting of six mules and four zebras being driven in the Transvaal, South Africa. The mules were being used to train the zebras

---

Thou Shalt Not . . .

In the Old Testament it states that it was forbidden to yoke an ox with an ass.

Bad Image

In the past the donkey has not always been well thought of throughout the world. The ancient Egyptians made his head and ears a symbol of ignorance, old Romans, when they met him, considered it a bad omen and to medieval Germans he stood for Thomas the unbeliever.

Harness This is usually made from one of three materials, webbing, buffalo hide or leather. In many ways, webbing is ideal for everyday use, being cheap, strong and easily maintained. Make sure, however, that the pad is fitted with a tree to keep the pressure off the spine of the donkey. Buffalo hide is strong and also comparatively cheap but has a tendency to stretch. It is, however, easily maintained and remains soft. Leather is the traditional material for harness and is strong, provided it is made from good leather, and is of good appearance. It requires more maintenance than the other materials and if neglected can become dangerously weakened. The best compromise is to use webbing for regular driving and leather for showing and best occasions.

Breast collars are more usual than full collars for donkeys as, due to the relative size of a donkey's head and neck, a full collar needs to be of the split type, buckled together at the top and these are not common. In no circumstances should a donkey, pony or horse be harnessed to a vehicle, with or without passengers, without a bridle, bit and preferably blinkers. Although animals may be trained to drive without blinkers, as do the Royal Horse Artillery, to remove the bridle of an animal whilst in the shafts is almost a guarantee of an accident.

The maintenance of harness is an important safety consideration. The main points to be checked are that the eyelets have not been pulled out of webbing harness and that leather does not show surface cracks when bent, that stitching has not rotted and that buckle tongs are not weakened by rust nor about to pull through the buckle. To keep harness in good condition sweat should be wiped off prior to saddle soaping and oiling or polishing. Rust should be cleaned off buckle tongs as this rots and cracks the leather. Webbing harness can be wiped clean with a cloth, rinsed in hot water and wrung dry.

Vehicles These may be of many different types but should all have certain characteristics. The weight that the shafts put on the donkey's back should be the minimum when in use, the balance should change as little as possible when going up or down hills and the size should be suitable for the animal. In the interest of safety, it is especially important that wheels, shafts and floor should be in good condition.

Transport This can be a problem when transporting the vehicle as well as the donkey. The simplest way is with the donkey in the front of a trailer and the vehicle at the back with its shafts over the tailboard. Small vehicles can also be carried on a roof rack with a trailer behind for the donkey or in the back of a pick-up truck. When show vehicles are roped, the paint should be protected with soft cloths.

> **Clipping**
>
> It may be advisable to trace clip. Where the coat is extra thick, a full clip may be necessary. Clipping the girth line is strongly recommended, as donkeys have little or no wither to hold the driving pad back in position, thus creating the problem of the hair getting trapped between the elbow and the girth, causing severe girth galls.

In Mexico donkeys are harnessed up and used to go out and pick up bait for fishing

Donkeys in Trouble

Bob Marley

For Bob Marley, 1 June 1985 was a lucky day. Our chief inspector for south Wales, who was in fact on holiday, received a desperate phone call at his home from a concerned sanctuary supporter, asking him to come immediately to a car park at the rear of the shopping area in Newent town, where her husband was endeavouring to detain a man with an ill-treated donkey.

By the time our inspector arrived, a large crowd had gathered around the poor donkey, who was tied to the car park fence with an enormous load on his back, held on with a makeshift harness made up of old car seat belts and sash cord, which had actually embedded themselves into the flesh of the donkey. His owner was a travelling man, using the donkey to carry his belongings.

Under pressure he agreed to remove the load when further sores were revealed. The veterinary surgeon, called to the scene by our inspector, agreed the donkey pack was unsuitable and causing distress and he immediately treated the sores, recommending further treatment and rest. The owner was informed that the donkey would need approximately three weeks' daily treatment, followed by several months' rest before he was fit to work again. Our inspector then threatened prosecution if he moved the donkey in its present condition, and after some arguing, Bob Marley was passed over to the sanctuary. ▶

MAUD AND EYO

Many new donkey owners do not realise what great problems the hoof can cause and, either through ignorance or lack of funds, a proper farrier is not employed and the donkey's hoofs are allowed to grow. At first the animal can cope with the extended hoof but as it grows longer it becomes misshapen and eventually curls round rather like an Arabian slipper; in extreme cases it can make three or four twists and achieve a total length of over 30cm (12in). This distortion causes great distress to the donkey, affecting his balance and producing a stretching of the tendons which is often irreversible.

The owners of Maud and Eyo found themselves in all sorts of problems. Originally they had only wanted one donkey but they were persuaded to accept two by the dealer who sold them and, as they already had one on their limited ground, they found they were totally unable to cope with three animals. In addition to the problem of feeding, they had not realised that Eyo was a stallion and, during the course of the year they were together, Maud, who was approximately fifteen years old, became pregnant. Luckily the owners discussed their problem with a local stud farm and the owner there recommended that the best way to try and solve the problem would be to send the donkeys to the Donkey Sanctuary. And so in June 1982 Maud and Eyo arrived. By this time their feet were at a critical stage, where, in the case of Maud, permanent crippling seemed inevitable. Up to a short time ago the policy of both veterinary surgeons and farriers was to remove a little of the hoof each week and allow the tendons to gradually tighten up, giving the donkey a chance to adjust to a new method of balancing and this is how Maud was treated. The current recommendation is to remove the unwanted hoof as soon as possible but this has to be extremely carefully supervised by both a veterinary surgeon and a farrier with a special knowledge of this technique. Today's farriers are being trained in this method and it would seem from recent cases admitted to the sanctuary that this does not cause the difficulties that such drastic action had previously been thought to cause. Great care must always be taken to see that the balance of the foot is maintained.

Both Maud and Eyo were very kind, gentle donkeys and were isolated together while their feet were attended to. However, Maud appeared in a great deal of distress and after two days we decided that they would have to be put in the special box that we use when stallions and mares come in together. This is a large, long airy box separated down the middle by wooden bars so that Maud and Eyo could talk to each other through the bars but each had a certain amount of privacy. Eyo of course, being a stallion, would have to be castrated as soon as he was strong enough and his feet were in a better condition, and Maud, although at this stage we were not sure she was pregnant, certainly appeared to be in a lot of discomfort. In fact, I was so worried about her that I set up a two-hour night-watch between myself and Jane MacNeill, our vet at that time. On the Saturday following their arrival I went in to see Maud at 10pm, Jane went in at midnight and 2am, and on each of the visits everything seemed perfectly in order. To my horror, when I went in at 4am I found Maud lying down in deep distress with a tiny, half-formed foal beside her. I ran to get Jane and, with her expert veterinary help, we were able to save Maud's life, but we both looked sadly at the pathetic little bundle in the corner, for which any form of help was impossible. Maud recovered fairly rapidly from the abortion but her feet continued giving her trouble and she stayed at Slade House Farm in the intensive care unit for over twelve months. As soon as Eyo had been castrated he rejoined her and they were both able to take it very easy, as use was gradually restored to their legs.

One of the most difficult problems was persuading Maud to walk. Her feet had hurt for so long that she seemed to have built up a psychological barrier to exercise. After her abortion, for medical reasons, she just had to keep moving and a new piece of equipment we had just purchased became invaluable. We adapted this machine, commonly known as a 'horse walker', to a 'donkey walker'. A circular strip of concrete is laid and a pivot is placed in the middle, from which long arms extend and the donkey's lead rein is attached to an arm. Behind each donkey is a second arm with a rubber flap on it. The motor is turned on and the 'arm' leads the donkey along. If the donkey slows

Bob Marley cont'd
▶

As Bob was in such poor condition, tired, footsore and in pain, our inspector took up the kind invitation of the lady who had reported his plight and lived locally, to care for the donkey. So Bob moved into a stable at her home. He was given a warm bath in a solution provided by the vet and antibiotic cream was applied to the severe cuts, sores and ulcerated areas.

After four weeks, Bob Marley was fit for the journey to the sanctuary and is now happily settled, peacefully grazing with his donkey friends, a well-deserved rest after his long ordeal.

Maud's terrible feet when she arrived

Rosie

A letter was received from a French student teacher and stated: 'They want to get rid of the donkey and I want to buy it for several reasons. If it were mine I would be able to have her hoofs cut, which they have not done for more than six months and it is a terrible sight – they are as long as a pair of shoes curling up in the air. Once her feet were walkable I would be able to take her out from the stable. She never goes out; she lives in a tiny hole. If you would take her from me I will get her. I hate to think they may sell her tonight and push her, half-crippled into the butchers' van for meat. She is standing day and night in a little corner isolated from the outside by a window covered by a plastic sheet. Please help.'

The student teacher, who was eighteen years old, sent us £5 and, with her help, we got the donkey, Rosie, out. Sadly for Rosie it was too late; her feet had not been treated for over four years in our estimation, and she had been totally deprived of any exercise for at least six months. We slowly started to feed her up, walk her gently every day and she had a large airy stable. However, despite all our care the damage had been done and she died five months later.

Maud and Eyo – good friends

or stops, the rubber flap gently propels the donkey from behind. Should the donkey stop altogether and dig his or her heels in, the machine is stopped. Maud and Eyo were put on the exerciser and received the greatest benefit from it. To start with Maud was in front and Eyo followed happily but Maud kept tripping over as she tried to look over her shoulder to see Eyo. The solution was to harness each donkey opposite the other and then, with the odd bray of communication, they exercised happily for half an hour a day.

By the time Maud and Eyo were ready to go out to one of the farms, we had just purchased our fifth unit and Maud and Eyo went to Town Barton. What a difference there was in these two little donkeys as they jauntily trotted up the ramp, when I recalled their arrival and their agonising, slow walk down the ramp to their new quarters; I could scarcely believe they were the same two donkeys. The lorry, which with all the partitions removed, can take between twelve and fifteen at a time, was loaded up throughout the day and over six trips were made. By 6pm that evening seventy-two donkeys had taken up residence at Town Barton and the tired and happy group of us stood watching them walk around their new, large, airy barn, enjoying, as donkeys always do, new surroundings and exploring every square inch of the beautiful new pasture that was available for them.

Maud and Eyo set off together and both were able to break into a trot as they surveyed their new field. They seemed rather disappointed that they could not get their heads far enough through the fence to nibble the hedge. They always seem to enjoy eating through the bars and we have to be careful when fencing to keep the fence far enough away to protect the hedge, so useful to wildlife and as a windbreak. Maud and Eyo decided we had got it right and regretfully trotted to the bottom of the field to see if there was any way they could paddle in the stream. Once again they were thwarted, but seemed pleased enough with their new home as they returned to the barn to sample the straw bedding, so lovingly and deeply laid for them.

Over the next few months the whole farm was fenced and special shelters built at strategic places. The total number of donkeys to be cared for at Town Barton was to be in the region of four hundred and so great care had to be taken in planning where the shelters should be placed. My son Paul wanted these built in concrete so that they could serve as winter as well as summer quarters and each was designed with a series of gates and tracks leading into three different big field areas. This meant that fields could be rested while the donkeys, still using the same shelter, had a track to another field which was ready for use. This rotation method allows the farm to be used with the minimum number of buildings.

Maud and Eyo have now settled in happily to a group consisting of the original seventy-two who arrived together, and it is hard to tell, as they gallop from shelter to field, that they had ever been in such terrible trouble. Let us hope they will have many happy years of life before them and, with constant care from the farrier, their dreadful foot problems should be a thing of the past.

ISLANDER

The word 'abandoned' is always emotive and when used in connection with a donkey is very disturbing indeed. When the sanctuary's attention was first drawn to the plight of an elderly donkey, abandoned for over eighteen years on a barren island off the west coast of Ireland, we were absolutely horrified. To add to the problems the island was extremely inaccessible, particularly during the winter, and although our inspectors went over and spoke to the worried lady who had reported this donkey's plight, they were unable to reach him due to the bad weather. The donkey had been left with only sheep as company when the original occupants were moved by the government back to the mainland.

The donkey had received only the most rudimentary care over all those years and had lived on poor grass and even seaweed. Shepherds visited the island occasionally to tend the sheep and even more occasionally would have a look at the donkey. Now, apparently he was in great trouble, scarcely able to walk and short of food. Our inspectors arranged with local fishermen that as soon as the weather permitted they would go across and bring the donkey back to the mainland, but when our inspectors returned the following month nothing had been done. After great pressure they managed to get the fishermen to go across and bring the donkey back. After a long search the actual owner of the donkey was found who signed him over to the sanctuary. Immediately this was done the little donkey was taken to a knowledgeable temporary home close at hand.

The inspectors named the donkey 'Islander', for obvious reasons, and immediately called a vet to see if it would be kinder to put him down as he was in such a terrible condition. The vet was a most humane man and, having examined Islander and heard of his history, said he felt that, despite his lameness, poor condition and extensive body parasites, with the right care he could improve. He said Islander had the spirit and will to live and should be given a chance of life. The sanctuary then faced the problem that to bring him home to Devon in his present condition would not be kind and a temporary home had to be arranged where he could have consistent skilled veterinary care.

It was nearly four months later, in July 1984, that he was declared fit to travel and our chief superintendent set off to Ireland with a specially adapted trailer to start the long journey home. The journey was done very slowly and carefully, with veterinary inspections en route. Fortunately, the sea crossing was calm and Islander travelled extremely well, arriving at the sanctuary with very little sign of travel stress, despite the immense distance covered.

On arrival at the sanctuary as the doors opened there stood at the top of the ramp a pathetic little figure, head down, eyes dull, bad feet. He had obviously suffered a great deal over the last years. Suddenly, from all the other donkeys around the yard a great bray of welcome arose and for the first time he lifted his head and looked around in wonder to see green fields and, for the first time in his life, other donkeys. With great dignity Islander walked off the lorry and joined his friends at the sanctuary.

Today Islander is hardly recognisable; thanks to regular veterinary and farriery care, he can now walk in reasonable comfort and he loves his companions at the Donkey Sanctuary.

Islander on arrival at the sanctuary . . .

. . . and after loving care and attention

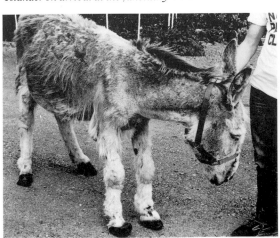

SPIDER

To almost all animals being in a market is a terrifying experience. Having been uprooted from familiar surroundings, the animal suddenly finds itself surrounded by other terrified animals being herded by blows and shouts. Spider, a four-month-old foal, was put into a Westcountry market in September 1979 and was surely no exception. He had been transported to market in a large box containing a mixture of horses, ponies and donkeys and up to the time of actually being herded into the pen, had managed to keep fairly close to his mother. However, unfortunately for Spider, his mother was herded into a separate section of the market and poor little Spider found himself alone, being consistently pushed and kicked by the other donkeys with him. Although he brayed pitifully for his mother, and could in fact hear his mother calling out to him, Spider never saw her again from that moment. About four hours later he found himself pushed into a small ring where he was poked and prodded with sticks whilst people began to bid for him.

At this point, Spider's luck began to change, as he was purchased for £28 by the Dartmoor Livestock Protection Society. The society was extremely worried by the conditions in this market, particularly for the young animals which had been abruptly separated from their mothers and were being sold unweaned, and it was only the fact that he went to a knowledgeable home that saved young Spider's life. The same society had previously rescued a donkey called Timothy who had been severely vandalised by having both his ears cut through. They had sent Timothy to us and had been delighted with his amazing recovery. From being so antisocial that he attacked every person and animal in sight, Timothy had settled down with the sanctuary and the Dartmoor Livestock Protection Society felt sure we could help Spider in a similar way. He was kept by them for approximately five weeks before being sent to the sanctuary. When he arrived he was unnamed and on seeing this pathetic little animal 'Spider' seemed a suitable name, as his life even then seemed to be hanging on a thread. He was extremely small and weak and his weaning had certainly taken its toll. We immediately set about continuing the skilled care he had been receiving and this, plus the love and attention he got, soon began to show results.

At about the same time that Spider came in another very poor donkey arrived, so thin we called him 'Bones'. As so often happens at the sanctuary, Spider, Bones and another little donkey called Jenny joined together and made a small group. All the donkeys are wormed on arrival, weighed and thereafter wormed regularly. A careful build-up feeding programme was instigated by the veterinary department and very, very slowly the donkeys began to put on weight. At first Spider had none of the energy normally found in young donkeys of his age, he would stand for hours, head down and eyes dull. Our joy when he began to behave more like a young colt was our reward. His little group had a special care box in the main yard. Each day they were taken out and exercised and the first time Spider found the energy to kick me, we all burst out cheering. His friends recovered slightly faster than Spider, so the donkeys had

Struck Down

Eeyore had become the focus of interest in the village of Balcombe; extremely well known, she was described in the press as the only mid-Sussex donkey ever to act in a play by Shakespeare. Unfortunately, according to the reports we received, Eeyore was badly injured by vandals in August 1984. The severe injury to Eeyore's leg left her hock broken with the danger that she would be permanently crippled and it was quite obvious to the veterinary surgeon in the area that she was going to need four to six months veterinary care.

The Donkey Sanctuary followed up the press report and visited the owner offering assistance and, within a few days, Eeyore arrived at the sanctuary. Our well-equipped hospital enabled X-rays to be taken and the leg to be plastered and re-plastered regularly as the damaged tarsal bones fused together. Eeyore soon became a great favourite with all the hospital staff and fortunately her owner had kept her in such good condition that she was able to overcome the obvious stress and shock caused by the incident and returned to live happily with her owner.

Dobbin

An urgent call for help was received on behalf of Dobbin. Due to circumstances, a two-year-old gelding had been permanently shut in and had become totally unmanageable. There was no question of Dobbin not being fed well enough, in fact to quote my inspector 'he had been fed like a racehorse!' Full of oats he became steamed up and constantly kicked at his stable door and bit or kicked anyone who approached him.

Our driver was warned how dangerous the donkey was when he called to collect him. Fortunately for all concerned our driver is extremely experienced at handling donkeys and Dobbin's owners were amazed at the apparent ease with which he allowed himself to be loaded onto the lorry.

Since his arrival here Dobbin has caused no problems and has settled down well in a group of donkeys, completely content to have friends of his own type and much more placid on the donkey diet he now receives.

to be fed individually to ensure Spider got his fair share. He loved his bran mash most and we were able to conceal the medication and the badly needed vitamins in the flavour of treacle or molasses. By the spring, the group was sufficiently fit to be able to graze outside during the day, although they were always brought in and stabled at night. Spider and his friends had to stay in our special unit at Slade House Farm for over a year before they were fit to be moved.

The farm chosen for Spider and his friends was Three Gates Farm in Dorset and there was no doubt that they absolutely loved their new home and spent many happy days galloping around. Spider began to develop well and under the careful feeding regime for the underweight donkeys, which consisted of approximately one-fifth of a bale of hay a day and a full handful of special barley nuts in the morning and evening, his coat soon began to shine and he became a very fit and able little donkey. Perhaps because he had lost his mother so early and had become a friend of humans, he always enjoyed following the manager, John, and his wife around, and took a great interest in all the activities of the farm.

Early one June morning when the grass was ready to mow and the weather looked set for the next few days, it was with a very happy heart that John, the manager, mounted the tractor and set off to mow the field. As always, Spider was leaning over the hedge watching with interest as the mower went past and there is no doubt at all that it was Spider who gave the terrified bray as the baby deer sprang to his feet a second too late as the mower passed. John stopped the machine and ran back absolutely horrified to find that one of the baby deer's legs had been severed just above the knee. Forgetting all thoughts of haymaking he picked up the small terrified animal and ran back to the farmhouse with it. Luckily the sanctuary vets are always within call and with their skill, and the patience and care of John and his wife, 'Bambi' survived and made his home in the sanctuary. Although the deer had only three legs it was amazing how he managed to get around and, having lived in the kitchen for the first three or four months, he then moved out into one of the stables and would happily lope along with the donkeys grazing during the day.

Spider thoroughly enjoyed his first winter at Three Gates. The new barn was quite enormous and right down the middle of the barn was stored the year's supply of straw and hay which formed a natural separation between the two sides. Spider, Jenny and Bones soon found their own favourite place where they could feed every day. Apart from liberal amounts of hay, they were fed extra nuts during the winter to keep their weight up and the donkeys were segregated into groups, depending on how much feed John and the veterinary surgeon decided was good for them. Spider thoroughly enjoyed being in the maximum feed area and it was quite obvious that he was almost fully recovered from his terrible and drastic start in life. Instead of the very quiet, pathetic, almost desperate little creature of some months before, here was a pushy young man who delighted in showing how quickly he could trot round the concrete yards outside the barn. Every donkey has access to fresh air in the

Spider

winter and concrete is very good for their hoofs as it keeps wearing them down naturally and keeps the foot from softening through standing on the straw bedding.

Jenny soon decided that Bones and Spider were getting a little too much for her and she began to wander off on her own more and more, while Bones and Spider thoroughly enjoyed the pushing and shoving so natural to young geldings of this age. Eventually John moved Jenny to a group of the older mares where she settled very happily. Spider and Bones, however, just could not wait for the end of the winter and when all the donkeys were let out again in April, they were the first two to go out

CRACKERS

Much of our work would be totally impossible without the continued support of the general public. Not only do we rely on them for funds, but we also rely on them to help us in our constant job of rescuing donkeys from trouble in all parts of the country. From a member of the public we first heard of the desperate plight of a little donkey who, because we rescued him at Christmas, we have called 'Crackers'. We know very little of Crackers' early background, but we do know that at the age of two he found himself tethered to a stake on some wasteland in the north of England in early November 1983. The length of the rope by which he was tethered was short and the amount of grazing available was almost nil. The weather was desperately cold, wet and windy, the very worst conditions to which a donkey can be subjected. In desperation, Crackers eventually managed to break free of his tether but, in doing so, inflicted a deep wound from the post on the inside of his hind legs. He then began to wander, looking for food, and apparently was seen for six weeks at various times, wandering around the small northern town, stopping the traffic on more than one occasion. Reports were made both to the police and the RSPCA, but neither was able to find the donkey. Eventually, being terrified of the traffic and near to death, he returned to within a mile of the wasteland where he had originally been tethered and here his luck changed. He lay exhausted outside the house of a member of the public who fortunately was not only a caring animal lover, but was also determined to do something about his pitiful condition. Giving him a feed of hay, she then rang the RSPCA, who in turn contacted the Donkey Sanctuary inspectors.

The story told over the telephone was almost unbelievable: the weather was about freezing, there was a light covering of snow on the fields and more was forecast. The inspectors realised the gravity of the situation and immediately postponed the private arrangements they had made and drove as quickly as possible to the area. They

arrived within two hours of the call on Friday 9 December. To say they were appalled was an understatement. Their experienced eyes told them how bad things were and, without a word, one of them climbed back in the car and drove back to get the donkey trailer. Very gently Crackers was loaded in and, supported by straps, he managed the journey to their house. I'm sure you can imagine his feelings when put into a warm stable, with deep straw, clear fresh water and a small warm feed of bran, oats and molasses, the first real meal he had received in many weeks.

He was found to be in a terrible condition and, following a telephone call to headquarters, it was agreed that a local vet be called in immediately for all the treatment necessary. This started before any attempt was made to move him. The local veterinary surgeon found that Crackers was suffering from very bad anaemia, had lung noises which he said were probably due to a previous bout of pneumonia which had not been treated, and a very, very bad wound on the hind leg which had now turned septic, sustained while escaping from his tether. In addition to this, he had an injury on the left eye, which had left it misted and he was full of worms and lice.

Crackers needed almost full-time nursing right through Christmas for nearly five weeks before he was declared fit by the veterinary surgeon to travel down to the sanctuary. For Crackers, he must have felt he was in heaven. Once he had got over his tetanus and antibiotic injections he was given special vitamin tablets, wormed, deloused and had his hoofs trimmed properly. Gradually, his feed was increased until he was eating ad-lib hay and two meals of bran, flaked maize and oats a day. Every night he was rugged to make sure he lost no body heat and energy, so desperately needed in his fight for survival during those early days.

There is no doubt that the loving care he received enabled him to make a miraculous return to health and what surprised everybody was the and canter round the fields. Visiting the farm very shortly after 'turn-out', the first donkey I noticed was Spider rolling vigorously in the sand heap that we put in every field for them. When Spider trotted across to say 'Hello', I almost had to laugh when patting him, for a great cloud of sand and anti-louse powder rose into the air. It was lovely to see Spider throw back his head and give a great bray of delight before galloping off to join Bones. It made my day to see such a happy, healthy little donkey and to think how different his fate might have been following that terrible day in the market.

immense friendliness of this little stallion, who had received such bad treatment previously at the hands of human beings. When Perry, the driver, arrived to pick him up to take him back to the sanctuary, he was greeted with the most unusual reception on his arrival. Normally, our inspectors are very pleased when our lorry arrives to pick up the animals they have rescued to take them back to the sanctuary, but in this particular case, such a bond of affection had sprung up that there were almost tears at the parting. Crackers was loaded extremely carefully into the new sanctuary lorry. This has been designed specially and, by placing the special padded sections to the positions required, it can provide a safe, comfortable travelling area for the donkey, padded on three sides and with a good supply of hay and water available on the fourth side. Crackers was also rugged up with the rugs provided for travelling donkeys and the long journey back to the sanctuary began on 13 January.

Perry drove very slowly with his precious cargo, stopping every hour to get in with the donkey to talk to him and make sure he had adequate water and hay. When Crackers arrived at the sanctuary he found a great welcome waiting for him. A box had been prepared for him in the hospital block, as we knew he would still need special treatment for some time to come. We couldn't believe how small he was when the big ramp of the lorry was opened and the little broken-coloured donkey's figure appeared at the top. He was still limping badly from the wound, although it was now no longer septic and giving him less trouble. But despite this having looked around the top of the ramp, he gave a large bray of joy before walking down to join us all. Despite his five weeks' care he was still pathetically thin and his head seemed far too big for his body. Gently he was led into the stable and no doubt he was delighted to see he had the same facilities as he had had at his previous stabling. As all donkeys do, he wandered slowly round the box, sniffing and nuzzling at everything until he was quite satisfied he knew exactly where he was. Then he came back to the door and put his head over to be petted and loved.

Being a stallion he could not be mixed with any of the other new donkey arrivals and, in any event, he was not well enough at this stage to even compete on a friendly basis for food. As he spent a great deal of his time either having to stand still or lying down with the pain in his leg, infra-red lamps were fixed up for him to keep him warm and each day he was taken for a short walk to keep his leg exercised.

Shortly after his arrival another little stallion called Daniel Chestnut came in and was put next door to Crackers and round the stable doors these two began to make firm friends. After six weeks it was decided that Crackers was fit to stand the castration operation, which both our veterinary surgeons strongly advised, as they felt his recovery could then continue without interruption. Crackers' improvement continued at an even faster pace once he had a friend. Crackers really enjoyed being groomed, obviously a pleasure he had never experienced before. He never fidgeted, no matter how many times the same area was brushed and at times leant on the groomer more and more heavily, eyes half shut and obviously enjoying every second. He soon trained Daniel into the donkey friendship act known as 'mutual grooming': they would stand for hours, head to tail, grooming each other's hair with their teeth. When they had both been passed as fit and sound by the veterinary staff, a big decision had to be made. Daniel was earmarked for the Slade Centre, but due to Crackers' malnutrition, eye damage and chronic lung problem, he would never be fit to join the *crème de la crème*. It was also obvious, however, that they could not be split and Crackers himself solved the problem by joining Daniel as the 'petting' donkey at the Slade Centre, not to give rides to the children, but just to be loved and petted, as this seems to be the one thing that Crackers really wants.

TIMOTHY

Some six years ago, Timothy was a happy normal gelding in his mid-twenties. We are told that he was given as a present to a young village boy when he gained his eleven plus exam. The boy had always wanted a donkey and his father already had a small well-fenced paddock near the main road.

When Timothy arrived there was great delight amongst the family and the boy visited Timothy every possible moment and they both got on really well. Then one evening the indescribable happened. A small group of boys from the village school, who had failed their exam, had become very jealous. As the boy was so attached to Timothy, they decided to attack him and five of the boys, one armed with a carving knife, crept up to his field one evening. Timothy had no reason to be afraid of the boys and had no sense of danger but his terror at what happened next can still be seen in his eyes. With four holding him down, one of the boys sliced savagely through one ear and then the other. In agonised terror Timothy flung them off and was still blundering desperately around the field, blood flowing down his eyes, when the unsuspecting owner arrived with his evening carrot. You can imagine the scene. First a vet came and managed to deaden the pain and then came the police but because the boys were so young a prosecution was not possible. The boy was heartbroken, Timothy would not let him anywhere near, rearing and kicking at the approach of anyone. His father was desperate and rang the Horse and Pony Protection Trust Society who collected Timothy and took him away from his scene of terror. They tended his wounds and, after a very difficult period of time, got a local farmer to put him in his field with some horses. Timothy, however, was no longer capable of being sociable with either people or animals and after a while the farmer had to advise the Horse and Pony Protection Trust Society that it was impossible for anyone to keep him. They realised they had a major temperament problem on their hands and rang us to see if we would take him as we had so much experience with donkeys.

When we unloaded him from the box my heart sank. We saw with horror his poor damaged ears; his lips were drawn back, his eyes red and angry and he was obviously emotionally disturbed. Gently we put him in a loosebox, took off his halter and left him in peace with hay and a bran mash. On entering to collect the bucket half an hour later, I thought my end had come. Timothy attacked me, not with his hind legs (which one gets used to) but with his front hoofs, rearing up and trying to hoof me under, eyes blazing, teeth bared. It's hard to appear calm on these occasions but knowing not to let him sense any fear I managed to slip out minus the bucket! After that it was always what we call a 'two-man box', one to put in the feed and the other to ward Timothy off!

Knowing how all donkeys are better in company, we tried introducing him to other geldings but he cared for them no more than for people and we frequently ended up rescuing the other gelding from the 'pairing box'. In despair the only answer seemed to be the ultimate one – to put him to sleep; to erase forever the terrible memories.

Then the miracle happened. Two very fat chocolate donkeys (called Henry and Henrietta) had come in. They were in the next stable to Timothy as Henry had been showing signs of extreme fatigue. One night on evening rounds Henry was found lying down, barely breathing, having suffered a massive heart attack. After phoning the vet I knelt beside him, massaging his heart to try to encourage the very weak beat. Henrietta became a real nuisance so I pushed her into the long corridor. By the time the vet arrived, Henry was unconscious and, despite injections and all the vet could do, we lost him. As I stumbled into the corridor half-blinded with tears I stopped in amazement. Timothy's head was extended over the door and gently nuzzling him was Henrietta! I just couldn't believe it! They both ignored me as I gently opened Timothy's door, Henrietta walked into his stable calmly and continued the nuzzling.

From that moment Timothy changed. Helped by Henrietta, he began to accept titbits and his attack with the front hoofs was turned into a morning hoof shake with Herb.

After Timothy and Henrietta had spent a few days together, we decided to let them out in the yard and with some trepidation, I opened the door. Henrietta led the way, followed by a quiet Timothy and together they explored every corner of the big yard. As soon as Henrietta's isolation period was over, we took them up to one of the fields and for two days they had the private use of it but they were able to talk to the donkeys in the next field over the fence. Henrietta was very firm with Timothy and at the first sign of bared teeth she would push him away from the donkey he was talking to! On the third day together, we allowed them into a group of donkeys, and now, with Henrietta always near him, he is living a happy, peaceful life again. He seems to have forgiven man for his inhumanity and would we, or could we, all do the same?

Timothy

Buffalo, a retired beach donkey, and the favourite donkey at the sanctuary until his death late in 1987

Doing the Donkey Work

DONKEY RIDES

Because of his gentleness and docility, combined with the strength of a pony, the donkey is chosen to give rides on the beach. To many young people this is their first opportunity to experience the thrill and adventure of riding. Hearts in mouths, they bump along, some cajoling the donkey to move faster, others just desperately clinging on until the far marker on the beach is rounded. Then, with squeals of delight intermingled with shrieks of genuine fear, the donkeys bear them back to their waiting parents at a faster pace! Donkeys are notorious for the slow walk out and the happy run home! Once back, the alarm for the nervous rider recedes, and cries of 'Oh just one more ride *please* Mum' can be heard. Many children fall in love with their mounts and the treasured donkey ride becomes the focal point of the day and indeed, the longest lasting memory of the holiday.

But life for a working donkey has never been easy; disturbed during the early morning hours while peacefully grazing by the arrival of a large lorry in the gate of the field, the donkeys would be harshly loaded up with shouts and crammed into the back of the evil-smelling vehicle. The journey to the beach would be a nightmare for many of the animals and it would almost be a relief to be herded onto the sand and tacked up ready for a day's work.

Ill-fitting tack can cause sores and discomfort during the day and the donkeys must have shrunk from the weight and the pain of the badly fitted saddles being tightly girthed. The day must have seemed never ending; large children, even adults, yanking on the reins and shouting, screaming, yelling, kicking and bumping on their backs as the donkeys made their painful way on the many rides, frequently beaten with sticks and, in the more recent years, prodded with electric goads to maintain their speed.

In the past compulsory rest breaks for the donkeys were not required and as dusk fell many would be almost too exhausted to mount the ramp of the lorry to return to their small paddocks. Perhaps Blackpool is most famous for its donkey rides, where they have been proud of their reputation for the care of the donkeys and, in fact, over one hundred years ago they designed a charter for the donkeys working on the beach. This charter was recently superseded by the rules laid down by the Riding Establishments Acts Committee used on all the other beaches in Britain.

Help Protect Beach Donkeys
(see page 183)

Suey's operator lost his licence and is no longer working and in the interests of the donkeys you may be able to help. Printed here is a simplification of the regulations relating to working donkeys. If you see these rules being broken, you can help the donkeys by reporting the operator to the local council office, where the operator's licences are issued or by ringing the sanctuary.

1 Every donkey must have at least one hour's rest midday for watering and feeding plus other short rests and *never* stay on the beach for more than nine hours in a day.
2 No one over 50kg (8st) may ride a donkey.
3 Mares with young foals should not work.
4 No sticks should be used.

At present there are approximately 240 donkeys working on Blackpool beach; for many of the owners it is a labour of love and has stayed in the same family for generations. There are twenty-eight donkey ranks ranging from Balmoral Road on the south shore of Blackpool to Bispham and all the donkey owners are allocated a pitch to start the season on. They then move in rota up and down the different pitches. Most seem to prefer the south pier stand and the donkeys seem to enjoy them all. Great care is taken to ensure that the winter quarters are as good as those provided during the summer and here Blackpool scores over many other seaside resorts.

Weston-super-Mare also has a large number of donkeys and one particular family, the Drews, have been keeping donkeys for over a hundred years in this area. However, conditions in the past have not been so good for the donkeys and great problems were experienced during the wintering of the donkeys, many of whom were turned away and had to forage on the local refuse dump. Once again though, conditions have now improved greatly and regular inspections here are met with co-operation rather than the earlier resentment.

Popular Phrases

The donkey is known for his hard labour and 'donkey work' is a common phrase. Likewise machinery has been named after him, eg 'donkey-engine' and 'donkey-pump'.

Prince and Ginger, retired Blackpool beach donkeys

Zorba

The bond between man and his working donkey is strong; a special relationship builds up where each depends totally on the other. On the island of Kea, off the coast of Greece, such a relationship has built up between Zorba and his owner. Zorba is a superb example of the Greek working donkey and he works, eats and almost sleeps with him! Zorba's stable is an integral part of the family house and there is no doubt he fares as well as the family. His work consists of carrying heavy milk churns for delivery from the cows scattered around the island to the newly built dairy. A heavy job but essential and as hard physically for the owner, lifting the heavy cans onto the special wooden saddle.

Ploughing practice for overseas students at Shuttleworth Agricultural College

AGRICULTURE

Donkeys used in the earlier days in agriculture would fare reasonably well, being regarded as one of the assets of the farm and therefore be treated with respect and kept in a good condition to enable the daily job to be done with the maximum efficiency.

There is a growing pressure from those interested in donkeys to try to introduce the donkey back into agriculture and provided the equipment the donkey is asked to pull, in regard to ploughing and harrowing, is correctly balanced and weighted the donkeys seem to enjoy this work particularly. The sanctuary took part in a recent ploughing association rally; the weather was so terrible that the tractors were bogged down and, in fact, it was only the donkeys who were able to complete their furrows.

It would be interesting to see donkeys able to play a more active part on smallholdings and as we have learned from the United States it is perfectly practical and possible for them to become extremely useful in this service. In the early days all around the sanctuary's grounds in Salcombe Regis donkeys played an important part. The south-facing cliffs were 'terraced' by the local farmers and early potatoes planted, taking advantage of the sheltered frost-free area. Donkeys did all the ploughing and carrying of the crops and Branscombe's early potatoes were well known. Once a week a team of sixteen donkeys pulled a large cart to Exeter bearing a large load of potatoes which were sold in the market. The donkeys were used to carrying seaweed at other times of the year and were also used by the smugglers, who regularly carried brandy up to Slade House itself! At one time an unwelcome visit from 'Ye Kings men' forced the smugglers to pour the brandy down the drains of the house.

Zorba and his owner in Greece

Spot the donkey! Overwork in Peru

THE DONKEY DERBY

Donkeys are also used for donkey derbys. Although these may be enjoyed by the riders, they are not very much fun for the donkeys, who are not natural racers. Once again, in the early days, these caused much abuse to the donkeys who were ridden by overweight riders and various methods, including sticks and even thistles under the saddle, were used to ensure the donkey's speedy action. Once again, a code of practice has been set up for donkey derbys which to some extent has alleviated the situation. However, the Donkey Sanctuary is not in favour of these derbys and, wherever possible, we keep a close eye on them to ensure the donkeys' welfare. Donkey racing has been proposed and has been carried out in certain parts of the country in a very limited way for some years. We feel even more strongly that this can only lead to donkeys being misused. Once betting is involved and money begins to change hands then the 'fun' side of the event becomes clouded by greed and ambition. We do not feel that the donkey can gain in any way by being used for racing; the normal gait of the domestic donkey is certainly not fast!

Jenny and Jilly Castle

Jenny is twenty-six and Jilly is thirty-two and for many years they worked the water mill at Carisbrook Castle on the Isle of Wight. This is not as bad as it sounds as apparently they enjoyed the work thoroughly and only spent fifteen minutes a day starting the mill up. During his lifetime Lord Louis Mountbatten took a great interest in both the donkeys and would no doubt have been delighted to know that they had now been retired to the Donkey Sanctuary.

STAGE STRUCK

I was born in Morecambe, Lancashire, a seaside resort so of course we boasted donkeys on the sands where donkey rides were part of a seaside holiday for both children and grown-ups. We played on the sands and sometimes would be given a free ride if business was a bit slack and because we were locals and knew the donkey men!

After all these years I can still recall the sound of the donkeys going home after their hard day's work and the sound of the harness jingling, the bells on their foreheads, their little hoofs gently tapping the sea-washed cobbles of the rampart as they trotted along on the way to their stables, their heads bobbing up and down. Sometimes we would run along beside them for a little way, patting them lovingly on their hindquarters and saying 'Goodnight Neddy!' They would blink their heavily lashed eyelids as much as to say 'Goodnight children – we'll be back tomorrow!' What a lovely childhood memory!

My next very friendly experience with a donkey was many, many years ago when I played Susan, the comedienne in *The Desert Song*. I was the girlfriend of Benny, the comedian. We made an entrance onto (supposedly) the edge of the desert and I was riding a donkey and Benny leading him. Now it's a well-known fact that animals don't always *want* to go on the stage when they are called upon to do so . . . but I always had a handful of sweets and never had any trouble until one night . . . the donkey wouldn't move. The only

sweets I had were cough tablets, chlorodyne lozenges to be exact, and as the donkey appeared to have no intention of moving, I gave him four, which he crunched very happily and seemed to enjoy. Off we trotted onto the centre stage, we started the scene and the donkey hiccupped, I was nearly thrown off but he just continued hiccupping . . . by now the audience were falling about laughing. I must admit, the scene had never *gone* so well although the audience couldn't hear a word we said for laughing. I made sure I had the usual Liquorice Allsorts for the next performance!

My third happy partnership with a donkey was in the London Palladium Show, *London Laughs*, in 1966. The finale of the first half of the show was a big concerted cockney scene where Harry Secombe and I rode on stage as a Pearly King and Queen in a lovely little cart pulled by a very lovable donkey. He was a dear animal, brought on to the side of the stage and harnessed in the cart just a few minutes before he was needed. He was never any trouble and the company all had goodies for him before he went on. I can't remember him ever 'misbehaving' himself on stage and you'll appreciate that is something one is always grateful for when working with animals. He did 'spend a penny' one night, just before we went on stage and we all thought that 'very professional'!

Thora Hird OBE

Carrying the peat in Ireland

WORK IN IRELAND

Donkeys in Southern Ireland are still working in many areas. They are used to carry peat from the bogs and, unfortunately, donkeys engaged in this way suffer quite severely, particularly from overgrown feet. On stopping an Irish peat farmer pulling his donkey and cart up the road the severely overgrown feet were pointed out to him and his answer was: 'To be sure they are long, how else would he walk through the bogs and peat if they didn't turn up at the top? If they were properly trimmed he'd sink straight down.' The donkey's legs were so deformed he was hardly able to walk at all.

Donkeys are also used for pulling milk floats and can regularly be seen in many of the south-western areas of Ireland. A certain number of donkeys are feral and range the hills in Southern Ireland but in about 1985 many of these were rounded up, slaughtered and sold for meat. The sanctuary has set up a small refuge under the care of our inspector in Southern Ireland, Paddy Barrett, and here those too old and sick to work any more can be cared for. Our inspector also arranges the castration of young stallions to prevent the unnecessary breeding of animals from poor stock.

Muffin the Mule

Muffin the Mule was a world-famous marionette character of the Hogarth Puppets. He appeared in the first children's programme on British television *For The Children* in 1946 which ran until 1954. Ann Hogarth manipulated Muffin, who would dance on top of the piano while Annette Mills played and sang.

Muffin the Mule became the nation's favourite personality and was probably the first star to be created by television anywhere in the world. The programme appeared on a Sunday tea-time and was not only watched by children but by mums and dads also. Muffin's signature tune was known to all:

We want Muffin, Muffin the Mule.
Dear old Muffin, playing the fool.
We want Muffin, everyone sing.
We want Muffin the Mule.

His co-stars of the Hogarth Puppet Circus included the penguin Mr Peregrine, Esq, Sally the Seal, Peter the Pup, Monty the Monkey and Louise the Lamb.

THE TWENTY-MULE TEAMS IN

The saga of the twenty-mule teams began with the discovery of borax in California in 1881. This mineral, used for thousands of years in ceramics and in the working of gold, previously had come from Tibet and Italy. Its discovery in California's Death Valley resulted in a rapid increase in the use of borax as a household cleanser in the United States. To meet public demand, a practical and economical method had to be devised for freighting borax ore from the 'mines' in Death Valley's vast dry lake beds to the railroad 165 miles away. William T. Coleman, owner of the old Harmony Borax Works near what is now Furnace Creek Ranch, took on this Herculean task.

He had seen eight- and twelve-mule teams hauling heavy loads and had observed that the payload increased disproportionately with each added pair of the animals. Experimenting, Coleman found that twenty mules could move 36 tons with relative ease. The route finally decided on, from Death Valley to the railroad at Mojave, covered 165 miles of raw, blistering, roadless mountains and desert. Coleman sent work crews out to hack, blast and sledgehammer a roadbed of sorts over this formidable wasteland. He counted on the wheels of his waggons to do the rest.

Such 'big teams' had been used before in the west on rare occasions but they were makeshift, thrown together for heavy jobs. To drive what soon became known as the twenty-mule teams, Coleman hired the most expert 'long-line skinners' in the business, along with their 'swampers' or brakemen helpers. The mules were hitched to single trees and double trees hooked into a 25m (80ft) chain which ran the length of the team and fastened directly onto the lead waggon.

Ed Stiles was the first man to haul borax out of Death Valley, driving a twelve-mule outfit from Eagle Borax Works to Daggett. When the outfit he drove was sold to Coleman's Amargosa Borax Works, Stiles went with it and he and Superintendent Perry formed the twenty-mule team by hitching a twelve-mule and an eight-mule team together in tandem. Stiles was probably the first man to drive a twenty-mule team between Harmony and Mojave.

The muleskinner drove his team from the 'box' of the first waggon, or, in rough going, from back of the 'nigh wheeler,' or left-hand animal nearest the wheel. His only means of controlling the teams were his voice and the 'jerkline,' a long rope running through the collar ring of each left-hand mule up to the leaders. A steady pull turned the team to the left, a series of jerks sent it to the right.

A sight which never failed to win admiration was that of the 'big team' taking a sharp turn. To keep the 25m (80ft) chain hitch from dragging at a tangent across a turn and pulling the waggons off the road, three mid-team pairs of mules, the 'eights', the 'sixes' and the 'pointers', were taught to leap nimbly over the chain and pull at almost right-angles to the direction of the turn. The manoeuvre required these particular mules to step along sideways in their forward progression, but it kept the chain lined up with the bend of the road until the turn was reached, whereupon the animals would fall back into normal positions again. It was a hazardous life. Added to the heat, desolation, rattlesnakes and general chance of injury, the great waggons themselves were a menace. Brakes gave way at times on steep grades. Then the 36ton juggernauts would thunder down

DEATH VALLEY, CALIFORNIA

the incline hard on the heels of the frantic mules, the muleskinner yelling and hoorawing at his team in a desperate effort to keep them outrunning the waggons. The twenty-mule teams could cover 16–18 miles a day. Camp was made on the desert each night. The one-way trip, from mine to railroad point, took about ten days.

For five years, from 1883 to 1889, the twenty-mule teams moved thousands of tons of borax ore out of Death Valley on a clockwork schedule. Then William Coleman's company failed and the old Harmony Borax Works closed forever. But the twenty-mule team was not to die entirely. Pacific Coast Borax Company, predecessor to United States Borax and Chemical Corporation, revived borax mining in Death Valley some time after Coleman abandoned it and took the 'big

team' as its trademark and corporation symbol. Throughout the first half of this century, the twenty-mule team hauling the original old waggons, was reassembled occasionally for promotional purposes.

Today, one set of waggons is still in running condition and can be seen at the visitors' viewing point on the edge of the Boron, California, open-pit mine. Two other sets are displayed at Furnace Creek Ranch in Death Valley, one in the Borax Museum and one at the entrance to the Ranch.

Borax Holdings Limited

A twenty-mule team in Death Valley, California

ON CALL – TUMBLEWEED, CLARENCE AND RUPERT

The telephone call from the animal agency came one sweltering June day. 'Would there be three amenable donkeys available for a commercial television advertisement?' They would have to be prepared to wear hats! As all our donkeys are dreadful 'hams' and delight in taking part in just about anything that happens outside their paddocks we said, well yes, we thought that three of ours would fit the bill.

The director came down in person to audition the boys, he arrived chauffeur driven in style, wearing only the briefest of shorts and an incredible suntan! Ours was his second call, the first being doomed, two of the trio interviewed had kicked out when asked to wave their tails in unison and were less than friendly at the other end, sadly. However, our clowns were soon peering down his camera lens whilst having pictures taken, two sported a beach hat with glee, Tumbleweed was not quite sure about a hat but was given the benefit of the doubt! Off went the director promising to keep in touch.

Shortly telephone calls began in earnest, wardrobe needed the circumference of ears and the size between, the agency arranged dates and times for filming, the beach location was fixed, and to our horror first call was for 7am on a beach an hour and a half away. Luckily this was amended to 8am after some consideration. July 1984 was the hottest on record for three-hundred years, as we all remember, and the 27th dawned sunny and promising a real scorcher. After frenzied packing of halters, head collars for the actual film, water, feeds, carrots, sugar lumps, peppermints for encouragement there was just room for swimsuits for ourselves! Three immaculately shampooed elegant fellows loaded into the trailer and off we went to the seaside.

There was a stiff breeze blowing off the sea which increased to what seemed gale force during the day, making the waves crash on the shore and every deckchair whip in the wind. The boys marched down purposefully towards the sand, eager to investigate this new world. As soon as they felt it beneath them of course they all wanted to roll, and get rid of the nice clean feel of their shampoo. To Rupert's disgust no grass grew here, so they soon lost interest!

The crew greeted us down on the beach in an area roped off by flapping bunting and warned my husband and myself and David, from the agency, to stand by for the first shots. Four or five men were busily engaged in erecting a large canvas shelter on sturdy poles for the donkeys.

Clarence viewed that with horror and indicated to the others that in no way was it wise to stand within yards of that huge floppy billowing monster! He had no intention of taking up hang-gliding, now or ever! Rupert plodded down to the water's edge (he who makes a dreadful scene at every puddle he is asked to drive past at home) and stared, and stared with ears almost touching his nose at this strange new place, and when power boats and even wind surfers and water-skiers passed he almost stood on tip-toe to watch them out of sight! Clarence and Tumbleweed were quite interested in preparations for filming and when the caterers set up a mobile food bar with coffee and buns they cheered up visibly! Rupert, finally bored with the shore, discovered a patch of wispy sour weed in a sand dune, sampled it with distaste and wandered back to his haynet.

By now the star had arrived, Su Pollard, of *Hi-De-Hi* fame. We soon found that her zany sense of humour is genuine when she cheerfully repeated the same tiny sequence, sipping tea and gesticulating over her shoulder at the appearance of three beach donkeys' heads over her windbreak for several hours! The actual positioning of those three heads over the windbreak was not quite so straightforward! The assistant producer was impressed to see Tumbleweed move to camera left, drop his nose over the windbreak and yelled 'lock it there!' (What a forlorn hope when dealing with any animal!) Rupert hastily bustled up to see what Tumbleweed was doing, and finding he was only looking at a 'prop' beach towel and a beachbag, deftly picked up both and swung them round! Whilst rescuing these and dusting off the sand he had disturbed (one man manipulated a broom all day for just this purpose) the assistant producer wilted, but struggled bravely on, only to wail when Clarence failed to 'lock it there' by about three feet! He continued to resist and held a silent protest, despite bribery, cajoling, pleas from Su Pollard, curses from everyone else, persisting in dropping his muzzle coyly just behind the dratted windbreak! In desperation the director began filming to make a start but soon after we were all relieved to be called to lunch. The assistant producer sternly insisted that the donkeys were to be back within three-quarters of an hour. The poor wardrobe mistress by this time had replaced Tumbleweed's straw beach hat three times (each time Rupert became bored he turned his attention to snatching a mouthful of Tumbleweed's hat, thereby pulling it down over his eyes).

They scampered back to the trailer in the car

park with delight and scoffed their feed surrounded by children demanding to know the cost of a ride! We were somewhat heartened by a delicious three course barbecue meal and were duly positioned when the team returned to work at 2pm. Miraculously we discovered that by ducking down behind the windbreak and flattening ourselves in the burning sand each side of Clarence he relaxed enough with tummy rubs and a finger tucked beneath his chin to keep his nose up for filming to proceed smoothly, encouraged by the director's non-stop stream of approving noises! At 4pm he announced he was satisfied, having studied the videos. The caterers carried down tea and dainty sandwiches, pastries and ice cold drinks which were so welcome to us having taken our faces out of the sand and awakened Tumbleweed who had dozed off! Encouraged by his success the director suggested that we now attempted what he delicately called 'the bum shots'. For this our trio were to swish their tails to a catchy musical tune played on a cassette recorder. They watched with interest whilst 'invisible' thread was gently circled round each tail in turn, the ends held by myself and a member of the crew crouched down in the sand to avoid shadows on the film! Away we went, waving to the music, only to find that one or the other thread slipped down, leaving two to tango instead of three! When the threads were correct Clarence moved away from camera range. The poor perspiring assistant director raced back and forth yelling instructions to the camera and orders to the donkeys who were fascinated by all the goings-on. In the middle of the perfect take Rupert's control finally gave way and a steaming heap of droppings cascaded on to the sand. Everyone cracked up and laughed so much that a halt was called for the day with assurances that we probably had enough film for a *ten second* advertisement!

We felt that a night in their own stable would be better than staying on location and be more restful for the boys so we wearily joined the race home from the beach with hundreds of holidaymakers.

Next morning our call was for 9am which was just a little less tiring, so with some trepidation we set off again, the weather promising to be even hotter! However to our delight the director reported a favourable response to the rushes from London, all we were required to do was sit in the shade in the car-park and await the arrival from London again, of three charming young men to 'match the legs'. In the final shot they were required to perform a dance routine!

The young men produced six artificial front legs and painstakingly the fur fabric was trimmed to the correct thickness and each limb carefully sprayed to match the donkeys' individual colouring, two roan, two skewbald and two grey. Such fantastic attention to the tiniest detail was what makes British television the finest in the world we were told. Tumbleweed and Rupert watched all this with interest but Clarence was convinced that his pair were to be *attached* and gave them a *very wide berth*!

At noon we were finally informed that we could go. Having downed their feeds the trio practically jammed three abreast scrambling into the box to go home and tell the others all about being a TV star.

David and Margaret Coles,
Donkey Breed Society Magazine

Role reversal!

DONKEYS AS GUARD DOGS

Are coyotes or dogs bothering your flock of sheep? Then consider the use of a guard donkey. Sheepraisers from Montana to Vermont are singing the praises of these long-eared critters.

Art and Marge Christensen run several hundred Targhee/Finn sheep in the foothills of the Ruby mountains in south-west Montana. Over the years they have tried a wide variety of predator controls including noise makers and guard dogs. None has been very successful. Finally, on the urging of John Conter, secretary of the American Council of Spotted Asses, they tried a guard donkey. Since introducing Small One to their flock they have had no losses.

'We had our last coyote kill two days before Small One, our guard donkey arrived. The government trapper has been out and he says the coyotes are still there. We still hear them yipping, but so far they haven't bothered our sheep,' says Marge.

But that's not the only reason the Christensens are pleased with their donkey. Art says they went up to gather the sheep and bring them down to the ranch and the donkey was nowhere in sight. They figured it was off eating somewhere instead of staying with the flock as it should. When they returned the sheep to the pasture, they spotted Small One on a hillside. An investigation found her literally standing over a sick ewe that had aborted four lambs. Marge says the donkey doubled in value in Art's eyes after that incident. A short time later her value shot up again. On a routine check of the sheep, the donkey again was not with the flock. A look around soon revealed her standing guard over a ewe with a newborn lamb.

What the Christensens like, too, is that the donkey lives with the sheep. She feeds with them during the day and beds down with them at night. 'That's the most important part,' says Art, 'because most coyotes attack at night and the donkey is right there to chase them off.'

According to Conter, the donkeys rarely kill a coyote, but they will bray, chase after, and strike out with their front feet. Dale and Marcia Brown in Vermont have seen their pair of guard donkeys drive off a pack of feral dogs by biting and kicking. One dog was kicked through the air and over the fence.

From Virginia, Zan Stuart reports one of his donkeys valiantly defended ninety-four fat lambs from an attack by a pair of German Shepherds. Although one lamb was killed before the shepherd arrived, the toll would have been much higher without the donkey.

Why are donkeys which are usually gentle, placid animals effective on predators? The key is the donkey's natural aggression towards strange canines. A female or jennet is preferred because they are the most protective. Jacks or stallions are not suitable because they can be very aggressive towards any smaller animal including lambs.

Most operators prefer to use one donkey with each flock of sheep. Especially in free-range situations they feel two or more donkeys might pal up and wander away from the sheep. Introducing a donkey to the sheep is the critical step. During the donkey's first two weeks with the flock, keep an eye on things but do not pet or handle the donkey. She must get lonesome enough that she 'adopts' the sheep. The fact that the donkey can live permanently with the sheep and eat as they do is one of the main advantages over dogs.

Judith E. Strom, United States of America

SUEY

Suey

Although the donkeys in Blackpool are well cared for, unfortunately, on other beaches they do not always fare so well and many have to be collected, exhausted from overwork and old age. This was the case with Suey. The operator she worked for was one of the worst kind. Once the season was over, all the donkeys were 'turned away' – they were literally herded into a rough field with no shelter and left to fend for themselves through the long winter. In Suey's group an added complication was the fact that there was a stallion amongst the team. This meant that all the younger mares, even those under two years old, inevitably got into foal.

Although the operator realised that Suey was elderly, he had not the knowledge to age her accurately by her teeth or he would have known that after that long hard winter she was well over thirty. Because of her age, she escaped the fate of the younger mares, but when they were collected by the owner at Easter, she was very thin, and her feet, which had not been trimmed, were long and distorted. One of the mares had foaled in the February, and while she was made to give rides, the foal was kept on the beach as an attraction for the public.

Normally Suey had enjoyed giving rides but this year she was almost exhausted before the season began. The saddles and bridles used by the operator were too large, having previously been used for ponies. The bit had to be wired up to keep it in place, causing sores on both her upper and lower jaws. A piece of baler twine used to tighten it, frequently cut into her.

The end to Suey's ordeal came one hot July Friday in the first week of the children's school holiday. She had been giving rides almost non-stop since early morning when a very large boy, well over the 50kg (8st) limit, insisted on riding her. Suey's knees buckled as he got on, but she got no sympathy from the operator who passed the boy his stick to 'Make the b----r go!' It was on the return journey that her knees buckled and she slowly collapsed on to the soft sand. Despite frequent blows from the now angry operator, her eyes remained closed. Fortunately the British public are animal lovers, and an angry crowd gathered. A rug was put over her by the operator as she was, in his words, 'spoiling the trade' and fortunately a bystander ran to the telephone and called the sanctuary.

It was some hours before we got there but as Suey was not fit to travel far she spent the night with a supporter of the sanctuary before undertaking the long journey to her new home. When the waggon doors were opened and I climbed in to her, I was met with the dullest, saddest eyes I had ever seen. The driver had put all the supports up for her journey, as her feet were so distorted and she had very little strength of her own. Gently we helped her down the ramp and her head lifted for a moment when she received the bray of welcome all new donkeys get on their arrival. Then she was led into her large airy box with a deep clean straw bedding, freshly shaken hay and cool clean water. Did I see just a little lifting of the head, a glint of interest in her eyes? By evening she was lying down, contentedly munching hay.

We left a full medical examination until the next day to give her time to recover. It was a very thorough veterinary check. She was thin, but not emaciated, and there was no sign of heart trouble or in fact anything to account for the long period of apparent unconsciousness. Perhaps she had just had enough. There were numerous sores and saddle galls which were treated every day and after a week she had her equine flu inoculation and anti-tetanus jab and was treated for parasites. It took a great deal of time to get her feet back to normal and we all spent many hours with her, bathing feet and sores in rotation. Never once did she attempt to kick us, despite our ministrations, which must have been very painful at times.

Gradually she began to walk without pain and, without the cruel tack, the sores began to heal and for Suey life became worth living again. She made friends with an elderly little mare called Jenny who moved in with her as her companion as soon as she was clear of lice and sores and had completed her isolation period. She still spends a great deal of time lying down. However, she is a happy donkey now, thoroughly enjoying her richly deserved retirement.

THE CLOVELLY DONKEYS

For many years in Clovelly donkeys were the only means of transport down the steep narrow and cobbled stepped streets leading to the quay. They were used to transport supplies and luggage to the New Inn and boarding houses and were also used by the postmen to deliver the Royal Mail.

Nowadays, more as a tourist attraction, donkeys are sometimes still used to carry the odd suitcase and occasionally give children rides during their off-duty hours.

Some of the retired donkeys from Clovelly have been taken in by the sanctuary; one being Chloe who is at the Donkey Sanctuary's Brookfield Farm thoroughly enjoying her retirement.

Donkeys at work in Clovelly, North Devon (Photographs reproduced by kind permission of the Beaford Archive)

ARRIVAL OF H.M.S. MAILS AT CLOVELLY

DONKEY SANCTUARY

Rest easy, friends
The hard part is over now
The toiling, sweltering days of
wind-whipped sand
Stinging dim, blinkered eyes
Of heedless, jabbing heels
Discordant voices
The perpetual retracing
of weary footsteps
Be still now – and feel glad
of the soft balm of grass
Against worn hoofs
Enjoy the gentle curve of meadowland
That sweeps into the distance
Where no discord
No jangling dissonance
No goading stick
Will ever again
Fall on your cross-marked shoulders.

Joan B. Howes
(Reproduced by kind permission of
Woman & Home)

HOME TO REST

The little donkey stands and looks around his new
  domain,
He feels so very happy now, he's very glad he
  came.

When at first they put him into that great big van,
He was so very frightened of every little bang.

He thought that men just hurt you and hit you
  with their hand,
But life at the sanctuary is nothing less than grand.

And when all the little children come to pat his
  head,
He listens very carefully to every word that's
  said.

He knows there's lots of love here, he can feel it
  in the air,
He knows he will spend his final days without a
  pain or care.

Gena Harrison

A-Z of Donkey Health

Abscesses An abscess is a pus-filled cavity and can occur anywhere in the body, though the commonest sites that a donkey owner will see are in the skin or in the foot (see Lameness). The abscess needs to be drained after prior lancing or bursting. It can be encouraged to 'point' (the stage at which it can be burst easily) by bathing with hand-hot salt water (one teaspoon in a pint of water). Once the abscess has burst it can be flushed out with salt water. It may be necessary to administer antibiotics at this stage and veterinary advice should always be sought.

Abscesses in the foot can result from a punctured sole or small foreign bodies working their way up the white line of the foot. This is the most common cause of foot lameness in donkeys. The abscess needs to be drained (by excavation of the foot) and this requires the attention of a veterinary surgeon or a qualified farrier. Topical application of gentian violet/tetracycline spray will usually suffice, after drainage is complete. However, it is sometimes necessary to poultice the foot with, eg Animalintex to help to draw out some of the pus. Occasionally, a deep abscess will break out at the coronary band. This will also require drainage and possibly antibiotic treatment.

Allergy see Sweet Itch, Urticaria, COPD

Alopecia This means loss of hair and usually occurs as a result of the donkey rubbing or biting itself because of irritation, eg lice infestation, sweet itch, ringworm, mange. Other causes of alopecia include hormonal imbalance, rain scald, photosensitisation and some metabolic diseases.

Anaemia Anaemia is a reduction in the number of red cells in the blood. This may be caused by (a) blood loss, (b) destruction of red blood cells by the body or (c) inability of the bone marrow to produce sufficient numbers of red blood cells. In all cases the donkey will be weak and depressed with pale mucous membranes.

Blood-loss anaemia can be the result of acute haemorrhage (obvious if external but not if the bleeding is internal), or it may be due to chronic blood loss which can occur in severe parasitism (in the intestines and on the skin).

Destruction of blood cells by the body (haemolysis) occurs normally within the body, but if excessive, can lead to anaemia and jaundice. Possible causes of this are certain types of poisoning (eg bracken), auto-immune disease or certain infections not found in the UK, eg equine infectious anaemia.

Bone marrow depression can result from chronic infections, iron deficiency, neoplasia or certain plant and drug toxicities. Veterinary advice should be sought.

Aneurysm The aneurysm is a dilatation of a blood vessel but the term is also sometimes used to describe the massive reaction to migrating *Strongylus vulgaris* larvae, found in the mesenteric arteries. This can lead to obstruction of blood vessels by dislodged blood clots, and consequent colic. If there is sufficient damage, the artery may rupture and the donkey may bleed to death.

Anorexia This term is used to describe the condition where a donkey will not eat. Appetite is an important indicator of a donkey's health and refusal to eat can be one of the first signs that he is unwell (though a good appetite is sometimes maintained in sick donkeys). Sudden onset may be due to colic, fever, pain especially in the mouth or feet or a sudden change in environment or feed. Some donkeys do have food preferences and if a particular food is refused, he may be willing to eat an alternative. Any donkey off his feed should be examined by a vet. If the condition persists, a state of hyperlipaemia can occur, particularly in fat donkeys, which will often prove fatal if not treated early enough.

Arthritis Quite common in older donkeys. There may be a generalised stiffness when first getting up but this often improves with gentle exercise. May also be a sequel to acute or chronic trauma to joints. Anti-inflammatory pain killers are often prescribed.

Botulism Has been reported in donkeys as well as horses, most recently as a result of feeding contaminated big bale silage. The feed is usually contaminated by infected rodents or birds which die and decompose within the feed and the toxin is dispersed. Signs are quite vague but there is extreme dullness, inability to swallow and therefore copious drooling of saliva from the mouth and muscular weakness leading to paralysis. The condition is nearly always fatal and is notoriously difficult to confirm by laboratory examination.

Bracken Poisoning Long-term ingestion of bracken (particularly in its green state) can lead to poisoning. This plant is usually only eaten if the pasture is poor. The plant has an enzyme which destroys thiamine in the donkey and this affects the brain leading to staggering, inco-ordination, weakness, emaciation and anaemia. Treatment with large doses of intravenous thiamine is required, as well as removal of the cause, though symptoms can occur long after the donkey is removed from the bracken. Horsetails have the same effect as bracken.

Broken Wind see COPD

Bruised Soles The soles of the feet can be bruised by traumatic injury such as walking over very stony ground when the soles are thin or flat. It can sometimes occur if the feet have been trimmed back too far. When the surface of the sole is scraped away a red discolouration, or bruise, can be seen. The condition improves as the horn of the sole grows and the bruising subsides. It may be necessary to provide protection of the soles in severe cases by bandaging the foot over some gamgee padding for a week or so. The padding should be checked and changed regularly to prevent the sole becoming infected and soft. The application of a gentian violet and tetracycline spray is often used to harden the horn and prevent infection.

Castration This surgical operation (also called gelding) involves the removal of the testicles from a stallion (jack) donkey. The operation is usually performed under general anaesthesia although it is sometimes possible to use sedation and local analgesia. It can be performed once the testicles are descended though it is usually preferable to wait until at least six months of age to give a general anaesthetic. The operation can be carried out at any time of the year if suitable facilities for surgery and post-operative care are available but most vets prefer to carry out the operation during spring or autumn when it is not too cold or wet and when there are less flies to aggravate the cast-

ration wound. Castration wounds are normally left open to allow drainage. Sometimes there is swelling around the wound which may extend to the sheath. The donkey should be encouraged to exercise in order to minimise the swelling.

Cataract This is an opacity in the lens of the eye and usually occurs in both eyes simultaneously. It is usually seen in old donkeys and is a senile change but it can occur in younger donkeys or as a sequel to trauma, infection or inflammation of the eye. As it progresses, it leads to impaired vision and ultimately to blindness in the affected eye.

Choke Food lodged in the oesophagus will lead to choke. The donkey will be unable to swallow, food may be regurgitated through the nose and, depending on the site of obstruction, there may be arching of the neck. The donkey is usually fairly distressed. Urgent veterinary attention should be sought. Treatment using a stomach tube passed through the nose to dislodge the obstruction is usually required and muscle relaxants may also be administered. The usual cause is from sugar beet which has not been properly soaked and this swells in the oesophagus and lodges there. Sugar beet should *always* be soaked for the required length of time. (Shreds should be soaked for twelve hours, pulp for eighteen hours, and pellets/nuts must be soaked for twenty-four hours before feeding.)

Colic This is a term used to describe abdominal pain. Signs are not always shown in donkeys at such an early stage as in horses and the symptoms are usually less violent. Signs of colic should thus be taken very seriously and urgent veterinary attention sought. Signs to look for are: acute loss of appetite, extreme dullness with low head carriage, restlessness, lying down a lot, rolling, looking at the belly, kicking at the flank, rapid pulse and breathing, constipation or diarrhoea. There are a number of different types of colic, which require different forms of treatment, some of which are potentially surgical. The main types of colic are:
1 Spasmodic – This is usually seen in nervous donkeys possibly after a change in environment. This type is the least serious and is usually very effectively treated with anti-spasmodic drugs.
2 Thrombo-embolic – This is caused by the occlusion of blood vessels to part of the gut and the most common cause of this is thought to be thrombi resulting from damage by migrating strongyle larvae. Regular worming is required to prevent this occurring.

3 Flatulent – This is due to a build-up of gas in the stomach or intestines particularly if a fermentable diet is being fed.

4 Impaction – This is caused by the build-up of hard, dry faeces, particularly in the caecum or colon, usually where the diameter of the intestine narrows at the pelvic flexure. Donkeys do normally need a diet that is high in fibre but if it is improperly digested or if there has been insufficient breakdown by chewing, or an inadequate intake of water, then an impaction can occur. Pain can be quite severe and affected donkeys will sometimes lie on their backs to relieve pain caused by the pull of the heavy intestine on the sensitive connective tissue in which it is suspended. This type of colic can usually be relieved by medical treatment alone, although recovery may take several days. Surgery may be necessary in some extreme cases that do not respond to more conservative treatment.

5 Obstruction – Other than impactions, which prevent the passage of faeces through the gut, obstructions can also occur as a result of twisting of the intestine, strangulation of part of the gut or a variety of other reasons. This type of colic nearly always requires surgical treatment. The pain is usually severe and if surgical facilities are not available then euthanasia may be recommended by the attending vet, on humane grounds.

6 Grass Sickness – This is a disease of equines, though not commonly seen in donkeys. The signs are those of a severe colic with profuse sweating, muscle tremors over the body and also, normally, a green discharge from the nose (regurgitated food). The cause is unknown but it affects the nervous control of the gut. There is no effective treatment and euthanasia is usually advised.

Donkeys suffering from other conditions which give rise to abdominal pain such as hepatitis, cystitis, pancreatitis or imminent foaling may also show signs of colic.

Congenital Deformities These are deformities which are present when the foal is born and can include undershot or overshot jaw, limb or spinal column deformities.

Conjunctivitis This is an inflammation of the conjunctiva, the membrane which covers the surface of the eye and inner eyelids. There is redness of the eye and usually there is a watery discharge (tears) which may later become thick and yellowish and the donkey may blink vigorously. In very severe cases the eye may be partially closed. The cause is usually a minor irritation, eg from dust in the hay or straw but is sometimes due to an infection or a foreign body in the eye (eg a piece of straw or a hay seed). A persistently runny eye will require veterinary treatment.

COPD Chronic Obstructive Pulmonary Disease, also known as broken wind, heaves, dust allergy or emphysema. This disease is similar to asthma in humans and is usually caused by an allergy, usually to fungal spores in the dust in hay or straw. The temperature of affected donkeys is usually normal although an episode may occur following any respiratory infection. Breathing is very laboured and wheezing can often be heard even without the aid of a stethoscope. Coughing is not common in donkeys, unlike horses. Affected donkeys are usually stabled and the condition is improved by turning them out and reducing exposure to dust. If they need to be housed, then bedding should be changed from straw to either peat, wood shavings or paper which are less dusty. Hay should be fed after soaking overnight to keep the dust down or a dust-free feed such as haylage can be given instead. The condition can usually be controlled by management alone but drugs to alleviate the bronchospasm can be useful in many cases. If the condition is truly allergic, the donkey will always be prone to it, so management changes will need to be maintained for the rest of the donkey's life.

Cough Donkeys are not often heard to cough even when severe lung lesions are present. It does occur, however, when there is irritation of the upper respiratory tract and in certain types of infection. A persistent cough should always be investigated by a veterinary surgeon. See also COPD, Lungworm, Pneumonia.

Cystitis Not very common but can occur in donkeys. It is an inflammation of the bladder and is characterised by frequent voiding of small amounts of urine, often with difficulty, and straining. There is also usually a fever and loss of appetite. The cause is usually an infection and requires treatment with antibiotics. Similar signs are also seen with calculi (stones) in the bladder or urethra and this condition may require surgery to correct.

Dermatophilus see Rain Scald and Mud Fever

Diarrhoea Causes of diarrhoea in donkeys can be (a) nervous, (b) dietary, (c) parasitic, (d) infectious, (e) inability to digest food properly. This inability can be caused by failure to chew food properly (eg bad teeth), inappropriate food (eg adult diet in young foal) or disease of the gut wall preventing ingress of dietary compounds.

Nervous donkeys which are easily upset will pass loose faeces from time to time but these become normal later when the donkey is allowed to settle down.

Whenever there is a sudden change in diet, diarrhoea can be precipitated. It is often seen when they are turned out to grass or if they are fed a high-protein feed. Foals can develop a nutritional diarrhoea due to an intolerance to milk. It can also occur when the mare has her 'foal heat' approximately one week after foaling. A reduction in milk intake and replacement with glucose/electrolyte solutions is usually beneficial.

Intestinal parasitism can give rise to chronic diarrhoea. Most commonly this is due to strongyle worm infections which regular worming should prevent. Infection with other species of worms or protozoan intestinal parasites may also cause diarrhoea.

Infections with certain bacteria (including salmonella) and viruses can cause both acute and chronic diarrhoea. The donkey is usually ill and may require intensive therapy with replacement fluids and probably antibiotics. See also Colic, Parascaris Infection, Salmonella, Strongyle Worm Infection, Strongyloides Infection, Tapeworms.

Dysphagia This means difficulty in eating and may be the result of a variety of causes. The most likely of these is pain in the mouth and this is often due to ulceration of the gums from sharp edges of the cheek teeth. This can be prevented by rasping the teeth regularly. Teeth may be loose or there may be an infection or foreign body in the mouth or pharynx. An inability to swallow will result in food being regurgitated down the nose and this will be seen as a greenish nasal discharge. This can also occur in choke, grass sickness, certain types of colic and certain conditions which affect the nervous system such as botulism, lead poisoning and rabies. See also Choke, Colic, Teeth, Weight Loss.

Ectropion This is where the skin of the lower eyelid is too long and the eyelid turns outwards giving a droopy eye appearance. It can also follow injury or swelling of the eyelid. If there is persistent inflammation or infection of the affected eye, then surgery is required to correct the condition.

Entropion This is a condition where the eyelid (upper or lower) turns inwards so that the eyelashes are rubbing on the surface of the eye. This causes intense irritation and damage to the eye and requires surgical correction under general anaesthetic. Usually a strip of skin is removed in order to return the eyelid to its normal position.

Equine Herpesvirus (rhinopneumonitis) This virus (EHV 1), of which there are two sub-types, is responsible for four different syndromes in equines. These are:

1 A respiratory form which is contagious and easily spread by nasal discharges. There is fever, dullness, nasal discharge and sometimes a cough.
2 Abortion usually in the latter part of gestation. Some infected mares will produce a live foal but this is usually weak and suffering from the third form of the disease.
3 Congenital rhinopneumonitis. Affected foals are weak at, or soon after, birth and refuse to suck. Treatment is usually unrewarding and most die within a few days.
4 Neurological disease. This may be preceded by respiratory signs. The hindquarters become unco-ordinated and there is sometimes urinary incontinence. In severe cases, the donkey may become recumbent.

The form most likely to be seen in donkeys is the respiratory disease and recovery from this is usually good although this may be complicated by infections by other organisms. There is a vaccine available which is mainly effective against abortion but the immunity it produces is not very strong and is rather short-lived.

Equine Influenza Equine flu is caused by a group of viruses known as the Myxoviruses, of which there are at least four sub-types. It is a highly contagious disease which is characterised by fever and nasal discharge with varying degrees of dullnesss and inappetence. The virus will also cause some inflammation of the heart and liver, so any strenuous exercise or stress should be avoided during the illness and for about a month afterwards. Recovery is usually good although secondary infections can be a problem. If the donkey is unwilling to eat, then this can lead to a condition known as hyperlipaemia which is very serious and can be very difficult to treat. It is possible (and recommended) to vaccinate against the commonly occurring strains of this virus. Two doses of vaccine are given initially, four to six weeks apart followed by boosters at least every year. It may be necessary to vaccinate at six-monthly intervals if the donkey is to mix with other equines, eg at shows, on a regular basis. Your veterinary surgeon will advise on the best regime for a particular individual. Following vaccination, exercise should be avoided for one week after a primary vaccine and three days after a booster vaccine. Flu-like symptoms are often seen in donkeys that are fully vaccinated. This is because there may be other strains of the virus not covered by the vaccine or the infection may be by a different type of virus (including equine herpesvirus). Occasionally, an animal may not respond adequately to the vaccine.

Eye Problems see Cataract, Conjunctivitis, Ectropion, Entropion

Fatty Liver see Hyperlipaemia

Feet Donkeys' feet are often neglected and, as they grow at a relatively rapid rate, they can soon become overgrown and twisted. In areas where the donkeys work on hard, rocky ground (such as in the Mediterranean countries) the rate of wear of hoof is approximately equal to its rate of growth so that their feet maintain a good shape and length. However, in this country, most donkeys lead a fairly sedentary life on soft ground and the hoofs can grow unchecked. They become very long and will start to curl up into 'Arabian slippers', particularly the front feet. If left uncorrected, they will become twisted. These deformities can be painful for the donkey and it may take months of trimming before a normal shaped hoof can be regained. Occasionally the deformity is so severe that it is impossible to obtain a normal foot. Regular trimming of hoofs is required every six to eight weeks. Donkeys are not normally shod but this may be necessary if the donkey is to do a lot of roadwork. Most lamenesses in donkeys are in the foot, the commonest causes being abscesses, thrush, laminitis, seedy toe and, of course, deformed feet.

Flies Flies are a nuisance throughout the summer. Not only do they cause annoyance and irritation but they are capable of spreading, and causing, disease. They are often found around the eyes and around wounds, feeding off the secretions there. The irritation delays the healing of wounds, and eggs, which develop into maggots, are often laid in the wound. This is called fly strike. Wounds should always be kept clean and, during the fly season, it is useful to apply an antibiotic powder which also contains an insecticide. Other flies (stable flies) can give painful bites which cause annoyance at the time and later give rise to swellings, sometimes with scabs, over the body. Various measures can be taken to reduce the numbers of flies around the donkey. Recently, fly tags which are marketed as ear tags for cattle, have been used successfully as fly repellents in donkeys. The fly tag is attached to a neck or head collar so that the tag is in contact with the skin. Insecticide is released from the tag into the coat and spreads over the body to a certain extent. Other products available include a pour-on insect repellent and washes. Some people use a fringed browband or a fine-meshed mask over the face to keep flies away from the donkey's eyes.

Grass Sickness see Colic

Heart Disease Clinical manifestations of heart disease are not commonly seen in donkeys, because they are not often asked to work hard (in the UK). Fairly severe heart murmurs can be heard in donkeys that appear to be normal as long as they are not subjected to strenuous exercise or a particularly stressful situation. When clinically affected, signs may include poor exercise tolerance, weakness, breathlessness and oedema usually noticeable as a build-up of fluid under the skin of the belly but it may also be present as fluid in the lungs or abdominal cavity. Rarely, a foal may be born with a congenital heart defect. In this case, the foal will be weak and stunted, breathless and may have a blue tinge to the gums.

Hydatid Cysts These are parasitic cysts which can be found usually in the liver but occasionally also in the lungs. They are the intermediate stage of the dog tapeworm, *Echinococcus granulosus*. A donkey is infected by eating pasture contaminated by an infected dog/fox etc which in turn was infected by scavenging infected horse (or possibly sheep) offal. Research is currently being undertaken into this disease in donkeys. Although clinical signs are not often seen in infected donkeys, if there are a large number of cysts present much of the liver tissue is destroyed. In these cases there may be signs of liver insufficiency.

Hyperlipaemia This is a particularly distressing condition which can be fatal if not treated at an early stage. It occurs, particularly in fat donkeys, when food intake has been drastically reduced over a period of time (which can be as short as three or four days). It may be a complication of another illness where appetite is reduced, eg colic, flu, laminitis, pneumonia, or the donkey may simply stop eating in response to a change in its environment.

When the energy intake is insufficient to meet the donkey's requirements, then fat reserves are mobilised and transported mainly to the liver but also to the kidneys and other organs. This response is so vigorous in donkeys (especially fat individuals) that large volumes of fat are present in the blood at this time and can interfere with circulation. The signs that are seen are related to impaired circulation of blood and to reduced functional ability of the organs, particularly the liver, in which vast quantities of fat have accumulated. Commonly, affected donkeys will be dull with low head carriage, have a drooping lower lip and may be dribbling, often standing for long periods over the water trough without drinking. There may be rapid breathing and a raised pulse rate and as the condition progresses, there is incoordination (the donkey looks drunk) and later recumbency. Hyperlipaemia should always be suspected following a period of anorexia when there is no improvement in the donkey's condition. It is easily diagnosed by taking a blood sample and allowing it to settle, the serum will have a distinct milky-white appearance.

Treatment can be very difficult, especially in the later stages and involves the repeated administration of fluids, glucose and bicarbonate either as a drench, by stomach tube or as an intravenous drip and daily injections of insulin are found to be helpful in many cases. The underlying cause of the anorexia should always be treated where possible. To attempt to prevent the development of hyperlipaemia in donkeys that will not eat, it may be useful to give a glucose drench twice daily (at least 115g (4oz) is required per day) unless the vet has advised that nothing is to be given by mouth. Appetite can often be stimulated by offering fresh grass rather than hay. Carrots, apples and other fresh vegetables may also be taken. It is a good idea to maintain an interest in the surroundings, so short walks (if capable of walking) to allow grazing can often be beneficial. Hyperlipaemia is ultimately fatal if left untreated.

Kidney Disease This is not commonly diagnosed in donkeys, particularly in the early stages. If only one kidney is affected, the remaining one can usually compensate. The most frequent causes of kidney disease in donkeys are fatty kidneys (associated with hyperlipaemia); kidney infections; kidney damage following chronic infections elsewhere in the body and cystic enlargement which may be either congenital or due to an obstruction further down the urinary tract. The clinical signs are due to infection, if present, and to the build-up of the toxic waste products which are usually filtered out by the kidneys. These accumulate in the blood causing uraemia which can be detected by blood tests. Symptoms include chronic weight loss, excessive drinking and urination, inappetence, dullness and fever if infection is present. Treatment which may be prescribed includes antibiotics, fluids and anabolic steroids. However, in old animals with long-standing kidney disease, the prognosis is poor and euthanasia is often recommended.

Lameness This is a common problem in donkeys. Most lamenesses are to be found in the foot (see Abscesses, Laminitis, Seedy Toe, Thrush, Mud Fever) but a variety of other musculo-skeletal conditions can be the cause. A lot of the traumatic and stress injuries that are common in horses are not often seen in donkeys because they are not usually required to perform the same type of work. Strained tendons do sometimes occur in donkeys and injuries to joints can result in bruising and swelling, the knees and fetlocks being most frequently affected.

Arthritis is not uncommon in old donkeys, often with new bone growth around the joints. A specific example of this is bone spavin which occurs in the hocks, usually in both legs and can be very painful initially. See also Arthritis, Spavin.

Fractures and dislocations can occur following traumatic injury. Depending on the site and nature of the fracture, treatment can be successful with either surgery or simply immobilisation of the limb in a plaster cast. However, certain types of limb fractures are not easily treated and it is kindest to relieve the donkey of suffering by euthanasia. Dislocation of the hip can occur in donkeys. Some individuals appear to have a shallow socket in the hip joint and this allows the leg to be dislocated more easily. It usually occurs after an awkward fall (the donkey may do the splits) and there is a sudden onset of severe lameness in the affected hind limb, which is reluctant to bear any weight.

Examination using X-rays is often required to establish the cause of lameness. Another aid to diagnosis is the use of temporary nerve blocks with local anaesthetic which can help to determine the site of lameness. See also Radial Paralysis, Stifle Lock, Stringhalt.

Laminitis Also known as founder or fever of the feet. This is an extremely painful condition of the feet and is due to congestion of the sensitive structures (laminae) within the foot. It is usually precipitated by the over-zealous introduction of high-quality feed (especially with a high-protein content) into the diet, or can occur following liver damage or illnesses accompanied by fever. Introduction of a new high-protein food should take place very gradually to avoid the likelihood of laminitis (and diarrhoea). All four feet can be affected although the front feet are almost invariably affected first. The donkey is reluctant to bear weight on any affected foot, often holding each one up in turn, and may try to take the weight on its heels or lie down. The feet are warm to the touch and the soles of the feet are extremely tender. If the condition becomes chronic, changes take place in the foot such that the pedal bone rotates downwards and can penetrate the sole in extreme cases. There may also be separation of the outer wall from the rest of the hoof. It is necessary, in these cases, to reshape the foot and the fitting of a wide-web shoe may be of benefit. The treatment of acute laminitis involves correction of the underlying cause particularly with respect to diet. Only hay or feeding straw should be fed with no concentrates and no grass unless it is of very poor quality. Pain-killers are administered and attempts are made to improve the circulation within the foot. This is done by soaking the feet in warm water (or alternate hot and cold bathing) and encouraging the donkey to walk unless there is rotation of the pedal bone. Deep, soft bedding such as peat (which also has a cooling effect on the feet) or wood shavings makes standing more comfortable for a donkey with laminitis. Feed additives containing biotin and methionine are useful as they stimulate new growth of horn.

Lice Donkeys are affected by both biting and sucking lice. It is contagious and is usually seen when donkeys are housed as the lice can survive in the buildings. Lice infestation causes intense irritation and by rubbing and biting, large areas of hair can be lost. Less severe infestation will give the coat a dull, scaly, unkempt ('lousy') appearance. In extreme cases the donkey may show a loss of condition and anaemia. Adult lice and the egg cases (nits) can often be seen in the coat but failure to find any does not necessarily preclude their presence. Insecticidal powders are usually used in the treatment of lice but it may be necessary to treat on a fortnightly basis to prevent re-infestation. Pour-on insecticides are often effective.

Liver Disease Liver lesions are quite common in donkeys but clinical signs are not seen until a large percentage of the organ is affected as the remaining healthy tissue can usually cope adequately. The most common causes of liver disease are:
1 Fatty liver and hyperlipaemia.
2 Ragwort poisoning.
3 Hydatid cysts.
4 Hepatitis – Caused by bacterial or viral infection.
5 Bile duct obstruction – May be a sequel to 2 or 3 (above) or may be due to the presence of parasites such as liver fluke or ascarid worms (not common).
Liver damage can usually (but not always) be detected from blood tests. In an acute condition, eg hepatitis there may be fever, abdominal pain, jaundice, dullness and anorexia. Chronic liver disease can cause jaundice, wasting, inappetence, oedema and diarrhoea. Neurological signs may be seen (as in ragwort poisoning) due to the build-up of ammonia in the blood, which is not being

processed to a less toxic form by the diseased liver. Treatment with antibiotics, anti-inflammatories, fluids, glucose, B vitamins and anabolic steroids may be useful in some cases. This may give the liver time to regenerate itself but chronic liver damage has a poor prognosis. See Hyperlipaemia, Hydatid Cysts, Ragwort Poisoning.

Lungworm The lungworm found in equines is called *Dictyocaulus arnfieldi*. The donkey is the natural host for this parasite and can harbour large numbers of lungworm without showing any clinical signs. The horse, however, produces a strong immune reaction to the parasite and this produces a chronic cough. Infected donkeys shed larvae in their dung but horses do not always and this makes diagnosis more difficult in the horse than the donkey. As the donkey can be a reservoir of infection, with no clinical signs, many horse owners are reluctant to graze their horses on the same pasture as donkeys. This need no longer be a problem as drugs are now available which are very efficient in treating lungworm. If both donkey and horse are wormed with a suitable product prior to introduction onto a *clean* pasture, then cross-infection is unlikely to occur. To be sure, it is advisable to have dung samples tested on three consecutive days to determine whether worming has been effective before moving the animals.

Mange Sarcoptic and psoroptic mange (not common in the UK) are caused by two types of mange mite. There is extreme irritation and hair loss with thick, scabby lesions over the body. The disease, if diagnosed, must be notified to the Ministry of Agriculture. Chorioptic mange is caused by another mange mite and affects the skin and hair around the fetlocks. It is uncommon in donkeys, as is demodectic mange.

Mastitis This is an inflammation of the udder usually as a result of infection. It is usually only seen in lactating mares but occasionally it can occur in the non-lactating udder. Some offspring, if not properly weaned, will continue to suckle a little for many years and these mares are also prone to mastitis. One or both sides of the udder are hot, swollen and painful and there may be oedema along the belly in front of the udder. The milk will change its appearance usually becoming thicker and pus-like or it may become grey and watery. Sometimes the milk is stained with blood. There may also be an accompanying fever with dullness and inappetence and the mare may vigorously resent handling of the udder. It is necessary to treat mastitis with antibiotics. Bathing the udder with warm water and stripping out the milk regularly will help to relieve the pain.

Mud Fever This is seen in donkeys which are kept in conditions which are wet and muddy underfoot. There is a moist inflammation of the skin from the fetlock down and this allows entry of bacteria especially the dermatophilus organism which is also responsible for rain scald. The lower legs may become swollen and tender and the donkey is often lame. Some also show signs of systemic illness and become dull and inappetent. It is essential to keep affected animals inside on dry bedding to allow the legs to dry out and to keep them clean using an antiseptic and possibly also anti-inflammatory agents can be applied. It may also be necessary to administer antibiotics by injection. See Rain Scald.

Nasal Discharge Discharges from the nostrils can be unilateral or bilateral and the type of discharge can be classified as follows:
1 Serous (watery) – which is usually very mild but which may progress to
2 Muco-purulent – which can be thick and white or creamy in colour.
3 Regurgitated food – a green discharge containing food as a result of vomiting or an inability to swallow (see Choke, Colic, Dysphagia, Grass Sickness).
4 Blood – either from frank haemorrhage or in conjuction with a mucoid or purulent discharge.
The most likely cause of a serous or muco-purulent discharge is an upper respiratory tract infection such as flu or equine herpesvirus infection and the discharge is usually bilateral (from both nostrils). Other causes include sinusitis, strangles, gutteral pouch infection, or the presence of a foreign body. These may cause a discharge from one or both nostrils. Blood from the nostrils may be due to ruptured blood vessels either in the back of the nose or possibly in the lungs. Occasionally there may be bleeding after a stomach tube has been passed through the nose. This may look rather dramatic but it is self-limiting and the bleeding usually stops quite quickly. Other possible causes of bloody nasal discharges are fungal infections or necrosis of the bones at the back of the nose, or rarely, a tumour may be involved. Donkeys with respiratory tract infections should be kept in a relatively dust-free environment as the condition can be exacerbated by irritation from dust in hay and straw.

Obesity This is a common problem in donkeys in this country but rarely encountered in countries where donkeys are required to work. The usual sites for deposition of fat in donkeys is on the neck, on either side of the chest wall – giving a 'saddle bag' appearance – and around the but-tocks. Fat is also stored in large quantities in the abdomen and surrounding various organs, especially the heart and kidneys. It is unhealthy for a donkey to be too fat. Exercise tolerance is reduced, there is extra strain on the heart and limbs, and the donkey is likely to develop hyperlipaemia much more quickly following a bout of anorexia.

Prevention is better than cure and it is preferable to control a donkey's diet before it becomes overweight than to have to embark on a long, often unrewarding slimming regime. The fat crest on the neck is notoriously difficult to remove and it is possible to have an otherwise very thin donkey that has retained its fat neck. A donkey that is not working, growing, pregnant, lactating, sick or thin does not usually require supplementation of the diet with concentrate feeds. Two kilos (4–5lb) of hay per day is sufficient for an average-sized donkey and should be fed in conjunction with an ad-lib supply of feeding straw, eg good-quality barley straw. In order to lose weight, the ration of hay may need to be reduced to 1kg (2–3lb) but ad-lib straw should always be available. If the donkey is at grass, grazing should be restricted, either by only using a small area of pasture at a time and eating this well down or by restricting the time allowed for grazing. Feeding straw can be made available at all times. Exercise should be encouraged. It is important not to try to lose weight too rapidly as this can also precipitate hyperlipaemia.

Oedema This is an accumulation of watery fluid in one or more of the body cavities or under the skin. The subcutaneous site is the one most likely to be seen in the donkey, particularly in the region of the belly, where it is called ventral oedema or around the area of a wound where there is a lot of tissue reaction. Fluid tends to accumulate on the underside of the body due to the effects of gravity. Ventral oedema can vary in size from a small patch to an area covering most of the lower belly and the raised area can be 5–7cm (2–3in) thick. When pressed with a finger, a depression is left in the affected area for a while. Usually this type of oedema is a result of local irritation such as lying on a wet, dirty bed. Other causes include impaired circulation due to heart or liver disease and it sometimes is associated with respiratory infections or parasitism. Other cases appear to have no obvious cause. Treatment involves frequent massaging of the area to mobilise the fluid and this can be aided by the use of diuretics.

Parascaris Infection This is the large roundworm of equines and generally only a problem in foals as resistance is developed in older donkeys. The eggs, which are passed in the dung of an infected foal, are sticky and very resistant so that they can survive for a long time in the environment. When a foal takes in mature eggs by mouth, the eggs hatch and the larvae thus released then migrate from the intestine to the liver and then later to the lungs. Once in the lungs, the larvae make their way up the airways and are eventually coughed up into the throat and swallowed. The larvae then develop in the intestine to the adult stage which are about 10–15cm (4–6in) long. These produce eggs which are passed in the dung and the life cycle is continued.

The presence of migrating larvae in the liver and lungs can give rise to signs associated with these organs and coughing with nasal discharge is a common sign. The presence of large numbers of adult worms in the gut can lead to impaction, colic and, rarely, rupture of the intestine. Other signs of infection include failure to gain weight, dull staring coat, pot-belly and, occasionally, nervous disturbances. Diagnosis can be confirmed by faecal examination to demonstrate the presence of ascarid eggs but these are not present in the dung until the foal is at least eleven weeks old. To control the occurrence of the disease, mares should be wormed prior to foaling, the foaling box should be thoroughly disinfected after each occupation, foals should be wormed from six weeks of age and, if possible, foals should not graze pasture which may have been contaminated by foals in the previous year.

Parasites Donkeys are commonly parasitised by internal (endo-) and external (ecto-) parasites. Ectoparasites are responsible for the majority of skin diseases which are characterised by itchiness. See Flies, Lice, Mange, Sweet Itch.

Insecticidal drugs are used to treat ectoparasites and can be administered in various forms: powders; pour-on liquids; sprays; or impregnated tags or collars.

Another itchy skin condition known as 'seat itch' can be caused by the irritation of eggs laid by the pinworm around the anus. This causes an infected donkey to rub its hindquarters on any available gate post, fence etc and can cause extensive skin damage particularly around the base of the tail. The pinworm is an endoparasite and can be controlled by routine worming. Donkeys should be regularly wormed to control the variety of endoparasites which they may harbour. These include strongyle worms, ascarid worms, lungworms and tapeworms. Lungworms and tapeworms require specific drugs for effective treatment. The larvae of bot flies can be present in the stomach of donkeys. They do not usually create a lot of problems unless they are present in large quantities when there may be inflamma-

tion and ulceration of the lining of the stomach. The adult bot flies lay their eggs on the hairs of the legs, abdomen and shoulders of the donkey and in so doing can cause annoyance. The eggs hatch when the donkey licks or bites the affected areas and are taken into the mouth from where they migrate to the stomach. Specific drugs are required to treat the bot larvae and this should take place at the end of the year after the first frosts have killed the adult flies and re-infection will not occur. Regular grooming may also reduce the number of eggs and larvae taken in by mouth. Other internal parasites of donkeys include hydatid cysts and the liver fluke, which is not common.

Photosensitisation This is a type of sunburn and is seen in some white and broken-coloured donkeys during the summer. Usually, only the pink, non-pigmented skin around the muzzle and face is affected, though it can occur on any unprotected area of non-pigmented skin. Some types of plants, eg St John's wort contain substances which make the donkey prone to photosensitisation. Liver disease may have the same effect in some cases. The affected areas become inflamed and later raw and scabby. Barrier creams can be used to keep the skin supple and provide protection from the sun. Severe cases should be kept inside when the sun is shining. An anti-bacterial, anti-inflammatory ointment can be used to reduce the inflammation and prevent bacterial infection of the damaged skin.

Pneumonia This is inflammation of the lungs and is usually the result of infection. It may follow an upper respiratory tract infection or a period of general malaise where the donkey's resistance to pathogenic organisms in the environment is lowered. The affected donkey is usually dull and inappetent with a high temperature, rapid shallow breathing and raised pulse rate. There may be a cough and a nasal discharge and the lungs will sound harsh, often with the presence of fluid in the chest. Antibiotic therapy is required together with supportive nutritional therapy to prevent hyperlipaemia occurring. The environment should be kept as dust free as possible.

Poisoning Most poisonings that occur in donkeys are the result of eating poisonous plants. Most common of these is ragwort poisoning but bracken and horsetail poisoning can also occur (see separate entries). Some plant poisons give rise to abdominal pain and diarrhoea, eg buttercups and acorns, and some will also produce nervous signs, eg nightshades, hemlock and laburnum. St John's wort is an example of a plant which causes photosensitisation and yew is extremely poisonous, affected animals usually being found dead.

Poisoning by chemical agents can also occur but is not common. Lead poisoning may be induced by the donkey licking objects coated with a lead-based paint. This will give rise to anaemia, weakness and neurological signs including inability to swallow. The feeding, to donkeys, of cattle feed containing the growth promoter, Monensin, can also lead to poisoning. Heart failure and death can occur if sufficient quantities are consumed.

Poisoning can occur from contaminated feed. The contaminant may be the toxin of a fungus, eg aflatoxin, or the fungus itself eg ergot of rye which can cause poor circulation and, later, gangrene of the extremities. Botulism is caused by the toxin of a bacterium *Clostridium botulinum*. See Botulism.

Quidding This is when a donkey will take food into the mouth, chew it and then spit it out. Sometimes improperly chewed food collects between the cheeks and the cheek teeth. It is usually a result of improper chewing due to pain in the mouth or restricted movement of the jaws. Teeth abnormalities are usually to blame, either because they are loose, or they have worn down irregularly. Regular examination of the mouth is to be recommended and rasping of the cheek teeth at least once a year should be carried out in donkeys over five years of age. See Teeth.

Radial Paralysis This is occasionally seen in donkeys. The affected forelimb is paralysed and the donkey is unable to advance the leg or take weight on it. The nerve may be damaged following fracture of the first rib or by pressure on the nerve from a lesion such as an abscess or tumour in the axilla or elsewhere along the nerve's path. A similar type of paralysis is very occasionally seen following a period of recumbency where pressure on the underneath limb can cause a temporary paralysis of the nerve. It may be compounded by inflammation of the muscles of the limb.

Ragwort Poisoning Ragwort is poisonous in both the fresh and the dried states but when fresh it is bitter and avoided by donkeys unless there is little else to eat. When dried, in hay for example, it is tasteless and readily eaten by donkeys. This is the usual means by which poisoning occurs. The effects are cumulative and large amounts may need to be taken in before clinical signs are seen. These may not appear until long after the intake of ragwort has stopped, often several months having elapsed. The poisonous components of the plant affect the liver and normal tissue is replaced by fibrous tissue. This is called cirrhosis of the liver

and is similar to the liver of a human alcoholic. Although the liver damage is chronic, the disease is usually presented with the sudden onset of nervous signs. There is blindness, staggering, aimless wandering, circling, head pressing and the donkey is very distressed. The symptoms are quite characteristic of the condition and can usually be confirmed from a blood test or a liver biopsy. Euthanasia in these cases is recommended as there is no treatment. If ragwort poisoning is suspected before clinical signs develop and a blood test shows abnormalities of liver function, then administration of B vitamins may be of some benefit. Ragwort is easily pulled out of the ground with its roots and every attempt should be made to clear pastures of this plant before it is at the seeding stage. Spraying with a herbicide may be necessary if there is heavy contamination of a pasture. Hay should never be made from fields where ragwort is present.

Rain Scald This is a skin condition which is caused by *Dermatophilus congolensis*, the organism which is also involved in mud fever. The condition can arise when the donkey has been standing in heavy driving rain and excessive wetting of the skin has occurred. This allows penetration of the organism into the skin causing a dermatitis. The hair is usually lost in small patches over the body leaving pink skin exposed which may become moist and scabby. The hair is often in tufts, matted with dried crusts and giving a 'paint brush' appearance. An affected donkey should be kept in the dry and mild cases will improve by doing this alone. Additionally, the skin may be washed with an antiseptic solution and severe cases may require antibiotic therapy.

Redworms see Strongyle Infection.

Rig A rig, also called a cryptorchid, is a male donkey in which either one or both testicles remain undescended at the age when it is expected that they should be in the scrotum. A rig can often be aggressive and difficult to handle and surgery to remove the retained testicle is usually advisable. Sometimes it will descend at a later date or following injection with hormones. It may be retained either within the abdomen or in the canal which connects the abdomen to the scrotum. The retained testicle is usually defective and, when in the abdomen, may rarely become cancerous. If no testicles are present in the scrotum and it is suspected that a donkey is a rig, then a fairly simple blood test can be performed to confirm or deny this.

Ringworm This is a highly contagious fungal infection of the skin. It can be spread by direct contact with affected animals or indirectly by brushes, tack, stables, clothes etc which have been in contact with the fungus. There are several different types of fungus that can cause ringworm in donkeys (and horses), with slightly different clinical signs, and some types can be transmitted from other species of animal, notably cattle. Some types can also infect humans. The skin lesions are variable but usually start as raised patches of skin on which the hair breaks to give round or irregular areas of hair loss, often with greyish scales or crusts. The lesions may be inflamed and moist and they are usually, but not always, itchy. They are often found around the head and in the saddle or girth region (if tack is used on the donkey) but they can occur anywhere on the body. To confirm the diagnosis of ringworm, a skin scraping is often taken by the vet. Infected donkeys should be isolated from other animals to prevent further spread of the disease. Treatment then involves the administration of anti-fungal drugs as a wash, or in the feed, or both. Brushes, tack, rugs and stables should also be treated with an anti-fungal preparation to prevent re-infection.

Salmonella Infection This is not a common problem in donkeys, particularly those that are kept on their own, but it may be suspected in cases of acute enteritis especially where there is blood present in the diarrhoea. Donkeys that recover from an acute infection may be left with a chronic diarrhoea and some may remain carriers of the disease without symptoms. These carriers may start to shed salmonella again after a period of stress, eg other illnesses, transportation, change of environment etc. The disease in young foals can be very serious and ultimately fatal. The foal is extremely dull and unwilling to suckle, usually having a very high temperature. There is also diarrhoea, pneumonia and later the joints may become swollen. Some foals may also have nervous signs. Fluid and antibiotic therapy is needed in these cases but affected foals usually do not survive. It is important that a newborn foal receives the first milk (colostrum) from his mother within a few hours of birth. The colostrum is a thick secretion which contains antibodies necessary for the foal to fight infections. After twenty-four hours of age, the foal cannot absorb these antibodies from the gut, so it is vital that colostrum is obtained within this time. Strict hygienic precautions must be taken when salmonella is suspected and affected donkeys should be kept in isolation. It should be remembered that humans can also be infected by salmonella, so cleanliness and disinfection is important after handling infected donkeys.

Sandcrack This is a crack in the hoof wall which extends down from the coronet. It is usually a sequel to an injury of the coronary band or from excessive dryness of the hoof wall possibly due to over-enthusiastic rasping. The donkey may be lame and rarely there may be evidence of infection underneath the crack. The crack can be prevented from spreading further down the wall by grooving the hoof wall and the weight-bearing surface of the hoof wall below the fissure may be pared away to reduce the pressure on the sandcrack. If lameness or infection is present, it may be beneficial to poultice the foot for a few days. The addition of biotin to the diet will encourage the growth of new horn.

Sarcoids These are skin tumours and are often seen in donkeys. It is thought that they may be caused by a viral infection which is possibly spread by flying insects. The condition is not, however, highly contagious although the incidence of the disease is probably higher where large numbers of donkeys are kept together. The lesions can grow rapidly from small nodules and can become very large – some can be several inches in diameter. Sarcoids can usually be felt as hard, rounded masses within the skin and some have a distinct 'neck' on them. Others are more invasive, are flatter and it is more difficult to feel a distinct edge to them as they spread into the surrounding tissues. They can occur on their own or in groups. A single sarcoid may, on closer examination, be found to be surrounded by multiple small satellite tumours. This type is the most difficult to treat and recurrence is common. As the sarcoid grows, it usually ulcerates through the skin and is easily traumatised and infected. The most common sites for the occurrence of sarcoids in donkeys are: the sheath in males; the udder in females; around the eyes, ears and nose; and on the brisket. The tumours can, however, be found anywhere on the body. When they occur in a position which is constantly in contact with another part of the body, eg the inside of the hind leg, then the sarcoid can spread to the area which is repeatedly touching it. A variety of methods are used to treat sarcoids and normally a combination of these is employed. Usually, a general anaesthetic is required for the operation. Some cases need only one treatment and do not recur, but others may require treatment on several occasions, especially if there are a lot of seedling tumours around the main one or if the sarcoid is particularly invasive. The commonest methods of treatment that are employed are surgical excision (cutting out); diathermy (using a concentrated source of heat); cryosurgery (freezing treatment); and injection into, and around, the tumour with BCG vaccine. BCG vaccine, used in humans against tuberculosis, will stimulate the body's immune system to destroy the tumour. Surgical excision alone can be used if the lesions are easy to remove with well-defined edges, but if there is a possibility that some of the tumour may be left behind or that smaller ones are growing around it, then it is advisable to use this method in conjunction with one of the others. The most effective method is to de-bulk the tumour using surgical excision or diathermy and then to freeze the base of the tumour to kill any residual tumour cells. BCG vaccine may be used either on its own or after prior treatment by another method. Following treatment with cryosurgery or BCG vaccine there is usually a fairly vigorous tissue reaction and the area may swell, exude pus and become scabby. This is the normal process of healing where dead tumour tissue is being rejected. Keep the wound clean and free from flies. Eventually the sarcoids will slough off and healthy, pink tissue will be left.

Seedy Toe In seedy toe, there is a separation of the wall of the hoof from the underlying structures and this gives rise to a cavity in the foot. The lesion usually occurs at the toe but can extend to either side. The cavity, which extends from the bearing surface of the foot, is filled with a crumbly type of horn. Dirt and debris can also accumulate in the space. If the material in the cavity exerts pressure on the sensitive structures of the foot, or if the cavity is very large, then the donkey may be lame. To treat seedy toe, the impacted material needs to be removed and the hole can be plugged, to prevent debris from re-entering the cavity. An antibiotic is often applied to the cavity to prevent infection. Supplementation of the diet with biotin will encourage new healthy hoof to grow. It is not known what causes seedy toe but it is sometimes associated with a previous attack of laminitis.

Sinusitis The paranasal sinuses of the donkey are cavities of the skull which are connected directly or indirectly with the nose. The roots of some of the cheek teeth extend into one of these cavities, the maxillary sinus. Infection of the paranasal sinuses can occur after an upper respiratory tract infection such as flu, or strangles, or from an infected tooth root. The affected sinus will become filled with mucus and/or pus and will usually discharge this through the nostril of that side. If the head is tapped over the sinuses, then the sound will be dull on the affected side. Treatment may require drilling a hole in the bone over the sinus and flushing out the cavity until the infection has resolved. An infected tooth may need to be removed. Antibiotics are also used. See also Nasal Discharge, Teeth.

Skin Diseases A number of skin diseases are common in donkeys and the causes may be parasitic, allergic, bacterial, fungal, metabolic, neoplastic or toxic. See Abscesses, Alopecia, Flies, Lice, Mange, Mud Fever, Oedema, Photosensitisation, Rain Scald, Ringworm, Sarcoid, Sweet Itch, Urticaria.

Spavin Bone spavin in donkeys is not uncommon. It is an osteoarthritis of the hock joint when new bone is deposited around the small bones of this joint. Its occurrence is not restricted to old donkeys and the cause is not fully understood. It may follow a period of inflammation of the joint and some people think that there is an inherited predisposition to the condition. There will be a progressive stiffness and lameness in the affected hind legs, usually both are affected but one may be worse than the other. The donkey may be seen to hold each affected leg up, in turn, but resents the hock being fully flexed and doing this will lead to a temporary increase in severity of the lameness. It may prove to be difficult to pick up the hind feet in order to trim them and the donkey may have difficulty in lifting the hind legs over a raised obstacle. A bony enlargement is occasionally seen on the inner aspect of the hock. With rest and time, possibly up to a year, the joint will settle down and some of the small bones of the joint may fuse together. The lameness improves gradually and the donkey will eventually be nearly sound, although strenuous work is not advisable. In horses, this process can be speeded up using a surgical technique called arthrodesis. As donkeys are not usually required to work, it is probably better to just rest them. Anti-inflammatory pain-killers can be used in the early, painful stages.

Stifle Lock The anatomy of the donkey's stifle (the equivalent of the human knee joint) is similar to that of the horse. The donkey is able to 'lock' this joint in order to support the weight of his body when standing by fixing the position of the patella (or knee cap). Problems arise when the animal is unable to unlock the joint properly at each step as it walks. Occasionally, the leg is completely locked and is dragged behind in an extended position. Veterinary attention is usually urgently required although a sudden fright may cause the donkey to jerk the leg back into position. More commonly, the condition in donkeys is seen as an abnormal hind-leg gait. The affected leg (or both legs) will have a jerky action and the condition may be confused with stringhalt. As the donkey walks, the leg will be held in extension for a longer than normal period of time and then 'snatched' up. This may or may not affect every stride. Usually the condition is seen in young, unfit or thin donkeys and once the muscles of the hind leg become more developed (by exercise and/or weight gain) the gait returns to normal. In some persistent or very severe cases, surgery is necessary and this is carried out on the conscious animal under local anaesthetic.

Strangles This disease is rarely seen these days, although it used to be very common. It is a highly contagious bacterial infection of the upper respiratory tract and the lymph glands of the head are usually swollen and purulent. There is fever, purulent discharges from the nose and eyes and a cough. The lymph nodes are enlarged and purulent and may interfere with swallowing. These later abscessate and burst, releasing the pus. The discharges are all highly infectious and an affected donkey should be isolated, along with its feed, buckets etc. Most affected animals recover and are immune to re-infection. Nursing care is very important as the donkey is unwilling to eat. Soft sloppy feeds can be offered; warm compresses can be applied to abscesses to encourage them to burst; and all discharges should be cleaned away to make the donkey more comfortable. Antibiotics, notably penicillin, are useful in the early stages. In rare cases, the infection may spread to other parts of the body and cause abscesses there (called 'bastard strangles'). The commonest sites are the abdominal lymph nodes, the liver and the spleen. This can give rise to intermittent abdominal pain and therefore signs of colic. Diagnosis and treatment of this condition is difficult.

Stringhalt This is a condition in which the nervous control of the hind legs is affected. There is a sudden snatching up of one or both hind legs when the donkey is walking and can be exacerbated by turning it in circles. The leg may be lifted high off the ground, sometimes as high as the belly. The cause is not known and there is no treatment but the condition is not painful. It can occur at any age and should not be confused with the locking stifle where the hind-leg action is slightly different.

Strongyle Worm Infection There are a number of species of strongyles (red worms) that can infect donkeys. Those causing the most damage are the large strongyles, particularly *Strongylus vulgaris*, due to the migration through the body by immature forms of these parasites. The small strongyles complete their life cycle in the large intestine and caecum (the donkey equivalent of our appendix) and cause less damage. The larvae of *Strongylus vulgaris* have a unique migratory route which involves travelling up the blood vessels of the intestine to one of the major arteries of the gut. They develop here for some time, causing damage to the blood vessels before returning to the intestine to complete their life cycle. There may be a massive reaction around affected blood vessels and blood clots and tissue sometimes break off and lodge in smaller blood vessels, causing an obstruction to blood flow. This can lead to colic. Sometimes the artery becomes dilated with thin walls which can burst but this is extremely rare (see Aneurysm, Colic). The other large strongyle species have their own migratory routes across the abdominal cavity and through the liver.

Donkeys acquire infections of a mixture of these worms by grazing contaminated pasture. Once the life cycle is complete in the donkey, eggs are produced and passed out onto the pasture where they hatch when conditions are favourable. These develop to larvae which are capable of infecting more donkeys and horses. Most donkeys harbour a number of these worms without showing signs of illness but, if left untreated, the numbers can build up to an unacceptably high level and clinical signs are seen. These include diarrhoea, chronic weight loss, poor condition, anaemia and sometimes colic. Occasionally, nervous signs are seen if migrating larvae get lost and travel to the brain.

It is normally recommended that donkeys are wormed every four to eight weeks depending on the number of equines grazing together and the type of drug used. This may be modified if an effective system of pasture management is also employed. This would involve rotation of paddocks being used, resting the pasture, picking up droppings and grazing with other species of animals, ie cattle or sheep, which are not affected by donkey worms. A worming and pasture management regime can be formulated for individual donkeys by your veterinary surgeon. It is usually advisable to change the wormer used from time to time to prevent the parasites from building up resistance to a particular drug.

Strongyloides Infection *Strongyloides westeri* is the threadworm of equines. It affects foals but rarely causes clinical signs other than diarrhoea in severe infections. Foals acquire the infection either through the mother's milk or from penetration of the skin by infective larvae. Treatment with most of the usual wormers is effective but some may need to be given at higher than normal dose rates.

Sunburn see Photosensitisation

Sweet Itch This is an allergic skin reaction to the bite of Culicoides midges. It occurs, in affected animals, every year from about April until Oc-

tober in England. There is an intense itching and
the donkey will usually rub the skin along its
mane, back and base of the tail, leading to hair
loss and red, inflamed, scabby skin which may
become thickened. It is possible to control this
condition by management alone but the use of
drugs which relieve irritation, such as corticosteroids, is also beneficial. The affected donkey,
or one that is known to be prone to the condition,
should be housed during the day, particularly
around dawn and dusk when the midges are most
active. Strong direct sunlight can aggravate the
inflamed skin, so this should be avoided. The
housing should be away from ponds or damp areas
where the insects breed. A thin sheet which covers
the donkey's back, mane and top of its head can
be fitted to provide a physical barrier to the insect.
A thin layer of liquid paraffin over the donkey's
back will also create a barrier but is very messy.
Insect repellents should be used in the stable and
on the donkey and impregnated cattle ear tags are
very useful for this purpose. They can be attached
to a collar or head collar but must be in contact
with the skin to be effective.

Tapeworms The tapeworm of donkeys and horses
is *Anoplocephala perfoliata*. It rarely causes clinical
disease but loss of condition, diarrhoea and colic
can be attributed to severe infestations. Infection
is by the eating of forage mites in which the
tapeworm has an intermediate stage of development. Treatment involves using a wormer which
has an activity against tapeworms. The intermediate stage of the dog tapeworm gives rise to
hydatid cysts in the liver. See Hydatid Cysts.

Teeth Problems The majority of problems associated with teeth can be related to uneven wear
of the cheek teeth as the donkey ages. Rough,
sharp edges can form on the outer edges of the
cheek teeth and can cause damage to the gums,
making the mouth painful and chewing difficult.
In extreme cases, the edges of the upper or lower
teeth can overlap their opposite numbers to such
an extent that sideways movement of the jaws is
restricted. To prevent this, the donkey's mouth
should be examined regularly and rasping of the
outer edges of the cheek teeth should be carried
out yearly from five years of age if necessary. The
front cheek tooth in either the upper or lower jaw
can overgrow the opposite one, forming a hook
which will need to be clipped off and this procedure sometimes requires a general anaesthetic.
Teeth may sometimes become loose in their soc-
kets usually in old donkeys or as the result of
infection, neoplasia or injury. Loose teeth should
be removed as they can be painful. Infections of
tooth roots can cause loosening of the tooth and

if its root is located in a paranasal sinus then
sinusitis can ensue. It is usually necessary to remove the offending tooth. In young donkeys,
there may be some pain associated with the loss
of temporary teeth and the eruption of permanent
teeth. The congenital conditions of over- or undershot jaw, where the upper and lower rows of incisor teeth do not meet, may make the grazing of
grass difficult although other feeds are usually
managed well. In an overshot jaw the upper jaw
projects too far forward and in an undershot jaw
the lower jaw is too long. In old donkeys the front
(incisor) teeth of the top jaw wear down, sometimes back to the gum. These donkeys may also
have difficulty in grazing. Abnormalities of the
teeth can lead to quidding (where partially chewed
food is spat out), colic, dribbling, reluctance to
eat, weight loss and in some cases sinusitis. See
Colic, Dysphagia, Quidding, Sinusitis, Weight
Loss.

Temperature The normal temperature of a donkey is 98.8°F but can vary between 98° and 99.5°F
in clinically normal donkeys. The temperature is
usually raised as the result of an infection but can
also be elevated if there is pain or following exercise. Healthy foals usually have a slightly higher
temperature than adults.

Tetanus This is a particularly distressing disease
in donkeys which can easily be prevented by
routine vaccination. The cause is a toxin produced
by the organism *Clostridium tetani* which normally
lives in the soil where it can survive for many
years. The organism can gain entry to the body
via wounds particularly small puncture wounds
which may not be immediately noticeable. As the
organism is in the soil, it is also normally found
in the donkey's digestive tract and can enter the
body by wounds or ulceration of the lining of the
tract including damage caused by heavy worm
burdens. Once inside the body, the organism mul-
tiplies and produces a toxin which affects the donkey's nervous system. Foals may be infected via
the navel cord at birth.

The toxin causes excessive nervous stimulation
of the muscles which go into spasm. The head is
usually affected first with rigid ears and restricted
movements of the jaws and the donkey may adopt
an anxious expression. The nostrils are dilated
and if the head is raised quickly the third eyelid
(the membrane at the inner corner of the eye)
flickers across the eye quite noticeably. The tail
is often raised and there may be profuse sweating
and over-sensitivity to touch and sound. There is
a progressive stiffness of the neck and leg muscles
and eventually the respiratory muscles become
affected. In advanced cases the limbs are held in

rigid extension and later there may be convulsions and the affected donkey will die from exhaustion and respiratory or heart failure. Treatment is possible in the early stages and will involve the administration of tetanus antiserum and antibiotics especially penicillin. It may be necessary to tranquillise the donkey and he should be kept in a dark quiet box to avoid over-stimulation of the senses. Nursing care is very important as the donkey is often unable to eat or drink properly.

It is simple to prevent the disease by following a routine vaccination programme. The vaccine (toxoid) will stimulate the donkey's immune system to produce its own antibodies to the disease and this may take several weeks to develop after an initial dose. The antiserum provides ready-made antibodies which are effective immediately and this is often administered to donkeys with wounds, where their vaccinations are not up to date, or if the wound is particularly deep or contaminated. A booster toxoid can be given at the same time. Vaccination can begin in foals at three to five months of age and a second dose is required four to six weeks later. A booster is required one year later and after this, booster injections should be given at one or two yearly intervals. Pregnant mares should receive a booster dose a month before foaling so that they can pass on a good level of antibodies to the foal in the colostrum. It may be advisable to give foals a dose of antiserum at birth and to treat the navel with an antibiotic or antiseptic as soon as possible after birth.

Thrush This is an infection of the frog of the donkey's foot which, if very severe, may spread to adjacent areas of the sole. The horn of the frog becomes soft, black and very smelly. Lameness is not always present, but, if severe, the condition can be very painful. Affected donkeys may be seen stamping their feet continuously. It is caused by standing in wet, dirty bedding or wet ground for long periods of time or if the feet are not cleaned out often enough. It is necessary to remove all the infected material and, if this is very extensive, a general anaesthetic is sometimes required. The foot should be kept clean and dry and an antibiotic is applied to the foot which may need to be kept bandaged initially. Spraying the feet with a gentian violet and antibiotic spray after trimming can help to keep the condition under control.

Urticaria This is an allergic reaction, usually to something that has been eaten or that has been in contact with the skin. The body and neck are covered with numerous small oedematous swellings which may merge to form larger plaques. The allergy may also affect other parts of the body, such as the lungs, and the donkey may be dull with laboured breathing and a rapid pulse rate. To treat the allergy corticosteroids and antihistamines are usually injected. If possible, the cause of the allergy should be identified and removed. Often the cause is a plant protein so donkeys at grass should be kept off the pasture until the condition is resolved.

Vaccinations Vaccination against specific diseases stimulates the donkey's immune system to produce antibodies to protect it from that disease. It is absolutely essential that all donkeys are vaccinated for tetanus and is highly recommended that vaccination against equine flu is carried out particularly if there are other donkeys or horses in the area. See Equine Herpesvirus, Equine Influenza and Tetanus.

Warts Some donkeys may be affected by multiple, small warts which are not the same as sarcoids but are also caused by a virus. Usually the warts drop off without treatment but occasionally it may be necessary to remove them surgically. If the disease is allowed to take its course, a recovered animal is usually immune to re-infection.

Weight Loss Weight loss can be a problem in some donkeys particularly old ones. It can follow a period of debilitation or stress when the intake of food is reduced. In donkeys which have lost weight the diet should be checked to ensure that it is adequate. If the diet is correct then other common causes of weight loss include teeth abnormalities (which prevent food being properly chewed), heavy worm burdens and liver or kidney disease.

Sometimes food intake is reduced in old donkeys that spend a lot of time standing around rather than eating. If this is the case more concentrates can be fed in the diet but these should always be introduced gradually to avoid diarrhoea and laminitis. Sugar beet is a useful feed for putting on weight, but should always be soaked before feeding (see Choke). Soya bean meal is also useful as it contains protein which is easily absorbed by the gut. Thin donkeys will often gain weight when turned out to grass but the quality of the grass is reduced later in the grazing season and good-quality hay is required to supplement the diet. Glucose licks are commercially available and are a useful additional source of energy as they are very palatable. If weight loss occurs too rapidly following an illness or an enforced diet, then hyperlipaemia may be a complication. See Anorexia, Hyperlipaemia, Kidney Disease, Parascaris Infection, Parasites, Quidding, Strongyle Worm Infections, Teeth Problems.

Wounds Wounds occur as the result of injury and may appear as bruising and swelling with intact skin or as open wounds of the skin. Fractures can also occur and these may or may not be accompanied by a skin wound. Minor skin wounds can usually be treated by keeping the wound clean and application of an antibiotic spray, powder or ointment. Extensive cuts in the skin may need to be stitched. Care should be taken with deep puncture wounds as they can heal quickly and seal in a deep infection leading to abscesses and infection of the underlying tissues. There is often a lot of reaction around wounds and there may be oedematous swelling and infection. Tetanus antiserum is usually administered to prevent the occurrence of tetanus and antibiotics are also often given. Bruising and inflammation can be eased by hot or cold bathing or the application of poultices. See Abscesses, Castration, Lameness, Oedema, Tetanus.

FURTHER READING

The following books are by Elisabeth Svendsen and are available from the Donkey Sanctuary:

Adult Books

Down Among the Donkeys –
 Hardback (Robert Hale, 1981)
Down Among the Donkeys – Paperback
 (Pan Books, 1981, reprinted 1985)
Twelve of My Favourite Donkeys
 (The Donkey Sanctuary, 1982,
 reprinted 1988)
In Defence of Donkeys (Whittet Books, 1985)
The Professional Handbook of the Donkey
 (The Donkey Sanctuary, 1986)
Donkey Years (Whittet Books, 1986)
A Week in the Life of the Donkey Sanctuary
 (Whittet Books, 1988)

Children's Books

*The Story of Eeyore the Naughtiest Donkey in
 the Sanctuary* (The Donkey Sanctuary, 1976,
 reprinted 1979, 1987)
Suey The Beach Donkey
 (The Donkey Sanctuary, 1977, reprinted 1986)
More Adventures of Eeyore
 (The Donkey Sanctuary, 1978)
Eeyore Helps the Children
 (The Donkey Sanctuary, 1981,
 reprinted 1986)
The Great Escape (Piccolo Books, 1981)
Jacko the Hurricane Donkey
 (The Donkey Sanctuary, 1982)
Eeyore and Christmas Crackers
 (The Donkey Sanctuary, 1984)
Eeyore Meets a Giant
 (The Donkey Sanctuary, 1987)

USEFUL ADDRESSES

United Kingdom
The Donkey Sanctuary Sidmouth Devon EX10 0NU
(Reg Charity No 264818)

The Slade Centre Sidmouth Devon EX10 0NU
(Reg Charity No 270551)

The International Donkey Protection Trust
Sidmouth Devon EX10 0NU
(Reg Charity No 271410)

Donkey Breed Society Secretary: Mr D. Demus
Manor Cottage South Thoresbry
Nr Alford Lincs LN13 0AS

British Mule Society Secretary: Mrs L. Travis
Hope Mount Farm Top of Hope Alston Field
Nr Ashbourne Derbyshire

Agricultural Development Advisory Service
(Midland & Western region)
Woodthorne Wergs Road Wolverhampton WV6 8TQ

Agricultural Development Advisory Service
(Eastern region)
Block C Government Buildings Brooklands Avenue
Cambridge CB2 2DR

Agricultural Development Advisory Service
(Northern region)
Block 2 Government Buildings Lawnswood
Leeds LS16 5PX

Agricultural Development Advisory Service (Wales)
Trawsgoed Aberystwyth Dyfed SY23 4HT

Agricultural Development Advisory Service
(South Eastern region)
Block A Government Offices Coley Park
Reading RG1 6DT

Agricultural Development Advisory Service
(South Western region)
Block 3 Government Buildings Burghill Road
Westbury-on-Trym Bristol BS10 6NJ

America
The American Donkey and Mule Society Inc
Mr and Mrs P Hutchins 2901 North Elm Street
Denton Texas 76201 USA

The Humane Society of the United States
2100 L Street NW Washington DC 20037 USA

Australia
Australian Donkey Breed Society: Jennifer Simpson
Booloumba Creek MS16 Maleny Queensland 4552
Australia

Australians for Animals
Private Bag 1 Bondi Junction 2022 NSW Australia

Canada
Canadian Donkey and Mule Association
Secretary: Mrs Sesse Halsall Greynose Farm
RR #2 Acton Ontario L7J 2L8 Canada

Denmark
Danish Donkey Society Secretary: Hanne Lissau
Teglgardsvej 121 3050 Humblebaek Denmark

Other Reading

Borwick, Robin. *People with Long Ears*
  (Cassell & Co Ltd, 1965)
Burbidge, Kath. *The Donkey Drivers*
  (Kath Burbidge, Australia, 1986)
Dent, Anthony. *Donkey: The Story of the Ass from East to West* (G. Harrap & Co, 1972)
Ellis, V. & Claxton. *Donkey Driving*
  (J. A. Allen, 1980)
Hutchins, Betsy & Paul. *The Definitive Donkey*
  (Hee-Haw Book Services, USA, 1981)
Morris, Dorothy. *Looking After a Donkey*
  (Whittet Books, 1988)
Simpson, Jenifer. *To Own a Donkey*
  (Angus & Robertson Publishers, 1985)
Swinfen, Avril. *The Irish Donkey*
  (The Mercier Press, 1969)
Walker, Stella. *Enamoured of an Ass*
  (Angus & Robertson Publishers, 1977)
Watney, M. *Royal Cavalcade*
  (T.A. Allen & Co, 1987)
de Wesselow, M. R. *Donkeys – their Care and Management* (Centaur Press Ltd, 1967)

Egypt
The Brooke Hospital for Animals (Cairo)
British Columbia House 1 Regent Street
London SW1Y 4PA England

Greece
Hellenic Animal Welfare Society
12 Pasteur Street Athens 602 Greece

Greek Animal Welfare Fund Ltd
11 Lower Barn Road Purley Surrey CR2 1HY England

Holland
Ver het Ned Ezelstamboek Buurtweg 161
2244 BJ Wassenaar Holland

Israel
The Society for the Prevention of Cruelty to Animals
30 Salame Road Jaffa Israel

Kenya
Kenya Society for the Prevention of Cruelty to Animals
Langata Road PO Box 24203 Nairobi Kenya

Mexico
Alecca AC (Association to Fight Cruelty to Animals)
Lope de Vega 316 Mexico 5DF

New Zealand
New Zealand Donkey Breed Society
Secretary: Mrs D. Holt
Wairere Horeke Northland New Zealand

North Africa
The Society for the Protection of Animals in
North Africa (SPANA)
15 Buckingham Gate London SW1E 6LB England

South Africa
Society for the Protection of Animals
Chambers Street Booysens Johannesburg 2091
Transvaal South Africa

South America
The Charles Darwin Research Station
Santa Cruz Galapagos Islands Ecuador South America

Spain
Asociacion para la Defensa de los Derechos del Animal
Gran Via 31 – 8° 28013 Madrid Spain

Switzerland
Swiss Donkey Society (SIGEF)
Im Bischoff 3314 Schalunen Switzerland

World-wide
The People's Trust for Endangered Species
Hamble House Meadrow Godalming Surrey
GU7 3XJ England

The World Society for the Protection of Animals
106 Jermyn Street London SW1Y 6EE England

International League for the Protection of Horses
PO Box No 166 67a Camden High Street
London NW1 7JL England

ACKNOWLEDGEMENTS

As well as those acknowledgements made within the text of this book, the author would like to thank the following for their contributions:

WHY A DONKEY?
International Donkey Protection Trust Trustee Robert Camac for the section on the origins and history of the donkey.

ACQUIRING A DONKEY
Donkey Sanctuary Trustee Rosalind de Wesselow and Betsy and Paul Hutchins for information for this chapter; Donkey Sanctuary employee Roy Harrington for 'Transport Laws'.

THEREBY HANGS A TAIL
Donkey Sanctuary inspectors Marjorie Monkhouse and Jay Duckworth for 'How Green Was My Missus' (*Donkey Breed Society Magazine*).

CARE OF THE DONKEY
Clive Scott; Rosalind de Wesselow; Dr David Sainsbury; Tom Williams; Gillian McCarthy; Paul and Betsy Hutchins; Donkey Sanctuary employees John Fowler and Bert Duncan.

DONKEYS AND MULES AT WAR
Major P.G. Malins MBE MC (retd) for his contribution to this chapter.

HELPING THE HANDICAPPED
Patricia Feather for her contribution to this chapter.

BREEDING AND SHOWING
Priscilla Kirby for the information on breeding; Joan Howard-Carter and Ursula Roberts for the information on showing and training.

INTERNATIONAL DONKEY PROTECTION TRUST
Dr D. Fielding for 'The Donkey – Four-leg Drive Rural Power'.

RIDING AND DRIVING
Vivian Ellis and Pamela Jermyn for their contribution to this chapter.

A-Z OF DONKEY HEALTH
The Veterinary Department of the Donkey Sanctuary for this chapter.

The author and publisher would also like to thank the following for supplying illustrations for this book. We apologise if acknowledgement to any photographer has been omitted.

Nicholas Toyne, pages 11, 26, 35, 38, 46, 50, 51, 55, 58, 75, 90, 91, 92, 95, 103, 107, 115, 119, 123, 163, 167, 183; Dorothy Morris, 22, 23, 63, 66, 75, 107, 111, 127, 152, 152, 153, 153; Sandra Harrington, 56, 57, 59, 59, 73, 93, 93, 95, 97, 109, 172, 173; Eve Bygrave, 13, 24, 33, 45, 52, 113, 185; Jennifer Johnson (for redrawn illustrations), 28, 30, 31, 67, 74, 76, 141; Steven Hyde, 2, 6, 10, 67, 102; Henry Phillips, 3, 21, 34, 177; Joan S. Byrne, 25, 27, 62, 71; Paul and Betsy Hutchins, 129, 129, 130, 131; June Evers, 138, 139, 143, 143, 174; Dr Colin P. Groves, 13, 14, 15, 15; Her Majesty The Queen, 9, 16, 17; Marylian Watney, 154, 156, 158; Major P. G. Malins, 81, 82, 86, 89, 89; Lise Kragh, 118, 119; the Beaford Archive, 184, 184; Asinerie du Val de Loir, 117, 181; Len Shepherd, 135, 146, 147; Roy Harrington, 133, 161, 164, 164; Judith E. Strom, 151, 155, 182; Chris Davis, 18; American Donkey & Mule Society, 159; Irene Williams, 39; the *Daily Telegraph*, 25; Daphne Cade, 43; Douglas Pickford, 37; Susan Davis, 48; Tom and Margaret Wetherell, 70; Pam Jermyn, 151; Henry Kirk, 84; Borax Holdings Limited, 178, 179; Wendy Boull, 110; Steve Cassidy, 109; Bob Camac, 175; J. A. Giddings, 125; Elizabeth and Keith Whiteman, 131; Kath Burbidge, 149.

INDEX

Page numbers in italic denote illustrations.